COOKING DIRTY

COOKING DIRTY

DIRTY

A STORY OF
LIFE, SEX, LOVE
AND DEATH
IN THE KITCHEN

JASON SHEEHAN

FARRAR, STRAUS AND GIROUX · NEW YORK

FARRAR, STRAUS AND GIROUX
18 West 18th Street, New York 10011

Distributed in Canada by Douglas & McIntyre Ltd.
Printed in the United States of America
First edition, 2009

Library of Congress Cataloging-in-Publication Data
Sheehan, Jason. Cooking dirty : a story of life, sex, love and death in the
kitchen / Jason Sheehan. — 1st ed.
     p.   cm.
   ISBN: 978-0-374-28921-8 (hardcover : alk. paper)
   1. Sheehan, Jason.   2. Cooks—United States—Biography.   3. Food
writers—United States—Biography.   I. Title.

TX649.A263A3 2009
641.5092—dc22
[B]

                                                        2008047158

Designed by Gretchen Achilles

www.fsgbooks.com

1   3   5   7   9   10   8   6   4   2

FOR EVERY CHEF WHO TRAINED ME, EVERY EDITOR WHO TOLERATED ME, ALL COOKS EVERYWHERE AND MOSTLY FOR MY TWO BEST GIRLS, LAURA VICTORIA AND PARKER FINN: IF THERE'S ANY GOOD IN ME THESE DAYS, IT'S ALL THEIR FAULT

What matters is what you don't know.
That's where they'll get you.

—PATTY CALHOUN

No matter where you go, there you are.

—BUCKAROO BANZAI

CONTENTS

COOKING DIRTY

PROLOGUE: FLORIDA, 1998

We had this superstition in the kitchen: On Fridays, no one counted heads. No one counted tables at the end of the night, no one counted covers. When the last table was cleared, the dupes were just left there, mounded up on the spike. You didn't look, not even in secret. No one even guessed. Bad things would happen if you did.

And even though no one looked, bad things happened anyway. Lane died on a Friday night due to complications of lifestyle—which is to say, he was shot by an acquaintance in a squabble over twenty dollars' worth of shitty brown horse. He wasn't found until Saturday morning; no one thought to call the restaurant to let us know that he wouldn't be coming in to work that day. He was just considered AWOL—a no-call/no-show that left the line a man short going into the early-bird rush.

This was Tampa, Florida, in the middle nineties—a bad time for cuisine, a worse place. It wasn't a great time for me, either. Worse for Lane, I guess, but everything is a matter of degrees. Of right and wrong places, right and wrong times.

Eventually, Lane's name was found in a late edition of the Tampa paper. Or maybe someone saw it on TV. I don't remember. In any event, we all found out, precisely too fucking late, that Lane was now fry-cooking in the sweet hereafter. The first hit was due in soon. And while there is a lot of voodoo in the air down in Florida, no one wanted to bet heavy on the long odds of Lane coming back as a zombie and retaking his place on the line. He'd been shit as a living cook anyhow. Being newly undead would probably only slow him worse than the smack had.

"This is why cooks should always have the decency to die in a public place," said Floyd, the kitchen manager and nominal chef. "That way, they make the morning paper and we'd know who isn't showing up for work."

In the kitchen, we discussed the best methods for dying in a spectacularly newsworthy fashion,* and Floyd promoted one of the afternoon prep crew into Lane's slot on the line. The FNG—the Fucking New Guy—went on fryers. It was my fourth night on the line at Jimmy's Crab Shack,† and no longer the F-ingest NG, I was brevetted to grill/steamer, working beside Sturgis, who was grill/top.

Saturday night, early, no one was able to find a rhythm. We kept getting popped, then stalled, taking five tables like BangBangBang-BangBang, then nothing for ten minutes. The FNG fell into the weeds—*dans la merde* even at this stuttering half-speed. Jimmy, the owner, was antsy on expo, alternating between giggling fits and bouts of screaming obscenity. Floyd rotated the line out for cigarettes. He had a speed pourer filled with rum and hurricane mix in his rack that he sucked at like a baby with a bottle, and he jumped on every check out of the printer as if it were the harbinger of the rush that steadfastly refused to come. It was difficult to see from the grill station at one end of the line to the fryers at the other because of the wavy heat-haze—the air squirming, like staring through aquarium water.

Five o'clock came and went. It seemed to me suddenly like there wasn't enough air on the line for all of us to breathe. I had chills. Cold flashes skittered up and down my spine while my front half baked. This being Florida and me being too young for menopause, I imagined it was malaria and stood firm, waiting for the hallucinations to

---

*The winner was falling naked from a plane or tall building onto the president, a local politician or a group of schoolchildren larger than six.

†Not the real name of the place I'm talking about, but close enough.

kick in. With the ventilation hood going full blast, Roberto and Chachi couldn't keep the pilots on their unused burners going so had to keep kissing them back to life—leaning over and blowing across the palms of their hands to get the flame from one to jump to the next with the gas turned all the way up. The alternative method: smacking a pan down on the grate at an angle and hard enough to catch a spark. They did it over and over again until Floyd yelled at them to quit it. After that, they fought over the galley radio. After that, they amused themselves by drinking the cooking wine (sieved through a coffee filter to separate out all the grease and floating crap and then mixed with orange soda) and pegging frozen mushroom caps at Jimmy whenever his back was turned.

At some point, Jimmy—in an attempt to catch whoever was throwing things at him, and half in the bag to begin with—spun around too fast, caught his foot on the edge of one of the kitchen mats and went down hard, his head spanging off the rounded edge of the expo table with a sound like someone throwing a melon at a gong. He was unconscious before he hit the floor.

There was an instant of shocked silence, then a crashing wave of laughter. Seeing anyone fall down is funny, but seeing a drunken fat man fall down beats all. One of the waitresses ran for the hostess (who also doubled as FOH manager), and she came at the best sprint she could manage in her stiletto heels and stirrup pants. The prep/runner crew treated Jimmy like any other heat casualty, breaking in a wing and descending like Stukas to drag him clear of the flow of service. It took four of them. Jimmy was a big man and moving him was like trying to roll a beached whale back into the sea.

They dumped him, loose-jointed, beside the cooler and calmly went back about their business. Jimmy's T-shirt (Pantera on that day, I think, black and sleeveless, making his thick, pasty-white arms look like they were made of lard) rode up over his hairy, pony-keg belly. His eyes were closed. There was no blood, which secretly disappointed us all.

Floyd spoke to the line. "No one cops to this. No one snitches."

He ordered Roberto to the wheel, shifted Dump, the roundsman, from second steamer (backing me) to second fryer (backing the new FNG), and vaulted the line to take Jimmy's place at expo himself.

As was only to be expected, that was when the real dinner hit finally came tumbling in. With the hostess seeing to Jimmy (and probably quietly looking to see how she could get at his wallet) the floor was left unmanaged. Waitresses double- and triple-sat their own sections in the absence of an egalitarian hand. The ticket machine began to spit. Like a pro, Roberto false-called a half dozen steaks to the grill, crabs to the steamers, and twenty-upped fries to get things rolling in anticipation of steaks going well-done and missed sides down the line, then started working actual tickets, hanging them ten at a time. The machine didn't stop. The paper strip grew long, drooping like a tongue, spooling out and down onto the floor. On the galley radio, the DJ came back from a commercial and kicked into the Misfits doing "Ballroom Blitz," and I—up to my wrists in meat and blood, crouching down at the lowboy trying to retrieve cheap-ass skirts and vac-pac T-bones from the dim interior—yelled that I'd kill the next cocksucking motherfucker that touched the dial. After that, we were in it, the machinery in motion.

Sturgis and I sang along with the radio, bouncing on our toes, burning energy while we had it and twirling tongs on our fingers like gunslingers before dropping them onto the steamer's bar handles. We shouted callbacks to Floyd with the strange, exaggerated politeness and house slang of the line: "Firing tables fifty-five, thirty, sixty-eight, thank you. Going on eight fillet. Four well, three middy, one rare. Working fourteen all day, hold six. Five strip up and down. Temps rare, rare, middy waiting on po fries, two well going baker, thank you. Wheel, new fires, please. We've got space."

We yelled at Roberto, at Floyd, at the radio and each other. We yelled at the runners to bring more compound butter and plates of oil (a cheap trick for getting those grill marks to char faster—dragging the steaks through cheap salad oil, which scorched up black and nutty in seconds), and when we weren't yelling, we were muttering, cursing, talking to the meat, the fire; begging and cajoling more heat out of the grills, bricking the steaks with iron weights, throwing them in the microwave to speed them along to temp, constantly poking and prodding and plating them to the rail; waiting for po—for starch—and veg and wrap.

Jimmy regained consciousness and sat glaze-eyed, staring and concussed on the floor until he was capable of standing without help. He retook expo like the marines taking a hill: lurching, wild-eyed and under fire. Floyd came back onto the line at the wheel. Roberto surrendered his position without a word, just turning and going straight back to his burners one step away with no interruption in the flow of orders. On fryers, the FNG was so deep in the weeds and lost that Dump had to crutch him full-time while I racked and emptied the stinking steamers, leaving dozens of pounds of crab legs and freezer-burned lobster tails and hundreds of clams to die in hotel pans under the heat lamps. The smell was . . . *staggering*.

Then the FNG passed out from the heat. The runners plunged onto the line, hip-checking their way through the chaos to drag him off.

Floyd shouted, "Hydrate that bitch!"

The FNG was dumped over a floor grate near the coolers and doused with ice water. He came to with a scream, sputtering and kicking, and while he recovered, another runner stood stage at his station, slicing bags of fries open with a silver butterfly knife he'd pulled out of his pocket and emptying them straight into the smoking fryers; fishing out an order at a time with long tongs and setting up sell plates under the lamps to catch up, his fist wrapped in a wet side towel to defend against the rivulets of hot oil that ran back down the grooves—another good trick, one that the FNG just hadn't had time yet to learn.

The night rolled on. Ice buckets were called for and installed at each station. You bent down and stuck your whole head in whenever you started to see fireworks—sure sign of an impending blackout. A plastic bottle of cornstarch made the rounds, everyone on the line dumping the stuff right down the front of our chef pants to soak up the sweat and keep the tackle from sticking. "Making pancakes," that was called, from the way the starch caked up on either side of one's ballsack.

I went down around nine. I felt it coming—the blackness squeezing into my head like heavy velvet. There was time enough to step back so I didn't topple over on the grill, then just the sensation of falling for miles.

Mark of one's perceived toughness: I was hydrated on the spot, Sturgis upending an ice bucket onto me while Floyd frantically waved off the runners. The floor was ankle-deep in shit—food scraps and packaging and dropped utensils and dirty towels. All the detritus of a killer service in a restaurant where people didn't care as much about what they were eating as they did about its being served fast, cheap and in gargantuan portions. I lay there on my back like I was trying to make a garbage angel, blinking, gasping and spitting. When I stood up again, I had a crab leg stuck in my hair.

Sturgis called me Crab Head from then on out.

I went right back to the grill—not because I was so tough or because I wanted to, but because I was too embarrassed to do anything else. I had to strip out of my chef coat and T-shirt because the water in them started to boil. The guys whistled at me. Sturgis rubbed my thin, bare belly. A runner brought me a dry jacket, and while I was shrugging into it, there was a sudden, odd quiet. The ticket machine had paused—first time since the rush had begun in earnest. We all stared as if it were our own hearts that'd stopped beating.

"Fire all!" Floyd yelled. "Hang 'em and bang 'em. Expo, all call."

We ran the rail, cooking everything in sight in one massive push to get ahead of the curve. And when it was done, Sturgis and I cooked through the last half hour of service on autopilot, going on gut and reflex with sore hands and boiling blood and eyes like broken windowpanes. Things were winding down, the siege broken, the fort once again saved from the Indians, whatever. We wiped down, wrapped and stored our station while the last of the straggling tables cleared, then gave the line over to the prep crew, who were also responsible for all the heavy cleaning. Four hours had snapped past like a minute.

This was The Life. The part they can't teach in culinary school, don't ever show on TV. The unscheduled death and disasters and heat and blistering adrenaline highs, the tunnel vision, the crashing din,

smell of calluses burning, crushing pressure and pure, raw joy of it all
as the entire rest of the world falls away and your whole universe becomes a small, hot steel box filled with knives and meat and fire;
everything turning on the next call, the next fire order, the twenty,
thirty, forty steaks in front of you and the hundreds on the way. This
was what made everything else forgivable. And I knew that if I could
just do this one thing, all night, every night, under the worst conditions and without fail, nothing else mattered.

Please, God, just this. The rest is only details.

We retired, with the rest of the crew, first to the dock to pass a
bowl around and hammer down cigarettes, then to the locker room
to change, then to the bathroom—transformed briefly into a white-
trash version of Studio 54 with ugly men in terrible clothing dry-
swallowing OxyContin tablets or tying off in the stalls with the
proficiency of practiced habit—then, finally, to the bar, where the air
tasted of tin and overworked air-conditioning machinery and the
hostess stood pouring restorative cocktails of pineapple juice and
well vodka into finger-smudged highball glasses.

It took a minimum of two drinks before any of us were able to get
it together enough to speak, three before what came out of our
mouths approached language. We talked about the night the way im-
pressionists painted, in splashes of color and hard, angular jive;
speaking in broken sentences, disjointed bursts of wasted rage mixed
with thumping bravado bouncing back and forth while we sat, all
clotted up around the service end of the bar in too few chairs as if,
even in an empty dining room, we strove to isolate ourselves from
where the customers—the enemy—sat and business was done.

Floyd sat slumped over with his arms folded on the bar top, head
resting on his crossed wrists. Sturgis and Chachi were chattering at
each other like monkeys, grooving on the same Colombian frequency. Roberto and I sat bracketing the FNG (who'd finished out the
night standing, which was noble enough), filling him with liquor and
trying to name him now that his cherry had been popped; running
down a list of funny Spanish words, French, kitchen slang, settling finally on Chupo—garbled Spanish for "I suck."

Jimmy came teetering out of the kitchen like a sea captain negotiating a rolling, rain-slick deck. The entire left side of his head had
swollen like he'd caught half a case of encephalitis, but he said nothing about it—seeming to have forgotten the mushroom-cap mutiny
entirely, like it was a hundred years ago and never that big a deal to
begin with. He squeezed my shoulder in passing, patted Roberto's
belly, grabbed Chupo by the back of the neck and shook him like a
puppy, telling him he'd done good, that he would be on the line again
tomorrow night, and that he shouldn't be drinking because he was
only eighteen, but if anyone outside the house said boo to him, to just
tell them he'd robbed a liquor store.

Jimmy made the rounds and ended up at the bar beside Floyd. I
watched him lay a hand gently on his top guy's back, between Floyd's
bony shoulders. They talked too quiet for me to hear, but Floyd
would raise his head only to answer direct questions, staring off into
some weird middle space between his eyes and the bar mirror when
he did, then settling his head back again onto his arms. He looked like
some wasted angel, a stick-skinny cherub, a galley saint—white as al-
abaster, beat to shit, spacey from the junk and exhausted. No one
lasted more than a few hours or a few days on the line at Jimmy's
Crab Shack. If you made it a month, you were almost like family.

Floyd had been holding down his post for two years.

LATER THAT NIGHT, full of house liquor and smelling like low tide on the
gutting flats, I went out back alone for a quiet smoke. Stumbling
through the large, darkened kitchen, my fingers trailing, bumping
along the tile walls, I went out onto the dock. There, away from the
insulating comfort of cooks, away from the furious noise and action
of the hot line, away from the familiarity of plastic ashtrays and ice-
frosted glasses, the language of kitchens, the screwheaded weirdness
and zapped-out combat-zone chic of being a working cook at the
ragged end of a long, bad night, all of reality came crashing back in on
me. Here was only the night, the dark, the green, fecund stink and distant highway roar, the wet pressure of just trying to breathe in this

swamp and the fat black cockroaches that crawled along the cement. Here was the realization of exactly how fast I'd fallen, and from
what middling height.

Suddenly, the thought of crawling back to my room and my alleged fiancée, of smoking cigarettes, lying slit-eyed on the couch, too
exhausted to sleep and watching another Spanish-dubbed version of
Red Dawn on Telemundo, was all just too much. Standing rigid, eyes
aching, feet throbbing, blood humming in the hollows behind my ears
to fill the sudden quiet, I stared up into the night and the stars.

And maybe this should've been one of those big moments. Maybe
I should've asked myself the big questions: *What's next, Jay?* or *How
in the fuck did you end up here?* It's possible that I even did. Tired as
I was, beaten cross-eyed like I was and just trying to catch my breath
among the roaches, cigarette dog-ends and hot trash stink, the scene
was certainly set for all manner of hammy self-indulgence.

This is my story. If I wanted, I could tell it exactly that way. I
could make myself appear deep, introspective or wise. If I wanted to
seem a tough guy, I'd just have me suck it up, light a fresh smoke and
stride off purposefully, bravely, into an ambiguous future.

But I'm none of those things. I'm not wise, I'm dumb. I'm not a
tough guy, I'm a coward. And the big questions? They all had small
and inconsequential answers that were the same every time I asked
them. I'd ended up where I did because of poor life choices and an
even worse sense of direction. What was next was another cigarette,
another drink at the bar, another rehashing of the night's action.

"Hey, remember when . . ."

"Or what about when Jimmy . . ."

What was next was a swift retreat back into the warm, close
embrace of a gang of cooks doing what cooks do best when there's
no more work to be done, which is everything possible to stall off
having to leave the orbit of their kitchens, the nocturnal world
and closed society of this thing of ours. To be in that—to be buried
and surrounded by it, regulated by it, protected by it—was a comfort.
It meant never having to be bothered by the big moments, the big
questions.

So whether I found clarity there on the dock that night is immaterial. Whether I looked deep into my soul, wept and gnashed my teeth over blown opportunities and potential pissed away, or simply stood for a minute or two or ten, lost in the quiet and hot, wet dark. What matters is what I did, and what I did was turn my back on the outside, square up my head and go back to the bar.

What's next? Tomorrow night's shift and tomorrow night's disasters.

And how the fuck did I end up here?

Because I couldn't remember ever wanting anything else.

FIRST IMPRESSIONS

When we were done talking, Angelo shook my hand, told me to come back tomorrow, and when I did, to come in through the back door.

To a kid, that's pretty exciting right from the start. I'd never walked in through the back door of anywhere except my parents' house; had never seen the inside, the back room, the inner workings, of anything.

Okay, so it wasn't like getting asked backstage at the rock show or being given a guided tour of the space shuttle. Just an invitation into the kitchen of Ferrara's Pizza on Cooper Road, a neighborhood joint fifteen minutes' walk from home. It wasn't even a job so much as a test. "You come," Angelo had said. "You like me, I like you, then maybe, eh?" He'd shrugged. "Then maybe you come back. Maybe not."

The next day, I came back. I remember the smell of ripe Dumpsters, acidic like hot tomatoes and yeasty like stale beer. I remember the intimate crunch of my shoes as I walked alone down into the alley/parking lot behind the place, cigarette butts strewn on the broken concrete and the sound of raised voices on the other side of the rickety screen door that let into the kitchen. I heard shouting that sounded happy and serious both at the same time—impossible for me to reconcile with the simple emotional architecture of my particular and quiet suburban upbringing, where shouting only ever meant something bad—and impossible to translate because it was in Italian.

I, of course, spoke not a word of Italian and (perhaps unwisely) had taken my first job in a place where Eyetie was the primary language. At the time, this seemed only a minor inconvenience.

I remember reaching for the door and feeling the dry heat baking through the screen on the palm of my outstretched hand.

Wow, I thought. *That's uncomfortable. Maybe the air conditioner isn't working.*

My second thought was that perhaps my choice (guided by my mother) in wearing a cadaverous blue button-down shirt and dark slacks with pointy-toed dress shoes to my first day of work had been a mistake.

But she'd been so proud, so happy. She'd insisted that—at least on their first day at a new job—everyone ought to dress as though they were attending a formal ball where one's clothing, carriage and grace would be studied with some rigor. Because one never truly knew what they were in for on their first day of anything, it was all a matter of first impressions. And Mom was a big believer in first impressions. I've seen pictures of myself when I was a small child, in the years before I had any control over how I dressed me, and have witnessed the full flowering of my mom's obsession with firsts. Coming home from the hospital, I looked like a small ham dressed for trick-or-treating in a Winnie-the-Pooh bunting complete with ears and paws. First day of school? Corduroy Toughskins and what appears to be a midget's dinner jacket. In my first-grade school picture I am wearing a plaid bow tie and cummerbund and a gap-toothed grin so wide and crazy I am frankly amazed I wasn't immediately prescribed something. At my First Communion, I looked like I should be serving drinks.

There is a treasured family photo of the four of us—Mom, Dad, me and my little brother, Brendan—posing on the edge of some mountain in the Adirondacks. It's the first mountain the four of us climbed together, according to my mother. Myself, I'd say it was probably just taken in the woodlot down at the end of the street where I grew up, except that the ground behind us in the picture seems to be slanting upward at some ridiculously steep angle, and none of us are actually standing. We are, in fact, clinging, crablike, with fingers and bootheels to a rock outcropping and quite plainly trying to keep from sliding off to our deaths.

In the picture, my mom and dad both look like teenagers. She's wearing shorts and hiking boots and pigtails and a look of manic, totally insane joy—an expression she wears, in one form or another, in every photo ever taken of her. He has a beard and a mustache, a flannel shirt, and the air of a man expecting to be eaten by a bear at any moment. Brendan is four years old so it doesn't matter what he's dressed in, but I have been attired in what appears to be a pair of miniature lederhosen like a tiny pitchman for European throat lozenges.

Anyway, Mom was big on firsts and big on dressing up for them. So it being 1988 and this being my first day of work, that was what I'd done—dolling myself up in my blue shirt with the too-large collar and poly-blend slacks and pointy shoes, looking like a short, skinny thrift-store version of the lead singer from Foreigner and having balked only at the addition of my best red leather tie. It was a pizza joint, I figured. A tie would just be overdoing it.

I pulled open the door and stepped inside. A radio was playing something unrecognizable and full of accordions. The air above and around the three double-deck pizza ovens was warped by the furnace heat radiating from them, like looking at the world through water, and everywhere else was thick with flour. It hung like a dusty cloud. The floor was gritty with it, every flat surface covered with it. The kitchen was a microcosm of motes and streamers, the thin stratus formations disturbed only by the passage of bodies through it and the suck of ventilating fans; a universe of flour that whitened everything it touched. To take a breath was to inhale whole galaxies of finely ground wheat, and the taste was like chalk on the tongue riding an olfactory wave of tomatoes, oregano and char. In two minutes, I'd sweated through my pretty blue shirt. After three, I was ready to pass out.

Angelo saw me standing there and broke out laughing, the cigarette in the corner of his mouth bobbing, the dusty skin around his
eyes wrinkling. Natalie, his wife, made a face like I was the funniest,
saddest thing she'd ever seen. And I just stood there, weaving in place
and sweating while the accordions honked and everyone in the
kitchen erupted in laughter and language I didn't understand.

Finally, Angelo took off his glasses and wiped at his eyes. He
pointed to a corner of the kitchen with a coatrack and some clean
aprons stacked on a shelf. "Jason. Go. Change," he said.

So I did.

MY MOM HAS THIS STORY she likes to tell. Well, not a story exactly. It's
more like an act, a shtick she falls back on whenever someone asks
her what I was like as a kid.

Jay used to be such a sweet boy. You remember that show Family Ties? *Well, Alex P. Keaton was his hero. He dressed like him,
acted like him. He was always more comfortable around adults,
you know? Very polite. Very smart. When he was little, he used to
dress up all the time. One day he'd put on an army helmet and a
backpack and be a soldier. The next day he'd wear this adorable little Boy Scout uniform and carry this bird book around with him.
And I'd always get a call from Mrs. So-and-So down the end of the
street and she'd say, "Cindy, Jason's running away again. And he's
dressed like a spaceman or something."*

*But he always came home, didn't he? He always came home
and he was always so sweet. See? Look at this . . .*

At which point she will unearth a box of pictures or, worse, a
framed-portrait collection of me through the years, from like five or
six years old on through maybe eighteen. It's an annual, one portrait
from every year, arranged in an oval around one central photo, larger
than all the others: a studio portrait of yours truly at eighteen looking
like King Dickweed in a turtleneck sweater and blue jeans, brown
leather jacket thrown jauntily over one shoulder, shot against a back-

drop of disco lights as though I'd been caught by the paparazzi on the dance floor of the Dork Club.* It has come to be known over the years as the Wheel O' Jay.

With the Wheel serving her like documentary evidence, she will run through the years with quick and practiced ease.

This one, he's what? Nine years old? Maybe eight?

I'm eight. She knows that perfectly well. And even if she didn't, you'd think the Cub Scout uniform and the manic, wild-eyed leer of total elementary school picture-day psychosis would be a dead giveaway.

Look at him here, she'll continue, her voice hard and nasal like Marge Gunderson from *Fargo* after a toot of helium. *Isn't he cute? That little tie and sweater vest. That was the year we all went to Atlantic City. To the boardwalk. He was so excited. And this one. Doesn't he look happy? He was twelve here. Our first cat had just died . . .*

Her affection for the photos starts to wane considerably by the late eighties, by the time I'd made it to high school. But still, she'll shrug, tap at the glass. She will claim that I was nothing short of a perfect little mama's boy until I reached my eighteenth birthday. An absolute angel, sweet as a gumdrop. Never mind that by eighteen, I'd already spent my first night in lockup, had already held and left three different jobs, had moved out (and subsequently back in) twice. She doesn't mention to guests making the rounds of the Wheel what it was like to stand up in the judge's chambers and agree to discipline a wayward son who was up on charges of possession of controlled substances, criminal trespassing and contributing to the delinquency of a foreign exchange student. She doesn't tell the story of how, in an effort to get me to quit smoking on my seventeenth birthday, she gave

---

*In that picture I'm wearing a slightly dazed and vacant look because, on the good advice of a friend, I'd gotten halfway shitfaced on most of a warm bottle of Wild Irish Rose before going to the studio. Mom has always claimed that I looked contemplative, as if caught thinking of something else the moment the shutter snapped or perhaps considering the gleam on the arc of the bright future stretching out before me. Truth is, I was just trying not to throw up.

me a pack of Marlboro Reds with a picture of my grandpa tucked inside the cellophane. He'd recently died of lung cancer (among other things), so the picture showed him in his casket. And she'd painstakingly written *Hi, grandpa!* in blue ballpoint pen on each individual cigarette, then somehow managed to get them all back in the pack.

Granted, that's a creepy thing for a mom to do, but catching me by the elbow on my way out the door on my way to my senior prom and pressing a twelve-pack of condoms into my hand—is that worse?

No. What's worse is that she'd wrapped them in pretty green paper. What's worse is that she'd known full well my date was already waiting in the car and would be sitting right next to me when I—thinking that she'd perhaps purchased me some sort of functional gift like a hip flask or a pistol—unwrapped her little present. What's worse is that the condoms she'd bought were ribbed.

She holds to her version of the past—the one in which I didn't go wrong until the day I left the nest, went away to college, fell in with a bad crowd. And while there is some truth to that rendering (I didn't discover amphetamines until college, for example, or their overachieving cousin, crystal methamphetamine, and while I might have been marginally screwed up before that magic moment, after it I was both screwed up and awake for days at a time), it really happened much sooner than that. If my opinion counts for anything in this (and I'm not entirely sure that it does), I would say that everything changed—that I changed—when Angelo told me to. Mom can say whatever she likes (and will, given the least excuse or opportunity), but I was there. I was the one in my skin and in that ridiculous blue dress shirt and in those pointy shoes, standing in the heat and floury clamor of the kitchen at Ferrara's, so when Ange wiped his eyes, pointed to the corner with the coatrack and aprons, and said, "Jason. Go. Change," I did. It was the first order I took from a chef, the first of a million to come.

I STRIPPED DOWN to a white T-shirt and tied on an apron. I tied it wrong and Natalie had to show me how to do it correctly—strings crossed in the back, tied in the front, the bib tucked inside. The shoes were still a problem, but since I wasn't going to work barefoot, I suffered with them. At least I looked like half a cook—the top half of one, crudely laced onto the bottom half of a short used-car salesman or the kind of guy who, in my town, would try to sell you shrimp or stolen stereos out of the back of a van.

My first duty was scraping sheet pans—using a bench scraper to flake off the skins of dried dough that'd stuck there after the trays had been pulled from the proofing box and the balls of raw dough removed, turned and laid in for a second rise in the humid air of the kitchen. Ferrara's Pizza went through an amazing number of sheet pans in a day, working a two-rise rotation that kept probably two hundred of them constantly moving from box to racks to dishwasher and back again. Fifty or more would be used to hold raw dough headed for the proofing box—the balls arranged in two rows of six, twelve to a tray, twenty-some trays to a box—and would stay in there overnight. In the morning, someone (not me) would strip the proofed dough, now all stiff and leathery, from the trays, turn it, move it to a new set of clean sheet pans, stack the dirty ones on the floor, and shove the pans of turned dough into open racks near the prep tables. The dirty pans would be scraped, cleaned and stacked, awaiting the next batch of raw dough, and as Angelo took ball after ball of proofed and risen dough from the pans in the open racks, these would begin to form a second stack of dirties.

That stack then became my responsibility—each pan needing to be scraped perfectly clean of dried-out dough because any trace of it left behind would collect in the dish machine's filter, eventually causing it to back up and flood the kitchen.

So I scraped the pans as best I could, but these were old pans, a *batterie de cuisine* that'd been in constant use for probably twenty years. They were warped, dented, buckled. There were pans whose sides had rolled, whose corners had pouched after thousands of violent, hurried probings with the sharp corner of a bench scraper. And each pock and ding and rough spot held flakes and dollops of dough; dough that sometimes came off easy like an old, dry scab, that sometimes turned to dust, that'd sometimes turned wet and gooey and would cling like a booger to anything it touched.

Each pan I finished on that first day I stacked on the loading end of the dishwasher until I had a mighty tower. I'd worked hard. I'd worked as fast as I was able, considering this was all completely new to me and I had no idea what exactly I was doing or how it fit into the grander scheme of Ferrara's nightly pizza production. I'd gotten the basic gist of the necessary interaction between scraper and tray pretty quickly; had developed something like a system about halfway through the stack, which involved a flashy double pass over the flat surfaces with the blade of the bench scraper and then a vigorous (if not particularly effective) assault on the edges, corners and rough spots with the handle of a spoon I'd pulled out of one of the drying racks. If nothing else, it made me look as though I was working hard and, after my inauspicious entry into the kitchen, looking like I knew what I was doing was very important to me.

It took me almost two hours to finish scraping fifty or maybe a hundred trays. When I was done, I figured they'd now become a dish-washer's responsibility, though I saw no dishwasher standing around anywhere, just waiting to jump in.

All around me, pizzas were being ordered and constructed with frightening speed. Things were being chopped and diced. The radio was playing and people were yelling and the ovens were cranked to their top settings, the doors left open, heat pouring out of them like liquid. The dinner rush was on and it was exciting, overwhelming. I felt lost, so I edged my way around the kitchen and stepped close to Angelo—wanting to learn how to throw dough, to ladle sauce and work the pizza stick (the big, flat, scorched wooden paddle with which pizzas were loaded and unloaded from the ovens), but terrified at the same time that I'd be asked to do anything other than to stand quietly in a corner and try not to faint. Timidly, I asked him what I could do next.

"Wash," he said without looking at me. "Run the machine." Then he made some strange stacking and lever-pulling motions with his hands, which were what passed for operating instructions for the dishwasher—a large, loud and (I assumed) expensive piece of industrial equipment full of spinning arms and harsh chemicals and boiling hot steam, which I was now expected to operate with some degree of expertise.

Again, I did my best, and again my best amounted to very little. I was quite pleased that I was even able to get the machine started, since I didn't even know how to work our dishwasher at home and most of my dealings with unfamiliar machinery (such as toasters, microwave ovens, my dad's Betamax or the lawn mower) involved pushing buttons or flipping switches at random until something unexpected—like a fire—happened. If nothing happened, I would get frustrated and resort immediately to violence, as if the toaster were deliberately trying to ruin my sandwich or the record player purposefully refusing to act as a centrifuge for the G.I. Joe action figures I'd taped to the turntable. Later, when my mom would demand to know who'd kicked the door off the broiling compartment of the oven or heaved my dad's good power drill up onto the patio roof, I'd pretend I had no idea what she was talking about. I'd tell her it was probably Bren, then calmly go back to smashing my old cassette player with a rock.

Anyway, I was considerably less pleased when, within minutes, I'd managed to flood the entire kitchen. Probably *pounds* of unscraped dough had swollen in contact with the hot water inside the machine and found their way to the drain screen. At the first sign of trouble (which announced itself in the form of a stinking geyser of drainwater shooting up from the machine's well), I panicked, jerked open the loading door in the side of the machine, and got a face full of superheated steam.

Natalie came to my rescue, indelicately muscling me aside and killing the machine with a quick stab at the big red button marked STOP that I'd entirely failed to notice. No one else in the kitchen even slowed down. Ignoring the floodwaters lapping at their boots and what I'd guess was probably a high and girlish screeching coming from me, they simply soldiered on, deconstructing fresh peppers, slicing pepperoni and throwing crusts with a focused concentration I initially took to be an intentional snub.

It wasn't. It was just that cooks—good cooks, in the middle of a solid hit—are monstrously single-minded creatures. When the rush is on, a cook *cooks*. He puts his head down and just burns. A flood ain't nothing till it gets so bad that it starts wetting his prep.

"Is okay," Natalie said to me, touching her fingertips to my chest, my arms, gently tapping and trying to calm me or something. "Is okay. Try again."

So I did. I ran the dish machine for the rest of the night, overflowing it at least twice more and kicking at its legs when no one was looking, but slowly figuring out its intricacies and what it could and couldn't do. It *could* wash an evenly spaced and carefully arranged load of sheet trays provided it was coddled along and not put under any sort of undue stress. It *couldn't* be made to work faster or better no matter what names I called it or how many times I hit it.

I found and cleaned the drain screen, familiarized myself with the machine's proper loading and unloading, played with all the buttons and switches, whose labels and settings had worn off ages ago. I was ready to walk out after the first disaster, but I was no quitter so figured I'd at least hang in until the end of the night, when I would no doubt be summarily fired.

EVENTUALLY IT WAS NINE O'CLOCK. My fancy, pointy shoes were ruined. I'd run out of obscenities to yell at the dish machine. I was hurting and exhausted and frustrated, soaked with sweat and dishwater from the top of my head to my kneecaps. I was embarrassed at how bad a job I'd done, sorry for repeatedly flooding this nice couple's kitchen, and I smelled *awful*. As the night wound down toward closing time, Natalie had shown me where the mop and bucket were kept, and I'd spent the final hour of my first day as a working man hopelessly trying to repair some of the damage I'd done. The combination of water from the dish machine and the flour that covered everything had coated the floor in a sticky, gloppy plaster, and my pointlessly swirling the mop around on the cracked cement floor was doing little more than moving gooey wads of gray-brown crap from one place to another.

One by one the cooks filed out, without a word, until just me and Ange and Natalie were left. I'd managed to corral most of the gunk near a central drain cut in the floor and was picking it up with my hands and depositing it in a garbage can because I couldn't figure out any other way of getting rid of it when Ange called me over to the back door. I went. I assumed this was it and told myself that I would be a man about it. Ange stepped outside onto the back stair. I followed. He held the door open for me. For a minute, he did nothing but look at me—squinting through the smoke from the Marlboro that was forever hanging from his lip. I remember how great the cool night air felt on every inch of me that was sore and steam-burned. I remember how much better everything smelled than me.

And I remember Angelo smiling, lacing his fingers behind his back, stretching his whip-thin frame until his spine cracked, and saying, "You're still here."

Now over the years, at the conclusion of many other bad nights, I've returned to that line in my head. I've never been sure if he meant that as a question (as in "What the hell are you still doing here?"), as an expression of his frank disbelief (as in "After what you did, I can't believe you're still here") or as a sort of existentialist's comment on the nature of really bad first days of work, like "Even after everything bad that's happened tonight, you are still here." Personally, I've always preferred the philosophical translation because it makes me seem somewhat heroic just for not giving up. And it makes Angelo seem like the sort of man who appreciated the quiet heroism of fifteen-year-olds too dumb to work a mop but also just too fucking stubborn to quit.

However he meant it, though, I looked back at him and repeated, "I'm still here."

Now, I thought. *Now he'll fire me.*

He nodded once, reached into the breast pocket of his T-shirt, took out a cigarette and forty bucks and handed both to me.

"That's good," he said. "Tomorrow, same time, okay?"

If I'd had a glass of water handy, I would've done a spit-take. "Really?"

He shrugged. "Tomorrow will be better."

I put the cash in my pocket and the cigarette in my mouth. He lit it for me with a battered Zippo. And then the two of us stood there, not talking, just smoking and feeling the cool night air.

I was in love. If I had to make a list of all the best moments of my life, then that one—standing there in the dark by the back door smoking a cigarette with Angelo—would be high up on the inventory. Maybe not at the top, but close. I swore hard that I'd do better tomorrow, and better than that the day after. I promised myself that I wasn't going to let this guy down, ever.

And I did, of course. A hundred times in probably my first month alone. But at the end of every night, I was still there.

On my first night, though, anything was still possible. All the small successes and failures of a highly checkered life were far, far away just then, so when I was finished with it, I flicked the butt of my cigarette out into the dark and stepped down onto the gravel of the alley. I started walking away.

"Hey," Angelo called after me. "Where you go? Finish the floor first, huh?" He jerked his shoulder back in the direction of the kitchen, back toward the clots of wet dough around the drain and the wreck of the dish machine.

I laughed, shrugged, and slunk back in past him. He stayed on the steps, lit another cigarette off the stump of the first, and stared off into the dark while the radio played quietly and Natalie counted out the day's receipts on the glass of the front counter. I picked up the mop again and heard Angelo from outside, yelling at me.

"Tomorrow, wear better shoes."

ALMOST FAMOUS

At this point, I would love to be able to say something along the lines of "And it was after this first inauspicious day and these encouraging words from my lifelong friend and mentor Angelo Ferrara that I knew for certain I wanted nothing more in my life than to become a chef."

I would then settle comfortably into a straight retelling of my smooth rise into the ranks of American über-chefs; how I struggled against some sort of externally presented adversity, overcame it with the help of Jesus and a good woman, then went on to get my own Food Network show, my own line of retail sauces and marinades and my own restaurant with two Michelin stars and a reputation for otherworldly excellence totally out of line with its location on a small Pacific island accessible only by hovercraft.

I'd love to be able to tell that story because that story would be familiar. There would be a clear beginning—a first day of work (very much like the one I have described), some words of encouragement from a trusted elder that would kindle my love affair with food. This would be followed by a juicy middle, the ubiquitous training montage; a breakdown, or a shark attack; and a scene in which I collapse, weeping, in the rain, then am found and comforted by a beautiful woman. After that, I am healed. My path becomes clear, and I follow it steadily toward ridiculous success. As with all tales like this, it would end with my best girl and me riding magical dinosaurs off into the sunset.

These kinds of stories are comfortable, recognizable, easy to follow. They're the kind of stories people like to read.

This is not one of those stories.

I feel like it's my responsibility as the teller of this story to say that if you're looking for some four-star confessional, for the cooking secrets of master chefs or some effervescent, champagne-and-twinkle-lights twaddle about bright knives, foie gras and sweaty love among the white jackets, go find another book. Plenty of other books out there deal with the glam end of cooking in what has become a grossly celebrity-driven industry. Books about food obsessions that come from clean, clinical and intellectual places. About cuisine that isn't born of pain and damage. About chefs who don't have any scars.

I know a lot of kitchens out there operate not at all like the hot, cramped asylums and dens of terrible iniquity that I came up through. I understand there are chefs who are true gentle geniuses. But I never knew any of them. I didn't work on their lines. And I can only tell my story and the stories of my guys—the ones I knew and worked beside, fought with, loved better than brothers (and the occasional sister), labored under, and eventually left behind like some kind of miserable, slinking Judas for a desk job, a byline and health insurance. My guys named their knives the way rock stars do their guitars, got butcher's diagrams of broken-down pigs tattooed on their asses, and went to jail for assaulting police dogs. They slept and screwed on the flour sacks in the basements of a thousand different restaurants; lifted waitresses (and sometimes customers) right up on the stainless and knocked the cutting boards loose; prepped cool, fat-slick lobes of foie gras with the skill of surgeons in restaurants where they never could've afforded to eat. They weren't pretty. They weren't nice. They smelled bad almost all the time. They weren't the guys you see on TV. They were the guys who make the guys on TV look *good*.

They were the guys who cook your dinner.

And after that first night at Ferrara's, I was one of them. My real story and the imaginary story I would like to tell may not have many similarities, but they do have one vital detail in common: love. I was hooked. I couldn't wait to get back into that kitchen. Like the guy who ends up staying forever with the girl who mercifully unburdens him of his virginity, I'd found true love on my very first try.

Just like my mom had said, you never know what can happen on your first day.

TRUTH: I was fifteen years old when I went to work for Ange and Natalie, but I didn't do it because I had any love for food or for cooking. The same is probably true of the majority of my peers—regardless of how their PR-spun bios might read. I know one who took his first kitchen job at sixteen because he had a crush on a waitress two years older than him. Another started washing dishes at fifteen because his boss let him keep a radio at his station and play heavy metal all night. Another did it to get off the family farm (where he now returns two or three times a year to clear the place out of expensive mushrooms and sugar beets and to fish the streams clean of trout). Another because it was either the corner diner or eventually taking his place beside his father at the factory where the old man had been working for twenty years.

I took my first cooking job for the basest of all possible reasons: because I needed money. I threw my lot in with Ange and Natalie just because Ange and Natalie were the first people I'd found who were willing to accept my fudged work permit and hire a fifteen-year-old kid whose only real skills were jerking off and quoting verbatim from *Star Wars*, *Star Trek*, *Star Blazers* and certain books on sailing and wilderness survival.

I didn't want to be a chef. I was fifteen years old. If I wanted to be anything, it was a pirate or, failing that, a rock star (that I couldn't play guitar and was hundreds of miles from the nearest ocean notwithstanding).

Still, by the time I was done with my first week as a working man, I'd at least gotten a feel for the rhythms and idiosyncrasies of the job. I could actually go an hour or more without anything terrible happening. In that hot, cramped, hectic kitchen, I was serving a purpose. Without me, sheet trays wouldn't get scraped. Dishes wouldn't get done. I liked to imagine that without me at my post, things in the kitchen would slow down, that the smooth operation of a crew who could, on a good night, serve out a couple hundred handmade pizzas would suffer.

Granted, without me there would've also been fewer messes, fewer catastrophic floods, fewer mushroom clouds of yeasty steam belching out of that damn ancient dish machine when some molecule of unscraped dough caused it to puke its guts up all over the floor and cease working for a half hour. I was becoming a skilled operator. I was becoming *important*. And if not important, at least it was nice to be expected somewhere.

Professional kitchens on the high end of the industry are staffed by small, private and extraordinarily well-trained armies and organized (in the best cases) along military lines. There are gods and generals, lieutenants and foot soldiers, all with vital jobs to do. But on the low end, kitchens are run like machines with people there only to serve the process, to carry out the necessary steps of fabrication whereby a bunch of produce, meat and dry stock is put into one end and, in short order, is turned into a pizza (or a cheeseburger or a churro or a sandwich) at the other. There is very little thought involved. No deviation from the process is allowed. At Ferrara's, dough was made the way it was because that was the way dough was made. Sauce was strained because the sauce needed straining. Beautifully circular logic, pat and simple.

And yet, those who work to service the machinery of production are not mindless automatons. Just the opposite. To be useful, you have to be a *smart* automaton. You have to be adaptable and always prepared to acquire new skills—sometimes in a very large hurry. Everything you learn today is based on something you learned yesterday, on the utilization of skills and reflexes hammered into you over weeks and years.

So I learned and I adapted. I became a better dough scraper so that the dish machine would upchuck with less frequency. With the dish machine upchucking less, I made less of a mess of the floors. With the floors less messy, I had more time for scraping trays.

See? A beautiful system.

Now, when the dish machine chugged to a stinking, sweaty halt, I could diagnose the problem with authority (gunk in the thingama- jig), decide on an effective course of action (first, kick machine; sec- ond, yell at machine; third, clean thingamajig) and effect repairs with expediency.

Being better at my job also gave me more time to escape the clamor and stand on the back step smoking cigarettes with Ange and the other cooks. Being outside got me, at least temporarily, out of the heat of the kitchen, and that was a big motivator. It also got me away from the kitchen radio, which was forever tuned to a station that, near as I could tell, played only one song that was twelve hours long, sung by a gay Italian man who'd recently been punched in the mouth, and prominently featured an accordion being played by a spastic and tone-deaf monkey.

After my first week's work at Ferrara's, a surprising thing hap- pened. There was a second one.

And I don't mean that there was a Friday, followed by a couple beers with Midge and Jimmy from accounts payable, a nice weekend of relaxation spent lounging on the couch, then a slow drift down into another Monday-morning commute.

No, there was Friday and Friday's work (differentiated from my first four days by its being as busy in one night as it had been in the last four all put together) and Friday's smoke on the back steps with Ange, and then, just like every previous day, there was Ange saying, "Come back tomorrow."

I remember thinking that perhaps the old man was addled. It was hot in that kitchen, after all. It'd been a very busy night. And Ange was, to my teenager's eyes, about three hundred years old. I thought maybe he'd forgotten it was Friday.

If I close my eyes now, I can actually see that little whelp of a fifteen-year-old me standing there on the back step beside Ange, about to utter six of the stupidest words he'd ever said. In my head, it's a black-and-white photo, the tall and ropy flour-dusted master in his white T-shirt and glasses towering, exhausted and despairingly, beside the pubescent apprentice with his stained tank top and over-large apron hanging down to his ankles—a picture not unlike the kind one might find hung on the wall of some midcity Italian theme restaurant serving unlimited breadsticks and Alfredo sauce from a bag. I can see me thinking, chewing carefully over my words, not sure exactly how to say what I'm about to say, until gently, stupidly and not without a little chiding humor in my voice, I simply spit it out: "Ange, it's Friday. Tomorrow's the weekend."

And Ange, he takes a long drag off his cigarette, then he sighs—the kind of sigh only a man who's been working every night for three hundred years can utter.

"Yeah," he says. "And the peoples got to eat on weekends, too."

The peoples got to eat. That pretty much summed up how my life was going to go for the next fifteen years.

AFTER A FEW WEEKS, I finally figured out that when Angelo said, "Come back tomorrow," it wasn't an order. It was a negotiation. If I needed a day off (provided it wasn't a Friday, Saturday or Sunday), all I had to do was ask or say, "No, Ange. I'll see you the day after. I got some stuff to do."

And by the time I'd figured that out, I wasn't just scraping trays and washing dishes. Rather than rolling in at a leisurely 4:30 or 5:00 in the evening, I was coming directly from school. I'd be at the back door by 3:15, having smoked two cigarettes on the way. And now I'd walk right in. With all but one of the ovens cold, the kitchen would seem downright chilly. Without the phone ringing and the cooks working and the pizzas coming and going, it felt almost placid—the antithetical calm of the house-not-yet-awake.

In these soft, cozy moments either Ange or Natalie would further my education by instructing me in my new duties. I would be told, for example, that from the way I used a mop, I'd apparently been raised in a barn by brain-damaged hillbillies. I just couldn't get the whole figure-eight swirl down no matter how many times Natalie showed me. When I mopped, it took almost an hour and the floor looked worse when I was done than when I'd started. When she mopped, it looked like she was dancing. She could do the whole floor, front and back, in about eight minutes, and when *she* was done, the floor wasn't just clean, it looked as though she'd laid and sealed new cement in her wake.

In frustration at my mopping abilities, Ange would send me off to fix the toilet in the bathroom. Which was funny because I knew less about plumbing than I did about mopping and I'm fairly sure I was the one who'd broken the toilet in the first place. The first time Ange had sent me in to see why the water wouldn't stop running, I'd taken the top off the tank, jiggled the little floaty thing, and the chain had snapped. I fixed it with a bent paper clip and never told Ange about it. After that, it broke once or twice a week, and every time I refixed it, Ange would look at me like I was some sort of toilet savant.

Actually, he looked at me like I was a walking coupon for $89 off a plumbing-service call, but whatever. A new chain costs about five bucks at any hardware store, but I kinda liked there being at least one thing I could be depended on to do right.

Ange taught me to turn the dough every afternoon—to take the young trays of first-risen dough from the cooler, scrape off each ball, and work it inside out with my hands. I remember him showing me how it was done, standing behind me (*towering* over me, all corded with hard muscles like beef jerky), then taking my wrists and making me do it myself. He would turn my hands just so when they needed to turn, training them with surprising delicacy to do a thing that his own hands knew to do without him even thinking. I remember the flour that dusted the dark hair on his forearms, the smell of his cigarettes, and the feel of the cold, leathery skin of the dough being slowly turned back inside itself; the strength of it, the elasticity, the chalky smell of flour cut by the bloom of the yeast, then the damp shininess of a finished ball set back on the tray, showing its newest, best skin to the world while it rested.

Natalie taught me how to assemble pizza boxes and would race me for fun. We would take a hundred boxes each—first one to finish wins—and she'd promise that if I ever beat her, she'd give me a raise. I would tell her I didn't need a raise. She would laugh, knowing she was in absolutely no danger of ever having to pay out. She'd regularly beat me by forty or fifty boxes (even when she had to stop in the middle to answer the phone or go to the store to pick up tomatoes), and even then I had the feeling she was going easy on me.

One day, Ange called me over to the prep table. He set down a flat of buttons (a box, low-sided and long, holding about ten pounds of mushrooms) and a knife on the cutting board and asked if I knew what to do. I'd been watching the cooks, so I said sure. I took out a mushroom, held it between my fingers, picked up the knife and went to town.

Ange stopped me after one, laying a hand on my wrist and tenderly taking the knife away.

"I just see a thing," he said. "I see that's a very bad idea, I think. Why not you go fix the bathroom."

I remember him standing at the prep table on the slow afternoons before the first dinner hit would come in; standing and swaying gently back and forth with a pack of Marlboros rolled in the sleeve of his T-shirt, a cigarette hanging from his lip, ash dangling precariously over the cutting board. Without looking, he could cut anything. His hand and his knife would move impossibly fast, the *tok tok tok* of the blade against the cutting board like a triple-time metronome, unwavering and sustained. And the whole time, he'd be smiling, singing quietly along under his breath with the never-ending song on the kitchen radio—a duet with the lisping Italian and his accordion-playing monkey.

I wanted, someday, to be that good with a knife. I wanted to be Angelo-fast. I wanted his hands, and though I didn't know where he went in his head when he sliced mushrooms or cored peppers, I wanted to see that place for myself, too.

Though it was apparent to Ange that I couldn't be trusted with a knife (at least not if he wanted to be able to send me home to my parents with all my fingers still attached), the job of shredding mozzarella did eventually fall to me.

The cheese came in ten-pound blocks shrink-wrapped in thick plastic covered with seals and declarations of its Italian heritage. The wrappings had to be split and peeled off, which I did with a butcher's saber—because when a kid looks to be in imminent danger of doing himself harm with an eight-inch chef's knife, the obvious solution is to arm him with a curved, hook-bladed, twenty-inch machete designed for the swift deconstruction of whole sides of beef.* I would joyously hack the cheese logs into manageable chunks, strip off the plastic and shred them through the attachment that screwed to the front of the massive floor-mount Hobart mixer.

My negligible fifteen-year-old's weight was barely enough to force down the handle that introduced the cheese to the shredding die, necessitating that I stand on tiptoe and actually muscle it through. I got big at Ferrara's thanks to that cheese, my own arms and shoulders growing muscled and hard as if they were carved out of pale, freckled wood.

Which was handy when, a couple months into my stint with Ange and Natalie, I was cornered by some older teenagers in the alley/parking lot that Ferrara's shared with Giehl's Deli next door (called Cooper Dell by generations of students who'd passed through Dake Middle and West Irondequoit High School just down Cooper Road in my hometown of Rochester, New York) and asked to remove my coat.

It wasn't a mugging, just play—just the bigger, stronger and older preying on the younger, smaller and weaker as if Cooper Dell, the alley, this whole stretch of glass- and cigarette-butt-littered real estate on the corner of Cooper and Titus was just an extension of the schoolyard and hallways down the road. Which was more or less the truth.

"Nice coat, Sheehan. Why don't you let me see it a minute?"

The biggest guy took a step closer. His friends were sniggering into their fists in the background, though I was only peripherally aware of them as an audience.

---

*Like any chef—current or former—I have a creepy fascination with knives, and like all chefs I came upon this infatuation early. Getting to spend my days playing with knives was a big part of what kept me going through the first years of my career, and until my late twenties my knives were the most valuable things I owned—worth, on average, triple what my car was at any given time.

I said no. Not defiantly, but incredulously, disbelievingly—like why would I take off my coat to let someone else see it? I grinned at the joke of it. A smile that no doubt looked like a challenge to the older boy's authority on this particular stretch of pavement.

"You saying no to me, *Sheehan*?" the older guy asked, spitting my name now and advancing another step. He was maybe a head taller than me, had long, thick arms, was wearing a shiny black jacket with a flaming muscle car silk-screened onto the back, and had random patches of stiff black hair on his face sprouting from amid fields of volcanic acne. He smelled like mayonnaise. I remember that, too. "Gimme that coat."

He pushed me then, palms popping flat into the hard softballs of my shoulders. Only then did I finally realize what this was. Every fight I'd ever seen (and the couple amateur tussles I'd been in prior to this moment) had all begun just like this. The push was like a flirtation before the main event. Like foreplay. My job, as I understood it, was now either to push the other guy back if I felt I was up to it, or to cry. To give in.

Instead, I skipped all reciprocal back-and-forth and any pretense at showmanship and just punched the guy in the head.

Frankly, it surprised both of us. I felt the bones in my hand crackle as I tagged him high on the cheek or forehead, then did it again, right ahead of the pain, and caught him in the eye and the bridge of the nose. My third punch was ineffectual as the older boy was already falling, staggering back from the point of impact, but my wild hook grazed his mouth, the bony knuckle of my ring finger catching on his protruding front teeth and splitting open like I'd punched a knife. The blood went everywhere.

And then it was done.

I walked away, shrugging the coat around my shoulders and turning toward the yellow glow of the streetlights at the alley's mouth, trailing blood from my hand.

Six twisting residential blocks away, I cut through a parking lot and hopped a fence into the playground of my old elementary school. I climbed up onto a splintery wood fort that looked as though it'd been constructed out of massive Lincoln Logs, lay down and chain-smoked three cigarettes until I got dizzy. Then I inspected my hand. I spat on my knuckles and smudged some of the caked blood away, finding the place where the tooth had cut me—a flap of skin lifted away from the bone as cleanly as if it'd been done with a scalpel. I pressed it into place and held it there until it stuck, then went wide-eyed at the pain when I tried to make a fist—two of my knuckles popping grudgingly back into place with a sensation unlike anything I'd ever felt before. A bone in the back of my hand buzzed uncomfortably. I wouldn't learn the name for that until years later: boxer's fracture. And by that time, I would've had plenty more.

When I got home, my mom cleaned and bandaged my hand. I told her I'd cut it at work and had been sent home early, even though it was late. I hoped she wouldn't call Ferrara's to check on my story, but Ange and Natalie spoke such broken English that they made the perfect alibi for almost anything.

ONE DAY, I QUIT. I don't know why except that maybe I'd finally just caused enough damage to these poor people and their business and was feeling bad about it. Or maybe the charm of my being the new guy had simply worn off and I was starting to actually be blamed for the things I was doing wrong.

After nine or ten months, I still hadn't learned how to toss a crust (which was only ever done for show anyhow) or, more usefully, how to stretch one across the lightly floured work board, mauling it with knuckles and fingertips until it thinned—more like sculpting than cooking. The only pizzas I'd ever been allowed to assemble were my own, and they were universally awful: too wet, too heavy, lopsided, unevenly risen—just bad in every conceivable way a pizza could be. There was an art to it, and if Angelo had the hands of an old master—a Monet or a Michelangelo—then I was just the kid drawing mustaches on the girls in the Freedent ads and crude pictures of stick figures humping.

Recently I'd graduated to occasional lessons from Ange on the proper implementation of the pizza stick—he no doubt seeing the advantage of having someone to watch the ovens for him in slow moments when he wanted to duck out for a smoke or to answer the phone, and me taking to it like a baby with a barbecue fork. Whenever the opportunity was offered, I would charge the ovens, plant myself squarely before their open, blistering maws and shuffle pizzas like crazy until someone made me stop.

But it wasn't enough. There was a hierarchy in the Ferrara's kitchen, one that valued things like talent and practice and skill and seniority over pure, blind desire. First there was Angelo, then Natalie, then the cooks, the family members who came and went with incomprehensible irregularity, the sporadic new hires who'd work for two days, a week, then vanish forever. And then, all the way at the bottom, there was me: dough-scraper and toilet-fixer, second-string cheese-shredder in my jeans and T-shirt.

The system at Ferrara's was not unlike that of a Japanese sushi kitchen run in the traditional Edo style, where one's potential value is based as much on patience and absolute loyalty as it is on desire. When training to become a sushi chef, a young apprentice might spend two or three years making rice. He'll never touch a fish. He'll never pick up a knife. Just rice, for month after month after month, until he knows rice like he knows his own pulse, his own breath.

Probably that apprentice will be washing dishes and sweeping floors and fixing the toilet, too. Probably he will carry a lot of tea. But rice—that's the important part. He will cook rice and scrape rice, carry rice, touch and taste and smell rice until rice becomes his entire world. He will live not just with rice, but *in* rice; in a universe made of grains. And rice will, at first, be fascinating because it's rice and rice is pretty cool stuff. It's finicky, fickle, as varied in its individuality as stars or snowflakes are, and does not brook idiocy or lack of care.

Soon, though, rice will become dull to the apprentice. Common. He will grow bored with rice, come to hate the rice because the rice represents the entirety of his labor. Then, one day, the rice will simply cease to be. It'll be just a thing, an extension of the apprentice's consciousness, requiring no thought or consideration. He'll be able to work magic with it then without even trying.

At which point he'll be handed the knife, shown the fish, and the practice will begin all over again.

The great sushi chefs, when they make hand rolls, the number of rice grains in them never varies by more than a few. They all point in the same direction. The chef knows how long he can and can't hold the fish because he knows the temperature of his blood and how quickly the warmth of his palm will start to cook the fish. A great pizza man will portion the dough by eye, rarely being off by more than a quarter ounce, one ball to another. His crusts will all stretch to the same circumference. They will rise with a precision that borders on legerdemain.

This knowledge and skill, this almost meditative expertise, is what is bought by the sort of dedication demanded of kitchen apprentices everywhere. Japanese, French, Italian—it's all the same. Desire is good. Desire is important because desire is all that you'll have to get you through the rough patches. Hard work? Also important. And the work will be impossibly hard sometimes because as much as apprenticeships are about training, they're also about weeding out the pussies, the bed wetters, the casual amateurs. Being a chef is the greatest job in the world—better than being a candy-taster, a Ferrari test-track driver or Santa Claus. If it wasn't hard, everyone would be one. So it's not enough to give only your time or your muscle to the job. That's just a given. *Of course* you're going to give that. It's not enough just to want it, because everyone around you will want it. If they didn't, they wouldn't be there, wherever there might be.

Most of all, the job requires your patience. First, scrape the trays. Run the dishes. Mop the floors. Turn the dough. First, make the rice. Everything that comes later—all wisdom—will come of these simple acts. And if you do right—if you learn your lessons, take your lumps, dedicate yourself to something larger and finer than yourself—in return you get perfect, beautiful crusts. You get red sauce that is the model of all other red sauces and a neighborhood pizza joint in the suburbs of a dying rust-belt city, a family restaurant that'll someday be turned into a chain pizzeria after you're gone and forgotten. I'm sorry, but there's nothing more promised than that. There are no guarantees. You might end up in The Bigs with the heavy hitters, the name guys on TV and in the bookstores. But probably you won't. You might end up like Angelo Ferrara, remembered fondly by some smart-mouth fuck like me, elevated, perhaps, beyond his due just because he didn't fire me when I deserved it.

MAYBE I'M OVERROMANTICIZING my time at Ferrara's—remembering it as better, sweeter, more moving and affecting than it really was. But I don't think so. I look back now from a distance of about two decades and I can still see the flour on Angelo's arms, the glasses pushed up on his forehead, the shine on the balls of freshly turned dough. I can still hear Natalie's voice in my head—her standing at the counter and trying to calm an irate customer whose pizza is taking too long, saying, "Sorry, we have a new Jason working today. Is okay. Go. Sit."

I can remember the heat—different from the heat I'd come to know as my natural environment in years to come, wetter and more fierce because it was so new to me—and the smell of the stone ovens working. I can remember blood on my hands and the milky-sour taste of good mozzarella (chunks of it pulled right off the damp blocks and popped into my mouth whenever I was hungry); the smell of yeast, alive and everywhere; accordion music and the supernal calm of winter nights on the back steps with cigarette smoke rising up like breath through the falling snow. Ferrara's is long gone now, replaced by a goddamn Domino's, of all fucking things. And I'm long gone from that time and place, too, replaced by just an older and marginally wiser version of that kid who dressed like Lou Gramm on his first day of work. But I remember it all like the live electricity of a fresh wound.

And that's what love is, isn't it?

LEARNING CURVE

got work as a cashier in a neighborhood grocery store and was fired shortly after for gross incompetence and for stealing. I wore a bow tie and a cummerbund and sold videos at the mall. I finished high school and painted houses with a bunch of pot smokers, burnouts and scam artists who were constantly on vacations courtesy of workmen's comp. Granted, they didn't really *go* anywhere, but would just take two weeks' pay on a bogus (but hard to disprove) back injury and sit around their dumpy apartments in their bathrobes watching game shows and tending to the marijuana plants in their closets.

By the time I was seventeen, I had a steady girlfriend who would eventually break my heart by going off to college and promptly fucking the guy who ran her orientation group. I'd also found a nice group of juvenile delinquents to call friends who'd take me in during my repeated attempts at leaving home. At one point, a whole bunch of us pooled our scant resources and procured for ourselves a stately old four-bedroom Victorian in downtown Rochester, just off Monroe Avenue, the city's high-water mark for punk rock, body piercing and freak culture.

Had we been even slightly more shrewd, it might've occurred to us that the place was curiously undervalued even for being just a couple doors down from a notorious mods-and-rockers neighborhood bar and facing a street better known for its tattoo parlors, drug deals and casual violence than any residential charm. But we were far too busy arguing over who was going to get what room, where the Nintendo was going to go, whether the bathtub was big enough to hold a full keg (plus ice) or were we going to have to start buying ponies, and where all our various Indian tapestries, incense holders, futons, blown guitar amps and thrift-store lamps would fit. On our first night, we were chased shrieking into the street by a veritable flood of fat, glossy brown cockroaches.

We jumped the lease, restrained ourselves (though only barely) from lighting the place on fire and split. Anything already moved into the house was called a loss and I ended up living in my car down by Lake Ontario for a while, sleeping out sometimes on the first green of a nearby golf course. It was summer so I called it camping, and a few years later, when my not-yet-wife, Laura, would come looking for me in Rochester in hopes of digging me out of whatever weird hole I'd crawled into, the beach and the first green were two of the places I took her. To me, it was like bringing her home—something that, at the time, I was unable to articulate, which was just one of the many reasons why she quickly left again, leaving me where she'd found me to ripen yet for a few more seasons.

I was trying to find myself. Anthony Bourdain once said that no one is born a chef; that the white jacket and solid black exec pants must be earned—preferably the hard way—and that people who tell you different are either fooling themselves or trying to sell you something. But, he continued, while no one is born with cooking "in their blood," there *are* those born and raised knowing how to eat well.

Personally, I disagree simply because I've never met anyone born to the table. Sure, I know people raised with money: people who grew up with family trips to Paris, fine meals in cloistered dining rooms and "educational" summers in Madrid or Baden-Baden. I know chefs who were the sons of chefs, who suckled on truffles and could use a knife before they could write their own names, others who grew up taking their meals from their home gardens and understood "slow food" not as a political movement, but simply as a way of life. But ask them, and every one with taste (rare enough) will talk of their coming to the table the way some people talk about losing their virginity—a combination of nervous anticipation, flat-out terror and a what-am-I-supposed-to-do-with-this-now? sense of utter, mortifying confusion.

Learning to eat well is the same as learning to fuck well or cook well. It's all about experimentation, error, humility before beauty, and training the senses to know good from bad. A real chef has to earn his stripes, no doubt. But so, too, I think, must the young gourmand. It's not enough to be bought a hooker on your eighteenth birthday. You've got to know what to do with her. It's not enough to be handed the lobster roll, plate of dripping, garlic-laden snails or Carolina barbecue. You've got to know where it came from and why. More important, perhaps, you've got to know where *you* came from and how you ended up where you are.

So there I was—a blue-collar, rust-belt diner kid; a beans-and-weenies, steak-and-potatoes simpleton. I knew nothing of food or restaurants or cooking or cuisine. At the time, I didn't even much care. I never went to France, never saw my grandmothers cook, never took much notice of what my own mother did in the kitchen every night. I didn't collect cookbooks, I collected comics. Unlike so many of my contemporaries who can go all Proust-and-his-madeleines over virtually anything from mom's scratch puttanesca to veal Orloff aboard the *QEII*, I have no ripe memory of any one particular dish or sauce or recipe that can, just by its bare mention, transport me home again. Whatever food epiphanies would eventually come to me were either years off yet or had come softly, to lie silently ticking close to my heart like little bombs with decades left on their timers.

Sure, Mom could fry a nice pork chop. She scalloped a mean potato and would occasionally become inspired to whip up thirty or forty gallons of the richest, most murderous cream of broccoli soup ever made. But through all of my childhood, food in our family had been exactly what it'd become to so many other families cut off from their culinary roots and traditions by feud, diaspora and the American Dream of suburban tract housing, a big TV and dinner from a can. It was just fuel, just sustenance on almost any given day. On holidays and special occasions when food was suddenly expected to be given primacy in the social ritual, we came to it like lapsed Catholics to an Easter service: with a small sense of wonder and awe at the fancy clothes and strangeness of it all.

When my dad would suddenly get an urge to fire up the backyard barbecue grill for the Fourth of July or Labor Day, there was always the possibility that—having forgotten some vital step in the preparation of the grill—he would blow himself up. On Thanksgiving morning when my mom would pull out the heavy plastic bag containing the disassembled pieces of the antique, hand-cranked food mill she used to make stuffing, we would all crowd around it like a family of chimps trying to assemble a bicycle.

The most commonly used spice in our kitchen when I was growing up was a gigantic tub of generic onion salt, which my dad put on almost everything, from breakfast eggs and potatoes to dinner steak and potatoes and plates of corned-beef hash out of the can—which is still one of my guiltiest culinary pleasures.

One of the sweetest, most endearing memories I have of my father as a young man was watching him come down the stairs in a stiff suit and tie, wearing his uncomfortable shoes, looking always as if he were headed to his prom or a funeral but, in any case, smiling and looking like a totally different man on those rare nights when he and my mom would go out for dinner without my brother and me. This hipped me to the idea that going out to eat was something special, something adult and powerful and meaningful. I remember the astringent, manly hospital smell of the cologne he wore. The clean pink of his skin when he was freshly shaved. The way his hands—calloused and battered and scarred, nails blacked out with blood blisters—looked so out of place poking from the cuffs of his fancy jacket.

Because the only restaurants I'd had any experience with at the time were diners, liminal, half-scary "family restaurants" filled with cheap wood paneling and cigarette smoke or fast-food outlets where you spoke your order into a giant clown head, I was worried for my dad that he'd feel out of place, overdressed; that he'd get made fun of. But I kept it to myself because their leaving always meant that the babysitter was coming, and our babysitter was a total pushover who let me eat ice cream for dinner.

FUNNY STORY: In the years before Laura and I were married, while we were still living in sin in various spots around the country, we would always try to fly back East for one of the two major holidays, Thanksgiving or Christmas. Obviously, we'd spent time visiting both sets of parents during the nonholiday season, and one of the things that always worried Laura about going and staying with my folks was the way they ate—which is to say, hardly at all. My parents are small people. They got together and made more small people: my brother and me. The house is small, the rooms are small, and at meals the portions are small. Always have been. Growing up, we all ate like tiny, wounded birds. It was just something I'd become accustomed to.

But holidays were different. At holidays (at least the way I remembered them), we ate from sunup till sundown, gorging ourselves nonstop, barely even pausing to breathe.

"Just wait," I told Laura while preparing for our first Christmas with my folks. "If there's one thing I can guarantee, it's that there'll be no shortage of things to eat."

Now, I don't want to give the wrong impression here. It's not like Laura is a big eater either. And I don't want anyone to infer from my words that she sits around all day eating bonbons or Crisco right out of the tub. When I say she was worried about there not being enough to eat, it was a very reasonable concern on her part because she'd already experienced Sheehan-style portion controls: two chicken breasts split among five people, a small ice cream bowl full of mashed potatoes for the table, an iceberg salad dressed from a bottle of Thousand Island that'd expired during the Carter administration— that kind of thing.

And I was nothing but reassuring, explaining to her over and over again how my folks would lay in enough supplies for a week and that it would all be consumed in one massive, gluttonous orgy on Christmas day. There would be baked goods and pastries, baked ham, sliced ham, mountains of mashed potatoes, bacon and eggs, more ham, cream of broccoli soup, potato salad, vegetables, ham. I described it like the miracle of the loaves and fishes, like the Christmas feast at the end of *A Christmas Carol*, complete with the biggest turkey in the city of London and figgy pudding for all.

She was skeptical, but took me at my word. It was the last time she ever made that mistake.

We came up from Laura's folks' place outside Philadelphia, driving in on Christmas Eve through the sort of hostile winter storm that blows through the area every year around the holidays yet never fails to shock and horrify all Western New Yorkers—most of whom have been born with a kind of weather autism that makes them incapable of remembering bad weather from one season to the next and unable to see the patterns that even dogs can. As a result, we arrived late and went to bed hungry because dinner was already done and everyone was exhausted.

"No problem," I told Laura. "Just wait until tomorrow morning."

Following me up the stairs, she nodded trustingly, gnawing a cold crust of dinner roll. We went to bed.

Christmas morning we woke to the smell of pine needles and cinnamon and fresh-brewed coffee (the one thing that my folks always did have plenty of on hand). Heading downstairs, I asked her if she was hungry. She gave me a look not unlike the looks I imagine were on the faces of those Uruguayan rugby players who crashed in the Andes and went cannibal.

"Don't worry," I said. "Let's go have breakfast."

One small coffee cake split five ways. One egg per person and two strips of bacon. Enough coffee for thirty cups apiece, orange juice served in doll glasses, and white toast thinly veneered in some bitter spread made from whipped olive oil.

Lunch was last night's cold ham leftovers made into sandwiches, which we missed because I'd dragged Laura out to try to get bagel dogs (a hot dog with cheese cooked inside a bagel) from a shop I remembered having good ones. It being Christmas Day, the shop was closed. No surprise. We ate candy bars from the gas station and made *Chronicles of Narnia* jokes about Edmund selling his soul for a handful of Turkish delight.

For dinner, my parents served the world's smallest turkey, roughly the size of three starlings stapled together, and roasted, limp green beans from a can, cream of broccoli soup and sides served in dishes better suited for dwarfs. We finished with one pie cut into a dozen tiny slivers.

"See?" I told her in bed that night. "Didn't I tell you there'd be enough to eat?" She had to cover her face with a pillow just so her bitter laughter wouldn't wake the neighbors.

The next night, Laura and I went out for dinner. And now, whenever we go to visit Rochester for Christmas, we pack as if for an extended polar expedition with no guarantee of resupply, loading down the bottom of one of our backpacks with snack foods, hiding beef jerky and PowerBars and granola and dried fruit in all our pockets.

I REMEMBER BEING LITTLE, watching cartoons on the living room floor and eating cold SpaghettiOs from the can, and my wonder at the microwave oven (one of the first on our block) Dad brought home from work one day.* I was amazed at how fast the thing could cook a potato. So was my mom. We ate baked potatoes for dinner for a week straight. Baked potatoes and bacon because she also no longer had to worry about hauling out the skillet, waiting for it to heat, the oil spattering all over the stovetop, and disposing of the drippings when I wasn't looking because I'd eat the stuff on bread if not watched like a hawk.

I will swear up and down that this whole cooking thing that I got myself into (and this whole food-writing thing that came later) was

---

*He was a mechanic and a traveling repairman for Sears—hence the beat-up hands. I was always in awe of his hands when I was a kid, always wanted a pair of my own someday just like his.

all just one big, colossal mistake, the unintended consequence of precocity, poor career planning and my absolute unwillingness to wear a tie or work someplace where my calling someone a goddamn cocksucker and threatening them with a really big knife would be considered grounds for anything more serious than a five-minute time-out on the loading dock.

I will tell you and anyone else who'll listen that I should've been an assembly-line worker, a machinist, the assistant manager of the corner Gas-n-Sip or an orthodontist. Orthodontists wear white coats just like chefs do. Orthodontists and chefs are both concerned about what's going into their customers' mouths. But you know what orthodontists have that (most) chefs don't? Boats. Big ones.*

I just didn't have it in me to look at teeth all day. But then I would've also sworn that nothing in particular was driving me toward the so-called culinary arts either; nothing in my makeup or personal history that had me kinked as a sensualist, a gastronaut, a fucking *foodie*.

And yet, and yet, and yet . . .

I had a whole second secret life even back then that I kept almost completely to myself; closeted like a small-town queer, hidden like a third nipple or a taste for stiff leather miniskirts and spanking.

When I was still little, every time Mom would take me shopping I would demand that she buy me cheese. A different cheese each time: aged cheddars, pearl mozzarella, individually wrapped Kraft singles, wedges of hard Parm, chèvre, baby Goudas in foil, Velveeta, expensive Muenster with that cool orange rind and farmer's cheeses, the stronger the better. It would be years before I would taste my first Brie or Vacherin or artisanal bleu, but it amazed me even then that one thing—"cheese"—could taste so many different ways, and yet the "cheese" traditionally employed in my mom's kitchen all tasted the same. Ditto "bread" (generic white sandwich) and "chocolate"

---

*For a brief time my mom had a serious hard-on for me becoming an orthodontist, because she knew an orthodontist through work. And do you know what that orthodontist had? All my parents' money and a really big motherfucking boat.

(Hershey's) and "butter" (read *margarine*) and the mayonnaise that wasn't mayonnaise at all, but some vile, whipped fluff called salad dressing that also wasn't salad dressing because my mom's refrigerator was where bottles of actual meant-to-go-on-top-of-lettuce salad dressing went to die.

In high school I would regularly ditch my last class before lunch so I'd have time to run down to the grocery store a few blocks away for sushi. Yeah, that's right: grocery-store sushi. Sometimes three or four times a week. And I was lucky. Growing up in Rochester meant growing up in the hometown of Wegmans, probably the best small family supermarket chain in the country.

Danny Wegman (who would later employ me during one of the darker points in my career) was and is something of a visionary. His stores were monuments, huge palaces of food where someone could find not only anything he wanted, but ten or twenty or thirty *other* things that he didn't even know existed but now must immediately taste. Tamales in a can. Plugrá. Irish brandy butter (which, just behind proper whiskey and the Pogues, is the greatest contribution of my people to world culture). Prosciutto. Japanese shrimp puffs. Focaccia. All of these things I had for the first time thanks to Wegmans. Same with all those cheeses. And grocery-store sushi packed in little black plastic clamshell to-go boxes with a smear of pasty wasabi and a strip of fake plastic grass for garnish. Smoked eel and *ebi*, *tamago*, *tekka maki* and California rolls—I would buy the box and eat my fish walking, picking rolls up with my fingers, mauling them in a puddle of soy or (horror) cocktail sauce. Obviously, it was terrible sushi— tasting, when it tasted of anything at all, like refrigerated air, shelf stabilizers and the rubber they use to make spatula blades.

But I loved it anyway, which fucked me up for years when it came to eating real sushi, because my best, most powerful memories of what sushi was supposed to taste like came from those afternoons strolling across the Wegmans parking lot, headed back toward school, jamming mushy rice and sticky nori and fake crab greedily into my mouth; rushing to finish it all before anyone saw me because this was still Rochester, after all, and in my neighborhood, fish got eaten only two ways: fried on Fridays with chips and washed down with six or eight Guinnesses so God didn't smite your heathen ass for accidentally having a cheeseburger, or caught on a fishing trip, gutted, scaled and burned to carbon on a backyard grill.

So even though Danny Wegman, with his big-city money and highfalutin notions, might offer raw fish for sale, it didn't mean anyone was supposed to actually *eat* the stuff. Do that and probably there was something wrong with you. Something shameful, to which the consumption of raw fish and "Oriental food" was just one clue.

I bought copies of *Gourmet* magazine on the sly, surreptitiously, like I was buying porno, like that scene from *American Graffiti* where the geek tries to buy whiskey.

"Can I help you, young man?"

"Why, yes, good shopkeep. I believe you can. I just need a few things here, so let me see . . . I'll take a carton of cigarettes, that home enema kit, a copy of *Screw*, a tube of Anal Eze, a bottle of Ten High, a pack of those Zig-Zags, some tampons, pocket comb . . . andacopy-of*Gourmet*magazineplease."

"What was that last one, son?"

"Copyof*Gourmet*magazineplease."

"One more time? I can't hear you."

"*Gourmet* magazine! A fucking copy of *Gourmet*! Just put it in the bag, old man. And stop looking at me like that, okay? It's not for me. It's for my"—*mom-dad-brother-grandma-friend*—"for my cousin. My girl cousin. From Canada. Magazines cost more up there, you know. Oh, and how 'bout throw in a twelve-pack of condoms, too. Ribbed, please."

ONE WEEK, quite to my surprise, the folks announced that we were going off to New York City on vacation. As with so much else in my life, I remember nothing about the trip except dinner—the tuxedoed waiters at the hotel restaurant, French service all the way, the whisper of soft-soled shoes on oxblood carpets and the flutter of hands suddenly appearing over my shoulder to clear plates and silver and drinks. I remember being told I could order anything I wanted and the way my parents—my plain old day-in/day-out, everyday suburbanite parents—looked like royalty under those lights, in the candle glow and warm halo of fawning attention from the staff. It was magic. The lobster came under a silver dome. The little pats of butter were molded into pictures of mermaids curled around their own tails. Desserts (which we didn't order) were wheeled around the dining room on a cart alongside cheeses even Danny Wegman had probably never heard of.

I'm sure I was a little bastard that whole trip, but for the two- or three-hour stretch we spent in that restaurant, I was happy—idiosyncratically at ease and engaged, and perhaps even smiling. All of which no doubt had my parents completely flummoxed and wondering whether I'd been hitting up the minibar when they weren't looking.

WHEN I WAS SIXTEEN OR SEVENTEEN, I convinced a bunch of my friends that we should all bake cookies and give them away as Christmas presents. Among my friends, this was not an easy sell. We could use my mom's kitchen, I told them. We'd save a bunch of money not having to buy flowers or stuffed animals or jewelry for girlfriends. Besides, I argued, chicks dig cookies, right? This'll get us *laid*.

The truth? I just really wanted to bake cookies. And frankly I was already starting to miss the bash and clamor of a working kitchen, so why not populate one of my own, at least for one day?

Around the same time, I started boosting my parents' car in the middle of the night—waiting until long after they'd gone to bed, then easing my way out the front door, going down the steps like a suburban ghost, popping the family station wagon into neutral and pushing the behemoth halfway up the street before daring to start the engine.

Sometimes I'd just drive. Sometimes I'd go to the diners and doughnut shops to hang out among the righteous drunks, the old men, taxi drivers and criminals. But most of the time I'd beeline it from my neighborhood in West Irondequoit into the heart of the city, to Hercules Chicken and Ribs, for barbecue.

The place was beautiful, all lit windows and bodies and clouds of thick, heavy, oily smoke; *jumping* at one, two o'clock in the morning, filled with big women in enormous hats and men dressed like fire-and-brimstone tent preachers gone wrong in sharkskin and leather, gold watches, pinkie rings, silk ties and stack-heeled ankle boots. The awnings were bright yellow and lit from within by some unnatural conflagration: kerosene fire maybe, a million captive fireflies, or just some kind of terrible static voodoo that was, in any event, irresistible to me, calling me down like a moth to a porch light. There was broken glass in the parking lot, bullet holes in the ceiling, and music drowned out by voices drowned out by laughter drowned out by shouting drowned out by the buzz in my head of being a kid who'd wandered into a right place that might've looked like a wrong place but was maybe the best place in the world for him just there and just then.

I couldn't quite understand why I wasn't stomped, beaten, thrown out on my ass. And while I have talked and bluffed and wormed and wheedled my way into many strange places since—everything from private Chinese poker clubs and Russian mob bars to locals-only karaoke joints, Ghanaian house restaurants, African goat butchers and the haute palaces of cuisine where my type (whatever the hell that is) are most plainly unwelcome—Hercules was my first.

Mine was the only white face in the house most nights, mine likely the only station wagon in the parking lot and certainly the only car with a stick-on Garfield in the window. I would show up alone, late at night, in a neighborhood that was one of the worst in a city full of bad ones, where most of the doors were boarded up like rotten teeth in a mean smile and even the boxing gym across the street had bars on the windows. And yet, I was unafraid. This was not because I'm some kind of knuckle-dragging badass. I'm about as tough as grilled cheese. But the way I figured, all these people were coming here for a reason. It wasn't to fuck with me. It was because they *knew* something. And I wanted to know what they knew, so I stood in line that first time same as all the rest of them, and ordered chicken and ribs, beans and greens, sweet tea. I waited. And when my food came? Well, then I understood, too.

It was barbecue, the be-all and end-all of American cuisine. And as with Danny Wegman's sushi, I know now that it was *terrible* barbecue, smoked in an old oil drum set up in the parking lot, the fire fed with two-by-fours or particleboard and whatever scrap lumber the pitmen could scrounge on top of what was probably an oakwood fire that made all the meat taste like blood and scotch and acetone. But that didn't matter because it was my first barbecue and I had no idea at the time that it was supposed to taste any different.

Also, this was the only barbecue there was.* It was here and nowhere else, and that was the secret—the thing all these people knew that I didn't. You do what you gotta do and you go where you gotta go for barbecue because once you get barbecue, for five minutes or ten minutes or an hour nothing else matters. You got barbecue. Everything is gonna be all right.

I spent maybe forty-five minutes there my first night and left with smoke in my blood, barbecue sauce in my hair and a lifelong addiction I pray I never shake.

After that, I went to Hercules a lot. The only people who ever even spoke to me were the girls who worked behind the counter and the big, sweating men in broad-shouldered suits who'd take my hand between their hard, dry palms and ask me if I wanted to get to know Jesus.

I'd say sure. But not tonight. And I'd ask if they had barbecue in their heaven since, from my experience, us mick Catholics had only fried fish, casseroles and beer.

---

*This, I've since discovered, was not entirely true. My dad reminded me recently that there was always Country Sweet Chicken & Ribs downtown—a place that made a name for itself (near as I can recall) by dipping all of its meats in a sauce made of honey and crushed red pepper flakes. Terrifying, right? But it was an honest regional barbecue derivative, native (like white hots and Schaller's burgers with hot sauce) only to the greater Rochester area.

"Boy," they'd say, "Jesus was a black man. Of course there's barbecue in heaven. It wouldn't be heaven without."

I WENT AWAY TO COLLEGE IN 1991, right on schedule, following a couple
of my more respectable high school buddies, John and Dan. We'd all
applied to the film school at Ithaca College, just a fast couple hours'
drive south from Rochester. And while this may have been a perfect
fit for them (what with their being smart, responsible, talented and, in
fact, *interested* in the celluloid arts), for me it was unwise in more
ways than I can even count.

But still, it was an out. Or so I thought. The rest of my delinquent
friends weren't doing much of anything. They were all, to a man, waiting around for their still–in–high school girlfriends to graduate, working dead-end jobs for rent and beer money, hanging out down in the
park or by the railroad tracks, drinking plastic bottles of no-brand
bourbon and lighting shit on fire, rolling into the back parking lot at
Ridge Billiards on fumes, trying to sell the stereos from their own
cars—their speakers, their floor mats—for a few bucks' cash to pay
off The Man. Some of them would end up in jail. A couple would be
dead. And most of the rest would simply settle, finding better company among Hooters waitresses and the beauty school dropouts
humping the pole down at the Klassy Cat, bars where they could have
their own personal beer steins hung on the wall and entry-level jobs
at Kodak or Xerox that must've looked both sweet and lifelong until
the day came that they weren't either anymore.

John got into the Roy H. Park School of Communications at
Ithaca College because he'd already been making films for years and
some of them were good.

Dan got into the Park School because he was a great writer, smart,
what Woody Allen would've been had Woody been a short, bespec-
tacled, working-class Polack. Dan's entrance interview, from what I
understand, ran like a tight ten-minute stand-up routine with the
school's representatives playing his unwitting straight men. When it
was done, he probably made them all balloon animals or something.

I got in because I wrote a good essay and because I had a couple letters of recommendation from high school English teachers who (at my suggestion) played me off like some kind of latent Andy Kaufman: brilliant, but wildly unstable and badly in need of the firm, guiding hand of a respectable faculty to keep me on track.

Getting them to write the letters had been an easy sell because they were at least half true (the "wildly unstable" part) and because those kindly teachers and I both saw my onrushing future the same way. At the time, I was just a couple of steps from the parking lot at Ridge Billiards myself.

DURING FRESHMAN ORIENTATION, the college threw an old-fashioned ice cream social. And though, like me, everyone was trying to act as though they were way too cool for that kind of thing, what was funny was watching the ebb and flow of the line as kids away from home for the first time—all flexing their new stick-on personas at each other and trying to come up with these wild, on-the-fly imagined histories of themselves that would free them from whatever they'd been in high school—would slink and sidle up to the counter where the ice cream was, quickly grab a bowl, and spoon it up like each bite was a last, frantic, comforting taste of their rapidly retreating childhoods.

Me? I had three bowls. But then, I really like ice cream.

That night, I think there was a dance, a band, some guy doing terrible David Letterman impressions. I chain-smoked half a pack of cigarettes on the back patio of a cafeteria building, sitting with Dan, who made hard and unusually cruel jokes all night to anyone who'd listen. I met a couple of the guys I'd be living with for the next several months, and all of us drifted off across the quad, hauling up in front of one of the school's picturesque fountains because there were girls there. Then more girls. Then just one girl, sitting close, knees to my knees and actually talking to me—one girl I was no doubt charming the socks off with the way I would smirk and snarl and stare at my boots every time she tried to catch my eye. She would tilt her head and look across at me quizzically through a red-brown fog of barely grown-out curls and I would look away, checking out some unusually shaped pebble on the ground or scrap of trash blowing by. She was pretty. And though I'm not at all shy, I've never really known what to do with pretty girls who want anything whatsoever to do with me.

"I bet I can tell you three things about yourself without even talking to you first," she said.

I shrugged coolly, lips pressed into a thin, tight line.

And then she did and she was right and I was impressed, though I would never have shown it. I'm not going to tell you what the three things were, but suffice it to say, she saw through the layered flannel shirts, torn blue jeans, combat boots and Mohawk to the huddled-up, ice-cream-sticky geek inside me. And that was impressive. I'd worked hard over the summer to finally beat my inner child into a sort of cringing submission. I thought I'd done a pretty good job.

When she was done reading my mind, I snorted, looked up at her (finally), and took a contemplative drag off my four hundredth cigarette of the night. "Okay," I said. "Okay, you're smart. Now if you could just put your feet behind your head, you'd be the perfect woman."

She smiled sweetly. "I can. Want to see?"

FOR WORK-STUDY, I was put into one of the cafeteria kitchens.

I walked in on my first day, ten minutes early, and was horrified. The kitchen was huge and filthy and smelled like an oyster midden buried under a pile of wet, smoldering hair. It looked like a sanitarium with everyone dressed in white smocks, shambling about aimlessly with looks of hopeless desperation on their faces. There were no knives, no pans,* no utensils that weren't blunt and smooth-edged, and, most noticeably, no actual food. What there was in place of food were boxes, bags, cans, bladders, mixes, concentrates, vac-pacs, cryos, pouches, powders, cartons and sacks.

---

*At the time, I didn't recognize hotel pans—the multisize baking and holding vessels cut for use in steam tables—as actual pans, only skillets, sautés and the like.

I found the quote/unquote Food Services Director I'd been instructed to report to, and he handed me a blank name tag, a short-sleeved polyester shirt, a pair of safety scissors with tape-wrapped handles and a hairnet without even looking at me. He pointed to an open shipping box set on one end of a rickety, gimp-legged prep table. The box was full of plastic freezer bags, their thawed, room-temperature contents all wet and red and sloshy.

"Dinner," he said. "Lasagna. Open the bags and pan 'em. Somebody'll be by to ship 'em into the ovens."

"I quit," I said, handed back the shirt, the scissors, the hairnet. I pocketed the name tag and walked out the door. Elapsed time: five minutes, give or take. The Food Services Director hadn't even seemed surprised.

I DO NOT RECALL MUCH ELSE about my year away at college. I quickly lost track of both Dan and John amid the scrum of campus life and the quick hustle of trying to find a peer group to call my own. I had a car, a knack for graft and an expertly chalked ID, so I was in charge of procuring supplies: a hundred beers and one medium pizza. I also always seemed to be the last man awake at the end of the night so I was in charge of collecting on debts—real and imagined. My friends thought it was insomnia or a high tolerance for shit lager. It was neither. It was amphetamines. We threw big parties that banged back and forth between all the cell-like cement rooms on our floor and always seemed to degenerate into drinking games that would end one step shy of an orgy. After a while I learned to always play to lose. More fun that way. Better stories come Monday morning.

I learned a few things, though none of these lessons (other than how to ask for a pack of cigarettes in Russian and how to mix an artful martini) came courtesy of the classroom. I learned that when everyone else on the floor is getting smashed on Rolling Rocks and a passed bottle of Southern Comfort after a long night of playing suck-and-blow with the girls from down on six, and then a collective decision is made that it would be a bonding experience to all go out and get tattoos, one should try to be the most sober guy in the room. For one, this will probably keep one from doing something dumb like getting a gigantic American eagle tattooed on one's ass. It'll also make it much easier to convince one's roommate—Chris, the accounting major from Acton, Mass.—to do something really cool like getting a gigantic American eagle tattooed on his ass.

I learned that when facing down four-to-one odds in a street fight, one should always try to joke one's way out of it or, when that fails, run like the devil knows you did it. No matter how pretty the girl is that you're trying to impress.

I learned that three of a kind beats a full house when the guy holding the eights and aces is too drunk to argue, and that when trying to decide whether to cheat on your high school girlfriend with whom you are trying to maintain a long-distance relationship, you should always cheat. Seriously, *always*.

Somewhere along the way, I forgot that I was also expected to go to class once in a while. My theory? I was doomed anyway, so why not enjoy the ride.

BY THE END OF FRESHMAN YEAR, John and Dan were already winning awards for their films, crewing for upperclassmen, lining up internships and generally doing all those things that make for a successful and career-oriented college experience. I, on the other hand, was spending all my time at the State Diner, crouching on the fold-down jump seats, guzzling black coffee and recording my jagged, inconsequential thoughts in notebooks. I'd decided at some point during the year that I wanted to be a writer, so was making a go of it. If I remember correctly, this mostly entailed sleeping till noon, stumbling dazedly around the campus, playing video games and trying to track down my dealer—a Cornell student who fancied himself a kind of latent beat poet but was too shy to read his work in public. Instead, he read his poems to me. I gave him enthusiastic encouragement, and in exchange he supplied me with black beauties and white cross, Benzedrine,* fat orange tabs of Dexedrine and, when that all ran out, crystal meth. The first bump I ever took I was crouched down between two cars in the side lot of the State Diner, and I remember thinking at the time what a bad idea this was. I recall thinking that there must be some way I can fake this, that I can *pretend* to hoover this shit up while actually, you know, *not*. It never occurred to me to simply say no.

I came to love both the chilling, fast, itchy ride to the top and the long, slow, bone-weary slide down the other end a day or two later. Thinking about it now, I can actually still feel the way the crank would mount my spine, spread out across my shoulders like wings, and open a direct circuit between brain and balls that made me twitch and fidget with fierce, uncontainable energy. If I close my eyes, I can still see the stuff—piss-yellow and crunchy like raw sugar—can still taste it the way someone who has recently beaten the flu can still taste the foul, tinny flavor of mucus in the back of the throat, can remember the way the pills would sometimes make my heart palpitate with anticipation even in the instant before I popped them into my mouth. It was good, except for those days when I would miscalculate my tolerances and end up asleep in the candy aisle of the twenty-four-hour grocery store at four in the morning or in the men's room throwing up blood because I'd ingested nothing but black coffee, cigarettes and cold medicine for the past ninety-six hours.

IN SCHOOL, when I could be bothered to attend, I was making films cobbled together from the cast-off work prints left behind on the floors or in the garbage cans of the film lab because I'd spent all my stock money and had convinced myself that constructing a ten-minute loop from other people's trash was a visionary statement.

My professors did not see it that way. Neither did anyone else. This was probably because they hadn't all been awake for the past

---

*Which wasn't actually Benzedrine, but probably just some no-name trucker crank. Though at the time, I had very little basis for comparison.

hundred-some hours, jangling themselves to pieces and chewing the points off the collars of their slightly used Swiss Army wool overcoats. I cursed them for their lack of vision, their inability to understand how beautifully the multiple leaders, the tight shot of the meat loaf on the cafeteria table, the long, underdeveloped pan across the night sky and the image of the crazed, laughing woman with the socks on her hands all blended together, then slept through most of my exams during finals week and woke up thinking that now might be an excellent time to leave.

I did want to go out with some style, though, which I thought to accomplish simply by vanishing without saying goodbye.

SEX, DRUGS AND KUNG PAO CHICKEN

y parents were, to say the least, disappointed by the way things had turned out. I'd been sort of teetering on the edge before, but now I was a full-blown loser: an unemployed college dropout with no money, no prospects, nowhere to live, and no plans for remedying any of these sad situations, either immediately or in the foreseeable future. Sitting there with them in the living room discussing my future a couple days after my slinking retreat from Ithaca, I was also all twitchy and sweating and short-tempered, unable to take a sip of coffee, light a cigarette or complete a sentence without breaking down into some foulmouthed rant about how I was going to have my revenge on those who'd done me wrong.

(This was not the drugs talking. This was the very distinct *lack* of drugs talking. Something that hadn't really occurred to me at the time: once I left Ithaca, I was also leaving behind my dealer and only dependable connection for chemical accelerants. I'd never learned how to cop in my hometown, and though at the time I probably could've figured out where to go and who to talk to if I tried, there was also a part of me—a small and easily bullied part of me—that didn't really want to. I mean, I wanted drugs. I wanted them quite badly. And if, at that moment, the Meth Fairy had twinkled in through the window, scattering little glassine bags and those old-fashioned McDonald's coffee stirrers in her wake, I would've been just as pleased as punch. But since I had no money and no motivation beyond the maddening itch of dependency, and since I hadn't yet been gut-hooked so solidly on the junk that I was sitting there mentally calculating the street value of Dad's stereo or Mom's collection of antique plates and silver, I'd simply been riding out the lack, having spent most of the preceding forty-eight or seventy-two hours doing little more than lying in bed, shaking, chain-smoking, playing Nintendo and watching the lizards crawl in under the door.)

The folks seemed only bemused by all of this, letting me go off on whatever weird jag occurred to me and nodding quietly until I'd settled down again, found another cigarette, found my lighter, my coffee, whatever. They allowed me to exhaust myself against the bulwarks of their patience, let me blame everyone I could think of for everything that'd gone wrong, let me rationalize and scheme, plot my comeback, list all the people who were going to be sorry when I was rich and famous and powerful (or at least able to walk from my bedroom to the bathroom without falling over), and when all that was done, they laid down the new plan.

I could move back in and stay for one month. I was to wake up at a reasonable hour, read the newspaper (paying particular attention to the help-wanted ads), and drink two pots of coffee on the couch like a sensible person. I was to find a job. It didn't matter to them what job I found so long as it had regular hours and a paycheck. I was also to look with some seriousness into enrolling at Monroe Community College.

At the end of the month, we'd talk again. If I'd accomplished *anything* in thirty days, we would discuss future arrangements. If not, we'd have nothing to talk about.

I felt this a rather cruel and abrupt way for them to be dealing with their prodigal son. I thought maybe I ought to explain everything—about the drugs, the poetry, the attempts at experimental filmmaking—but when I tried, it all came out wrong.

"Thanks" was what I actually said. "I'll see what I can do."

Inside of a week, I was back in the restaurant business.

CHINA TOWN WAS OWNED BY TWO BROTHERS, who we'll call Barney and Jake. The place wasn't actually called China Town. The brothers weren't actually named Barney and Jake. And I'm not even sure they were brothers. But I'm changing the names out of consideration for the real guys and their real restaurant because I liked the two of them quite a lot.

China Town was known for many things. At one time, by reputation, anyone could drink at the bar there, provided they were able to come up with some form of identification. A driver's license was fine, of course. Passport. Library card. Video store membership. An old baseball card with a picture of a player on it who looked vaguely like the customer presenting it.

Needless to say, this open and generous policy at the bar had gotten the bar in Dutch with the cops on numerous occasions, though charges never stuck. Lucky for them, they had among their coterie of semiregulars my uncle Rick, the lawyer. Rick had defended the house in court before, mostly against complaints of serving underage patrons gigantic umbrella drinks full of rum and tropical fruit, so he ate free in their dining room. He drank top-shelf scotch from the bar. And when there came a day that his broke, dumb-ass college-dropout nephew found himself suddenly in need of quick, no-questions-asked employment, Rick was right there.

Rick called me up at my parents' house, told me to find a clean white shirt, a pair of black pants and a tie, put them on and meet him in front of the place in an hour. This I did, and when I got there, he was already waiting.

"Okay, here's how this is going to go . . . ," he said.

We went up the long, narrow, steep flight of stairs to the bar/ restaurant on the second floor. It was quiet and smelled like old beer, sour breath, smoke and flowers. It smelled like kung pao chicken. At the landing, we pushed through a heavy door and stepped into China Town proper—big, ornate dining room to the right, surprisingly large and well-stocked bar to the left, cavernous kitchen in the back. The dining room was like a leftover movie set from some flashy seventies chop-socky movie—something right out of Quentin Tarantino's wet dreams, all deep, plush booths, red lacquer, curling dragons and furry whorehouse chandeliers—and the bar looked like the kind of place a man went to be killed for disappointing his Triad masters.

The place was unoccupied except for an old Chinese bartender, two men playing go at the far end of the bar by the TV, and Barney and Jake (both Chinese; Barney small and thin and tidy in an immaculate tuxedo; Jake tall and fat and sweating through a silk shirt, its collar wilting under the pressure of his jowls), who sat at the first table in the dining room, counting a huge stack of receipts and hissing angrily at each other like two mismatched cats.

They both bounced to their feet when they saw Rick come in, though. They bowed, snapped fingers at the bartender, who stirred reluctantly to life and wordlessly poured four tiny glasses of plum wine.

We drank. Rick introduced me. I dutifully shook hands and said nothing. Then the three of them headed to the dining room's farthest corner.

"Wait at the bar," said Rick, the defense attorney who represented this place in court against charges of serving minors, to his then nineteen-year-old nephew. "Have a drink. Relax."

I sat. The bartender asked what I'd like. Actually, he just grunted, inclining his head slightly toward the bottles ranked in tiers behind him—least possible expenditure of effort—but I got the idea. I asked for a gin gimlet, two limes. He stared silently out at me from beneath thick, expressive eyebrows, giving me a look like I'd just asked for three fingers of what-the-fuck.

"Beer," I said.

He nudged open a cooler with his foot, set a cold, unopened Tsingtao in front of me, and shambled off, panting and apparently exhausted by the effort. I popped the top with my lighter and nursed the beer while I waited. It took a surprisingly long time. I just tried to look cool, like I belonged in this place where I most assuredly did not.

After a while, Rick shot me a quick glance and cut his eyes toward the door. I nodded, rooted around in my pocket, and slipped a crumpled five across the bar for the beer. It was all the money I had. Rick was laughing, joking with the guys, shaking hands as they bowed reflexively like those toy birds that drink the water. I've always loved those things.

I stood waiting for him on the sidewalk beneath China Town's front windows with the sweet-and-sour scent of the place still clinging to my skin. Finally he came out.

"Five nights a week," Rick said. "Sundays and Mondays off, okay? They're going to pay you eight hours a night out of the register, five an hour, which should get you on your feet. Plus whatever tips you make. If it's slow and you don't make any tips, Barney'll give you a little extra for being a good kid. Also, they do some parties and things here. Private stuff. That'll be good for a few bucks, too."

I nodded. "When do I start?"

"You started twenty minutes ago. First thing you gotta do is go upstairs and tell that bartender you're in charge of the bar now."

"You mean fire him?"

"No . . ." Rick shook his head, recoiling and looking hurt, almost offended at the notion of putting me in such an uncomfortable position right off the bat. "Jake'll find something for him to do, I'm sure. But that's your bar now. You're in charge."

WALKING BACK UP THE STAIRS, I'd thought maybe there'd be violence. I figured that Barney and Jake would have to back me up, but when I walked back into the bar, they were nowhere to be found. It was just me and the bartender, Michael, and the two regulars, who'd prudently taken their game into the dining room.

Michael had been working at China Town a long time. There were things he understood that it would take me years to. So when I laid things out for him, he just shook his head and asked if he could stay for the rest of the night—offering to show me where the glasses were and how to work the cash register and so forth. Having been expecting incredulity, yelling demands for explanations I was totally unprepared to give, I told him I'd appreciate that. But oddly, telling him he didn't have to bother coming back tomorrow was like punching a baby in the face. He went down without any fight at all.

THERE HAD BEEN ONE CLASS at Ithaca that I never skipped. It was a night bartending course concerned mostly with the rote memorization of about two hundred common cocktails and the practice of a perfect, unjiggered one-ounce pour. In this, I'd graduated top of my class. You know who came in second? That girl who could put both her feet behind her head. We'd each missed one drink on the final test, but she'd missed the woo-woo and I'd missed the pink squirrel, and because the woo-woo was the more common of the two (and the simpler to assemble), I'd decided I was better than her and named myself valedictorian.

That night, Michael and I worked four hours together. We served a total of maybe half a dozen customers. The first drink I poured was an Alabama Slammer for an old man wearing a scarf and small rimless glasses who sat with a young, silent Asian girl beside him, drinking Cokes with lemon. I messed up the slammer but he didn't seem to notice. I suspect he was just fucking with me anyhow—pulling the most obscure drink he could think of out of his ass and asking the new kid to make it. But who cares? He left a ten-dollar tip.

By ten o'clock the dining room was dark and the seats at the bar all empty. Out of nowhere, Jake suddenly appeared, standing at the far end by the TV and back stairs, leaning heavily on the rail. Michael poured him a plum wine and walked it down to him. Jake sipped it, and when Michael leaned over and started speaking in hurried, hushed Chinese, Jake dismissed him with a hiss, waving his hand toward the door. Michael slunk off without another word.

To me he said, "We're closed. Go home. Be back tomorrow at five, five-thirty, whatever." He reached into his jacket with one hand, knocked back the rest of his drink with the other, and came up with a thin fold of twenties from an inside pocket, which he pushed across the bar to me with one thick finger.

"Here," he said. "Now go."

It was eighty dollars—five an hour for eight hours, of which I'd worked four, plus the promised little bit extra. Counting my few tips, I'd made more than a hundred bucks for doing little more than standing in one place and not falling asleep on my feet. Not bad considering I'd walked in just a few hours ago with my last five-spot in my pocket.

I tucked the cash into my shirt pocket and took the bottle of plum wine down from where Michael had left it on the back bar. I poured Jake a fresh one. "I'll see you tomorrow, boss."

He nodded, his head down, pouchy eyes tracing the grain of the bar. He ran a finger around the rim of the glass, then picked it up and drank without comment.

I left him there alone and went out to celebrate.

FROM THE START, the waitresses refused to give me their drink orders in English. As at Ferrara's, I thought this was a snub, some sort of clannish disinclination to accept me, the sole white kid on staff, into the family.

And again, this (mostly) wasn't the case. The truth was, none of the waitresses spoke English. This complicated things at the bar. They would come up and start rattling off calls in Cantonese and I would just stand there, staring through them, thinking about boxing or television or pie. For me, it was like trying to make sense of a cat describing a seven and seven or taking instructions from one of the adults in a Charlie Brown cartoon. For them, it must've been like talking to a wall, like trying to get a two-year-old to make a passable gin and tonic.

English is almost never the primary language of the kitchen, the dish-pit or the dock. On the floor, at the bar and in the owner's office, speaking English may be an advantage and being able to fake it a requirement, but in the back of the house, it is almost a detriment. Spanish, obviously, is big. French, too. Chinese is handy. Russian. Vietnamese. And on the line, cooks speak a patois that would give any linguist the vapors—a constantly evolving multilingual mish-

mash of house slang and obscenity, truncated in-jokes, World War II
and Vietnam-era military jargon, Spanish, English and butchered
Frog, liberally spiced by whatever the prevailing ethnicity of that particular kitchen might be. In later years, I would work in kitchens
where the dish room couldn't talk to the pastry department except
through translators, where the floor was virtually incapable of com-
municating with the chef and the line grooved to its own vernacular
as dense and impenetrable as mud—a secret guild cant wherein the
knowing of it served as proof of belonging, loyalty and bitter, hard-
won experience. I would work in places where the only common language wasn't even a language at all, but the simplified set of symbols
and shorthand that ticked out constantly from the printer: the clock
slashes of table position, SPEC-this and VIP-that, abbreviations of
complicated names (OE and POIV and XMAS and REO), and always
the red letters—FIRE, FIRE, FIRE.

At the China Town bar, we tried pantomime. We tried pointing
and yelling. We tried that trick where they'd talk louder and faster
and I'd talk louder and slower, really enunciating: "I . . . can't . . .
fucking . . . understand . . . you."

We settled on a compromise of phonetics, brand recognition and
slapdash Chinglish, developed on the spot and poorly understood by
all involved. I learned the Chinese words for certain common cocktails, for "another round" and "stupid idiot asshole," which was more
or less my name for my first few weeks on the job. The waitresses
learned to parrot back words to me such as *Mickey-robe* and *vodka
martini.* And whatever that didn't cover, we handled with charades,
educated guesses and a complex system of hand signals that allowed
us to communicate simple requests like "up" or "on the rocks" but
failed utterly when it came to expressing more complicated, reflexive, emotional phrasing like "This guy would like you to make his
drink in a clean glass, please" or "Screw this shit. I'm going home until someone here learns to speak my language."

One night I heard one of the waitresses speaking pretty good
English in the dining room, then coming to the bar and pretending
that I was just making up my own gibberish dialect whenever I

spoke. She was older than all the other girls on the floor by about eight hundred years, looked like she'd been preserved in cider vinegar and salt and was the only Asian woman I've ever seen with a perm. Her head was like a small, shriveled apple crowned with a Texas-schoolmarm Barbie wig, and when I confronted her about having heard her speak English in the dining room, she looked straight at me, furrowed her tiny, fierce eyebrows, and said simply, "I hate you every day."

Come to find out, she was Michael-the-former-bartender's sister, so I guess I had that coming.

THE CHINA TOWN REGULARS came for one or another highly personal reason. Gary came to hit on the waitresses and to play epic games of go with Jake that could last for hours. Mary came to have two glasses of wine and spout off about her Baptist faith. We were all heathens in her eyes, and it was her mission to convert us. When that didn't work, she'd have a bowl of egg-drop soup and talk about growing up in the South, eating pickled watermelon rind and chitlins and barbecue. Whenever she cooked a big meal, she'd bring bags of leftovers in for the other regulars, and for me and Barney and Jake, so we could all sit around the bar of a Chinese restaurant in upstate New York eating smoked pork shoulder, collard greens, okra and beans and cold slices of rhubarb or sweet potato pie.

Mary was a nurse who worked in the geriatric critical-care ward at the hospital down the street. Her job was to watch over people while they died. Food and her faith were her shield against the depredations of such grim business, providing her moments of joy in a life spent lived at the ends of other lives.

Joe the lawyer came to watch the news after work with no distractions. He would sit, drinking Chinese beer in silence, riveted by the phosphorescent glow of the cheap bar TV, then get up and leave. On a good night, not a single word would pass between us.

Tom, on the other hand, came for the conversation. He and I would talk all night if it was slow, our exchanges ranging wildly from sports (about which I knew just enough to hold up one end of a lop-sided discussion) to politics to science to cars to women. And if we ever ran out of things to talk about, I'd make fun of his mustache—a big, sandy-blond thing that looked glued onto his babyish face and made him appear to strangers like a creepy seventies porn star on the make.

Tom wore a wedding ring but never seemed in any hurry to get home. I only found out later that he'd been recently (and brutally) divorced; lost his wife, his kids, everything but the big, empty house. We were company, and company was all Tom wanted.

One night, Tom came with a date for dinner. They sat in the dining room and were treated like visiting royalty, lavished with food and wine and (after much whispered debate at the bar as to the appropriateness of the gesture) the special dirty fortune cookies that Barney bought in bulk from some Asian company, containing such cockeyed wisdom as "Two lovers is better on one hand" and "Confucius say: Man suck own dick never much lonely."

I don't know what fortunes Tom and his lady ended up getting, but they'd laughed, so we all figured we'd chosen right.

IF I POURED FIFTY DRINKS, beers included, it was a busy night. A hundred at the upstairs bar was almost unheard of. For long stretches—hours at a time, and sometimes whole days—not a single customer was seated in the dining room.

On the surface, it seemed like the simplest job ever. But my job was not to tend bar. It was to *look* like I was tending bar in those hours between the much more engaging and interesting duties I performed for Barney and Jake along the periphery of the restaurant business.

For example, China Town was the only restaurant I knew of then that got liquor deliveries at eleven o'clock on Tuesday nights. It was the only place I knew that took its delivery from the back of a beat-up, wheezing panel van with the name of some Asian produce company still showing ghostly through several coats of whitewash and spray paint. The owners did their ordering standing in the dark in the small parking lot outside the back door, pointing at cases of wine and whiskey and rum stacked up inside the truck while the driver totted up the list on a cocktail napkin or scrap of newspaper. The negotiations were conducted squatting on the pavement in the glow of the truck's headlights, stacks of bills thrown down onto the ground. My job was to stand in the doorway, a skinny, five-foot-six-inch Irishman armed with a baseball bat.

Sometimes I was told to leave the bat and go watch the front door—to sit just inside the glass and not allow anyone in under any circumstances for forty-five minutes. I was never told explicitly what I was supposed to do if someone *did* try to come in. Was I supposed to warn Barney and Jake? Call for help? Politely ask them to fuck off?

So some Tuesdays I watched the front, guarding against detachments of imaginary tongs or, worse, cops. Some Tuesdays I watched Barney's or Jake's back while he did his business—me slouching coolly against the doorframe with the Louisville Slugger near at hand, eyeballing the "helpers" the drivers would sometimes bring with them and giving them my best sleepy-eyed, heavy-lidded, I'm-so-bad-this-whole-scene-bores-me Steve McQueen stare. And on other nights I'd stand there the same way, but with a murderous little Vietnamese cook from the kitchen (a mean fucker, short but ropy, banded with hard muscle and covered in jailhouse tattoos, who never said a word to me in English except to call me Fuckhead or Mayonnaise Face) and two or three of his crew. They never did anything except squat, loose-limbed and menacing, in a tight group just outside the door. Squat and smoke. Squat and smoke and stare silently out at the truck driver and whoever he'd brought along with him. The head cook's tattoos were black and smudgy, but easy enough to read even in the dark because no matter how poorly it's rendered, a swastika is still a swastika and KILL spelled out across the knuckles is tough to mistake for anything else. He had spiderwebs inked on the sharp points of his elbows, a dragon on his neck, and though the only time I would ever see him for any length of time outside of the back parking lot was when he and the crew would sit down at the bar at the end of the night, he would *still* call me Fuckhead or Mayonnaise Face, even when I was lining up free Tsingtaos for him and his boys.

On the one night that the bunch of them were inspired to actually stand, they were even scarier—something in the way they uncoiled from the ground, flowing to their feet like water and advancing on Jake's back slowly but with unquestionable purpose.

The trigger for this unprecedented show of quiet force was the driver of the panel van. He'd been hunkered down across from Jake, the two of them quietly doing their business, when suddenly, and in the middle of negotiations, he'd yelped, thrown down a wad of bills, and leaped to his feet with his hands raised. His helpers— three of them, who'd been hanging around the truck's back door giving the four of us hanging around by the restaurant's back door the stink-eye—scrambled, shouting, to their feet and hurried to see what the trouble was. Meanwhile, me and the V.C. had simply strolled over quietly, casually as can be, as if merely curious about what was going to happen next. Like, what's happening here, Cool Breeze? Is someone going to apologize to the boss or are you all gonna end up as tomorrow's short rib special? Make your move.

It wasn't me saying this, of course. It was our numbers, and mostly, Vietnamese Hitler, who stood there smiling all the way back to his molars like he was anxious to get things started so he could eat someone's heart. I wasn't saying anything at all, because I was too busy cursing myself. In the excitement of the moment, I'd forgotten my bat. I'd also forgotten to mention to anyone that I had absolutely no desire to get my teeth stomped out in some kind of cheapjack gang war behind a Chinese restaurant for five bucks an hour.

Ten an hour, maybe. But in any event, if I was going to get my ass kicked, I wanted a fucking raise.

Once the sides were arranged, Jake sighed as if this whole thing—this whole *misunderstanding*, whatever it was—was just deeply disappointing to him. Then he turned his back on all of it and started walking away, passing straight through our little defensive line, heading for the back door. This made me exceedingly nervous because, every once in a while, there'd be a night when two trucks would show up for the liquor delivery rather than the usual one. On those nights, Jake or Barney would come back inside, tell me to close the door, lock it, and walk away. "Business," they'd say, shrugging. "Let them settle it themselves."

We'd all go upstairs, have a drink, wait five or ten or fifteen minutes, and when we went back down, there'd be one truck again. I never asked how such complications in the supply chain got resolved.

That night, the driver of the delivery truck only let Jake get about halfway to the door before yelling something. It was either a concession or an apology, since everyone suddenly relaxed and reached for their cigarettes. Jake shrugged, turned around, came back and finished his business. The cases got unloaded. Money changed hands.

And when it was all done, Jake took the pack of Marlboros out of my shirt pocket without asking and lit one for himself. "You forgot your stick," he said.

"There were only four of them. I figured I didn't need it."

I hadn't meant it to be funny when I said it, but, on hearing it, Jake exploded with laughter. So much that he had to bend over to catch his breath. He yelled to the cooks in Chinese, repeating what I'd said, holding up four fingers and making a swinging motion with his own invisible bat.

I TOOK TO WEARING most of a tuxedo to work every day, having bought three or four pleated, bone-colored shirts off the dead man's rack at the thrift store and augmenting them with black trousers trimmed in satin, a black bow tie, and the cummerbund I used to wear when I was selling videos at the mall. When it was slow, I'd stand at the end of the bar smoking cigarettes, drinking Chinese beer out of tall, elegantly curved pilsner glasses and watching the news or boxing or *The Simpsons* on TV.

I was enamored of the decaying glamour, the soured class, the cracked veneer of luxury China Town had. On the rare nights when the house was busy, when the bar grew inexplicably crowded and the dining room loud with trade; when Barney and Jake moved smilingly through the throngs like they were on rails, calling everyone by name; when the whole place filled with the sounds and smells of business— laughter, fried rice, call whiskey, raised voices, smoke and fragrant puffs of steam coming from plates uncovered at table, the silver domes lifted and miniature mushroom clouds blooming toward the ceiling—I could almost convince myself that I was *somewhere* when, really, I was nowhere at all.

I had one regular who'd come in to play chess with me, a professor of history from one of the local universities who, after three or four beers, would admit to a passionate love for dead historical figures like Marie Antoinette or Mao Tse-tung and an absolute loathing for his students. When the professor one day mysteriously stopped coming to the bar, I learned to play go instead. Like chess, go is one of those games that takes two minutes to learn and several lifetimes to master. When I say "I learned to play go," what I mean is I learned how to open the enamel box Jake kept his gear in, unroll the board and set the little black and white stones in their places, and that I learned how to do all that with just one hand so as to leave my other free for smoking and drinking, which is the only reason I'd "learned to play go" in the first place—to have something to do with my right hand during the long, slow hours that was healthier than what my left hand was doing. I needed an anchor for my vices, and like baccarat, snapping away at a typewriter in a crowded bull pen, or counting enormous stacks of money, playing go just makes one's bad habits look cooler.

When I discovered that Barney and Jake would bet on anything, I found myself another pastime: losing money to Barney and Jake.

There was a tree in front of China Town. From a table set against the second-floor windows, you could look out and be eye level with the branches. Come autumn, Barney and Jake would do exactly that: sit at the table and watch the tree, sometimes for hours at a stretch. They were betting on which leaf would fall next.

If more than one table was occupied in the dining room, they'd bet on which would finish first. They'd bet on customers sitting down at the bar, guessing how many drinks they'd have and leaving it to me to keep count. No matter what number I gave, one of them won and one of them lost, and the loser always blamed me for doing something wrong. When Jake noticed that I liked watching boxing, he would bet against me on the fights. Whether I wanted to or not.

In this way my nights at China Town got considerably longer. Barney and Jake irregularly ran a small, very private casino operation out of a rarely (legally) used private back room off the bar. The three-table concern alternately offered poker, *pai gow*, blackjack, roulette or craps depending on who was playing and what their favorite game was. Play didn't start up until well after midnight (I'd actually had no clue this even went on until the first night I was asked to stick around) and would go for hours. The room would be blue with cigar smoke, crowded with sector cops, bent lawyers, rich suckers, regulars and friends of the house, all squaring their cards, tapping their chips or watching the little white ball go round and round. I was drafted to provide drink service—locking the front door, standing behind the bar and making ghostly passes through the back room every twenty minutes or so, moving silent as a geisha.

If a space was open at a table, I'd sometimes be asked to play. You'd think I would've been smarter than that, but I wasn't. I developed a half-decent system for five-dollar roulette but never had the pool of available cash necessary to make it pay. Barney offered me house credit, secured against my paychecks. You'd think I would've been smarter than that, too. Again, you'd be wrong. I ended up working a month for free after one bad night and, not long after, got skunked again playing Chinese three-tier poker all night and ended up owing the brothers another three weeks.

My only saving grace was the ponies, straight bets on long shots, always to win. One lucky horse could pay for a lot of bad afternoons.

Still, as it slowly became apparent to the brothers that the proverbial luck of the Irish only held for such things as horse racing or drunkenly falling down a long flight of stairs and getting up without a scratch,* but *not* for life's more important pastimes like love, war and (most notably) card playing, I was invited to sit in more often. As it slowly became apparent to me that I had precisely zero skill at such things, I started to beg off—saying I was tired of giving back money I hadn't even earned yet. Jake's solution? I just needed to make more money.

This, as it turned out, was easy because on Sunday nights (and occasionally some other nights as well) China Town hosted private parties in a dim, mildew-smelling, bunkerish banquet space in the basement. A full bar was down there, with a dance floor only slightly warped by the damp, a DJ booth, seating for about a hundred. It was used for Chinese wedding receptions (a couple of which I'd worked), festival celebrations, birthdays of regulars, things like that. But on Sunday nights (*some* Sunday nights), it was reserved for the Sunshine Club.

"The fuck's a Sunshine Club?" I asked Jake, imagining a gathering of granola-eating, unicorn-humping hippie Girl Scouts or mob of elder queers.

Jake just smiled like someone'd fishhooked him in the jowls and pulled. "Sunday at seven. And wear a clean shirt."

THE SUNSHINE CLUB turned out to be a loose association of swingers, wife-swappers, closet fetishists, bi-curious dry-humpers, and gangbang enthusiasts who, in a city such as Rochester, which still clung to the tatters of its historical small-town puritanism with fierce zeal, were lucky to have found each other at all. That they had to "find each other" repeatedly at my bar, at the darkened back tables, or in the empty DJ booth in the basement of China Town every couple of Sundays was, depending on how you look at it, either a measure of the desperation of rust-belt perverts and sexual freethinkers or just another example of how weird a job my gig at China Town was.

---

*A trick I performed twice while in their employ, though not ever the full flight or when anything more than mildly buzzed. These stories tend to grow in the telling.

Club members didn't need much in the way of atmosphere or ambience to get down. A warm room with a lock on the door was enough. They'd bring their own music to plug into our PA, their own decorations, and ask only that the lights be kept dim and the whole party be treated like a lock-in. In other words, once things got rolling, the doors would be bolted until a certain hour. No one in and no one out.

Such a party (or succession of parties, as things would turn out) does need drinks, though. A lot of them, served strong and fast and with no fuss, to lubricate the cogs of fringe social interaction and blackjack the inhibitions of those who might normally be unwilling to get bent over a bar table and aggressively rear-ended in public.

Prior to my being handed the gig, Michael (remember him?) had been acting in this capacity. And while, under normal circumstances, someone who gets their kicks being finger-banged by strangers in a grotty basement or being led around by a leather strap tied around their ballsack is not really in much of a position to comment on the comportment of others, Barney and Jake had been getting some complaints about Michael's behavior from the swingers. Apparently, some nights he would refuse to serve anything but beers—claiming he had no liquor while standing before a fully stocked wall of bottles, then saying that he wasn't being paid enough to do anything but crack bottles. He would try to engage certain members in long conversations about their chosen kink or lifestyle, which was not what these people were coming in for. Most annoyingly, he'd started begging for tips—a massive bringdown in any service situation. My first duty upon being given the Sunshine Club nights by Jake was to fire Michael.

Again.

THE SUNSHINE CLUB IN ROCHESTER, NEW YORK, was heavily populated by what I would politely call *veteran* swingers. It wasn't exactly Girls Gone Wild, with stupid-drunk coeds taking their tops off and tongue-kissing each other, beautiful people posing nude on the banquettes or hordes of hard, tight, morally challenged underwear models tenderly exploring their sexuality in full view of me behind the bar. The parties would start around seven or eight and require at least two hours of drinking and fully clothed flirtatious socializing before anything fun happened at all, which made the parties rather like a corporate meet and greet or faculty luncheon that, at a certain point, was destined to go totally sideways.

Still, no matter how open-minded and accepting a cat might be (and I am just about as open-minded and accepting as cats come), seeing some gray-haired captain of industry squeezed into a pair of assless chaps and a black leather Brando–in–*The Wild One* motorcycle hat strutting around the dance floor and cavorting disreputably with some thirty-year-old hustler already blown out on poppers and clinging desperately to that last shred of his youth is going to start to demoralize you after the tenth or twentieth or fiftieth iteration. If you're me, it's going to put you, oddly enough, in the mind-set of fierce, almost hysterical, monogamy because anything—even a state so biologically unnatural as sexual exclusivity—is better than suddenly finding yourself alone with your fetishes at thirty and having to spend your Sunday nights in the basement of a Chinese restaurant hoping to get ass-fucked by Thurston Howell III just to prove you still got it.

ON SUNSHINE CLUB NIGHTS, the number of bodies and volume of heavy breathing was enough to raise the temperature twenty degrees, when the shaded half-windows up along the ceiling would fog and sweat and the cigarette smoke would pool around the lights in the sound-proofed ceiling like antigravity milk. Some nights I'd make three and four hundred dollars in tips that were almost like hush money so I'd just forget the things I'd seen: frantic pansexual groping in the booths, dry-humping orgies on the dance floor and wholly unnatural things done with my bar garnishes. Some nights—totally in violation of my bosses' orders and plain common sense—I would duck out from behind the bar and follow a couple of the younger, hipper Sunshine regulars across the dance floor, dodging knots of revelers and stepping around impassioned adulterers breaking their vows two and three at a clip, until we reached a narrow back door that let into a mostly unused access hallway. There, we'd do tiny toots of meth or cocaine off the fat pad between thumb and index finger. And though weed, amyl nitrite, and Nembutal weren't really my thing, I'd do those, too. At least I wasn't walking around in a black leather gimp mask, licking rum off the nipples of senior citizens, or sliding a hundred across the bar to settle up my tab at the end of the night and only then noticing the crust of dried semen on my knuckles. Everything's relative, I guess.

I WAS GOING BAMBOO, slowly but surely, my body becoming acclimated to the distinctly Asian rhythms of the place—to the hours, the smells, the background chatter of a language that was not my own. I'd grown to feel comfortable and at ease at China Town—behind the bar and in the dining room, passing through the kitchen to get to the coolers to retrieve limes, lemons, oranges and pineapples for garnish; spelunking through the dark basement corridors to get to the liquor room. Now, when it was my turn to watch Jake's or Barney's back, I adopted the same casual squat of the kitchen crew: loose-limbed, elbows on my knees, cigarette in my hand, staring flat and dead-eyed across the dark parking lot. I learned, out of necessity, to use chopsticks at China Town. And though to this day I still hold them wrong (as would a clumsy child or, worse, snapping away like some kind of retarded lobster, with quickness but no grace), during staff meals I could hold my own—reaching into the communal pot or platter to snag the best bits before they were all eaten, sucking on chicken feet in day-old brown sauce, eating scraps of pork or beef deemed unfit for public consumption or whole chicken and duck eggs, hard-boiled and tossed in soy sauce. To my *gwailo*, white-barbarian palate, these were some of the best meals I'd ever eaten.

The cooks at China Town made the best salt-and-pepper shrimp I've ever had, even to this day. These were served whole, shell-on, crusted in a crispy, fried paste of salt and pepper, and I would eat them with my fingers—taking them by the fistful from the platter brought out from the kitchen and set on the bar, transferring them to a plate and eating them all night between drink orders until my lips were dry and flaking and my breath terrible with shrimp funk.

For reasons I never understood, the other employees dreaded salt-and-pepper-shrimp day like they were being served hot Super Balls in used motor oil. I, on the other hand, could not stomach their favorite: cold omelets of kitchen scraps that the cooks made by cracking and scrambling eggs into a pot of boiling stock and dumping in whatever they could find kicking around the lowboys—old meat, dead vegetable ends, highly questionable shellfish, cigarette butts, fingernail clippings. It tasted like eating the raft that floats on top of a clarifying consommé, and on those days I would subsist on fortune cookies and the bowls of crispy noodles put out on the bar, dipped in plum sauce.

MY FRIEND STACY drank at the China Town bar sometimes. She was loud when sober, but get two or three shots of well tequila into her and she was like a walking bullhorn with platinum-blond hair, blood-red lips and a crazy streak that bordered on clinical. She was the kind of girl who made a man want to drink whiskey and invest in a tranquilizer pistol, and one night she came rolling into the bar after work to tell me she had a friend I should get to know—a girl who might meet at least some of the weirdly byzantine requirements I'd developed for consideration of serious female companionship after several months of basement debauchery at China Town.

"She's your dream girl, Jay," Stacy insisted, smiling and cackling crazily. "Her name's Samantha and I can't wait for you to meet her."

It should be said in Stacy's defense that Sam did meet many of my alluded-to impossible standards. For example, she owned no Eagles CDs (which was grounds for automatic disqualification as girlfriend material, no appeal allowed), had perfectly normal-sized nipples (which I saw on our first quasi-date at Ridge Billiards, to which she wore shit-stomper Doc Martens and a homespun sundress, nothing else), and beyond that, smoked, drank, fought and fucked like a boroughs-bred hellion—sometimes all at once.

She had a shaved head and two nasty scars, both gotten at the point of a knife wielded in anger and in her direction; a killer music collection (mostly shoplifted) that ran the gamut from CBGB New York punk and hardcore to Lou Reed to drifty, art-rock proto-goth like Dead Can Dance and the Cocteau Twins; and a tendency to strip naked in public, usually while we were walking home together after closing the bar. Together we made an interesting picture: Weegee crossed with Leibovitz, both of us starvation-thin, dark-eyed and sallow, her stark raving naked but for her Docs and piercings, me in some dead man's tuxedo.

In the first year, Sam would make two serious attempts on my life and dislocate my jaw (accidentally) in a fight over who starred in *Are You Being Served?* on the BBC. Five years later, I would come within a hairsbreadth of marrying her but end up in the hospital instead, with her and my best friend, David, standing, concerned but not exactly grief-stricken, by my bedside. She was, at that point, in love with David. But I'll save that story for its proper place.

After being introduced by Stacy, Sam and I managed a few weeks of near normalcy, living first in her attic room on Dartmouth Street atop a sort of punk-rock commune, then for a while in a studio apartment off Goodman, on the first floor of a house otherwise occupied by a mostly deaf German woman who was impressed, I think, with my wearing a tuxedo to work. This arrangement lasted several months and might've gone on longer if only Sam and I had managed to pay the rent. When this eventually came to a head, we moved again—packing our things into bursting cardboard boxes and trash bags, slinking out under the icy Teutonic gaze of our landlady, and hauling our few pathetic belongings down the street to the old Hungerford building.

In a thoroughly toxic part of the city, the Hungerford Building had, in former incarnations, been a shoe factory and a fruit warehouse, part of Rochester's lost industrial infrastructure, but was now being rented out piecemeal to artists, sculptors, young computer programmers, playwrights, dancers and bums—not one of whom could admit to living there even though nearly every one of them did. Eighty dollars a month secured us a large, airy, squarish space on the third floor, accessible only by a groaning freight elevator, with cement floors, huge windows, hastily erected walls made from bare drywall, and no running water. We had rights to the communal bathroom down the hall and sporadic electricity. Phone service was the battered public telephone across the parking lot. My car was broken into twice in our first month there. The first time, the thieves politely smashed only the little triangular demi-window on the back passenger's side and took my toolbox, pool cue and an eight-inch sheath knife I kept tucked into the springs under the driver's seat. The second time, with nothing much else to steal, the fuckers smashed in the windshield and took my dress shoes and half a sandwich I'd left on the front seat.

CHINA TOWN IS GONE NOW, replaced by God-knows-what during one of the periodic gentrifications of downtown Rochester. I don't know what became of Barney, of Jake, of Vietnamese Hitler or any of my regulars.

At the end, Sam would come in and we'd drink Molsons and watch TV like we were at home, close the place, buy a bottle of peppermint schnapps out of the register, get loaded and end up down on the beach, swimming naked, walking beneath the creepy shadow of the Jack Rabbit—one of the oldest still-operating wooden roller coasters in the country, a holdover from the days when Rochester's Seabreeze Amusement Park rivaled Coney Island as a playground for East Coast swells.

But finally, I'd had enough. "This is it, Jake. My last night."

I wanted to explain to him that I had plans, things I wanted to see and do; that this was supposed to have been an interim job—just something to get me back on my feet, put a little money in my pocket. I'd come in hoping to work a few weeks, tops, until something better came along. That had been more than two years ago. Nothing better had come. Not that I'd been looking . . .

Jake just told me to leave, paid me out, slumped down at the bar and turned to watch the TV.

A couple of days later, I was back to pick up a few things—books, a pair of boots, stuff I'd left behind. I walked up the long flight of stairs and into the bar. Barney and Jake were both standing there, talking with the customers, laughing and raising their drinks. Everyone was having a great time.

When Jake stepped aside, I could see behind the bar. Michael was there in a tuxedo, bow tie done tight, polishing a glass like he'd never left. He smiled when he saw me—a vicious, murderous, hateful smile that spoke of years of patience, of waiting. He was back; I was gone. To him, that must have seemed like victory.

I turned and walked out without my things. On the street, I took a deep breath that smelled nothing like kung pao chicken and had a feeling that I'd escaped something, and just in time.

WILL WORK NIGHTS

When the alarm goes off, it drags me out of a dream of potatoes. Nothing weird, just potatoes. Peeling potatoes, shredding potatoes, ricing them, running them across the naked blade of the mandolin.

Mandolins* have always scared me. They're dangerous contraptions, terribly unstable, bloodthirsty. Slip on the mandolin and you won't just nick yourself. There'll be a nice waffle-cut piece of your palm lying on the cutting board, an inch-long piece of skin dangling from the blade.

In my dream, I'd been running a sack of potatoes through the mandolin, cutting them finer and finer. Had I kept at it, I knew I would've ended up hurting myself. In my dream, I hadn't been able to stop. Only the bleating of the alarm had saved my dream-me's knuckles.

I've got a cigarette lit before my eyes are even open. Sam reaches over and sets our heavy clay ashtray on my chest.

"You awake?" she asks.

"No."

"Ten more minutes?"

---

*Those wobbly little machines with the slanted metal base and exposed cutting die that cooks use for making all those nice julienne veggies, gaufrette potatoes, paper-thin slices for chips, or maybe a delicious lyonnaise. Essentially, you take the vegetable of your choice, hold it tightly in your bare hand, then rub it back and forth over a bare razor until it has been reduced to a pile of artistic slices. There's not a cook out there who hasn't given up some skin and blood to the damn thing.

I think about it while holding my breath, first drag held deep in my lungs.

"No," I decide, huffing out an angry storm front of cigarette smoke toward the ceiling. "Better not. How long was I asleep?"

"About an hour. You going to take a shower?"

"No." I set the ashtray aside and sit up, groaning, my back and legs still sore, my feet burning. I'd fallen asleep in my clothes. My boots were outside. They smell like death, my boots—like I'd taken them off a corpse, and not a fresh one. My boots are no longer allowed inside.

"Hungry?"

"No."

"You should eat."

"No."

"Really, you should."

As a compromise, I take four ibuprofen and swallow them with a mouthful of warm Mountain Dew. I light another cigarette. Sam has retreated to the corner of the futon bed—our only piece of furniture—and is watching a BBC comedy, *Are You Being Served?*, on PBS, on our twelve-inch black-and-white TV with the rabbit ears and the missing volume knob. The TV sits on top of a milk crate. She's going through the laundry stacked on the floor. I'm staring at my feet, wondering why in the hell they hurt so bad. It's ten minutes after nine at night.

"What?" I ask.

"What?" Sam repeats.

"Did you ask me something?"

"No."

Shrugging. "I gotta go, baby."

"I know. See you in the morning?"

"I'll try not to wake you."

She turns. "No, Jay. Wake me, okay? Just wake me up. I won't mind."

I smile, know she's lying. "Okay. I'll wake you."

I stand up, strip off my T-shirt, change into my black one with the faded white Misfits skull. To get my blood moving, I jump in place, swing my arms, crack my neck. My feet are killing me. I roll my shoulders and the joints make popping sounds like squeezing a roll of Bubble Wrap. I kiss the girl and head for the door.

It's the most we've talked in a couple weeks. I'm feeling good.

AFTER I LEFT CHINA TOWN, Sam and I had hit on the idea of a road trip, a big, no-holds-barred, high-speed cross-country romp, conceived in the Kerouacian mode (which is to say, drunk), and executed with little planning, less money, and absolutely zero understanding of what was waiting for us out there in the great, wide whatsis. We'd bummed our way through many states, slept in the car, picked fights, begged for change, gone all the way to California, to Mexico, to California again.

Now, we were back. Sam was working days, I can't remember where. I was working nights in a roadhouse diner just down the hill and around the corner from her folks' house, where we were staying in a barely converted one-room apartment/solarium. It was not an ideal situation, but it was lovely. We were living, more or less, in a glass house, looking out over nothing but wooded slopes and a small stream that burbled with a placidity completely lost on me. Neither of us had anything like a plan for moving on.

I SHOW UP AT THE RESTAURANT a half hour early for the start of my 10:00 p.m. shift, and the dinner crew is already anxious to clock out for the night.

I am precise to a fault about clocking in, always showing up twenty or thirty minutes early and performing all the necessary preshift investigations: making sure the bread racks have been pulled around close to the kitchen door, that the stock in the coolers has been moved into night positions, that all the inserts in the cold tables have been topped and backed up and that at least a dozen cold beers are hidden under the trash bags out in the little stockade enclosure behind the restaurant where the Dumpsters live.

I check the stock levels in the walk-ins and freezer, look at pars and paperwork that I'm barely able to read—spreadsheeted portion breakdowns and prep lists prepared for and by managers but containing, I believe, some arcane wisdom just slightly beyond my ken. Frustrated, I turn away from the clipboards and weigh back stock and breakouts by eye and experience, by a simple comparison: knowing what a full cooler looks like at the beginning of a night, knowing what a wreck of one looks like at the end of one. After just a few months on this job, I can judge an entire walk-in at a glance; know almost without looking where we are going to be short, where we are long. It's all about supply lines and dispersion of supplies. Who will need what, when, and in what quantities. I do the grunt math in my head and, inevitably, find our stock lacking. Not wanting to be caught light, I razor open cardboard boxes full of brown, waxy bags of frozen fries, pull fifty extra pounds of burger patties, forty dozen more eggs, a flat of frozen steaks out to thaw. It's a Friday night and it's going to be bad. They all are.

Only after all this business is done (plus various odds and ends) do I clock myself in and punch the cards for all my guys. Most of them will roll in sometime in the next half hour; straggling in one at a time, coming from wherever they go when they're not at work, from whatever they do when they're not here—which is not stuff any of us much care to talk about. Stumbling drunk, sometimes bloodied, stinking of beer and skank and the kind of troubled debauchery that only the very desperate or very creative can find before Letterman's opening monologue is over, they come because they are mercenaries: well paid for doing a job no one else wants.

But it's my responsibility to have them all here on time, and under my watch they're never late. At least not on paper.

I'VE LEARNED NOT TO STEP across the border separating the line proper from the rest of the kitchen until I have to. When I do, the switch flips—turning the house over from dinner shift to night shift. And I am careful in timing my move onto the line because—at least until my boys start rolling in—I'm alone here.

As soon as I step in, the dinner crew will walk off. Immediately. No matter what they're doing. They could be in the middle of a hit, halfway through flipping an egg, whatever. They walk, and the line becomes mine. So I must be cautious: make sure a party of ten didn't just get seated, make sure there's not more than a couple of easy checks on the slide, make sure nothing is on fire.

The dinner crew has good reason for their peevishness. I mean besides their all being a bunch of pussy little bitches who wouldn't know a hard night's work if it snuck up and fucked 'em, they're mostly company men—loyal guys who've been in this galley a long time, who've clawed their way into this sweet two-to-ten slot through years of responsible, dedicated labor. They believe that this ought to make them characters deserving of some respect, and they often take spiteful offense at the night crew's complete and total dismissal of them.

When working, they look like bored extras cast in some kind of industrial training film about the joys of teamwork and proper food handling. They all have to wear these totally gay polo shirts, hats, hairnets and latex rectal-exam gloves. We wear whatever we want, whatever we wake up in, and look, for the most part, like the infield crowd at Talladega or the crew of a hip pirate ship—all tattoos and earrings and boots and long knives and gold teeth.

They have to actually show up on time. Because I have faith that, unless dead or in handcuffs, my guys will all arrive eventually, they get here when they get here. As I was once trusted when I first started this gig, I now trust them. We don't let each other down.

The dinner crew is expected to be clean, sober and presentable while working; to restrain their more base impulses and behave, at all times, in a polite and respectable fashion. As for us, we have a twelve-inch-long, heavily veined, and anatomically improbable foam dick that we keep in a box and slap down onto the omelets of customers who, for one reason or another, piss us off. We have our own schedules, ashtrays in the kitchen, beers out by the Dumpster, and beyond even the usual restaurant-industry friction between front of the house and back of the house, crew and bosses—the sometimes genial, sometimes abrasive back-and-forth about who has the harder job, who's smart and who's dumb—we have an unmitigated disdain for anyone who's not One of Us. It's a tribal thing: Us versus Them. And Them are anyone who ain't Us: customers, waitstaff, management, dinner crew.

FOUR COOKS ARE NOW permanently in the night brigade; four guys who rotate a single night off a week, then me, who gets none. In the beginning, I was part of someone else's night brigade, but turnover in this galley is high, so now it is my kitchen, my crew. There's Juan, who runs my fryers. James is my roundsman, my jack-of-all-trades. Freddy usually works the grill. Hero does eggs on the flat.

Juan is Mexican, heavily muscled, big, and aggressively pansexual by way of unwelcome assault. He will dry-hump anything—waiters, waitresses, busboys, produce boxes, doorframes. When he wants his fryers to work faster, he mounts them—grabbing their hot, oily flanks bare-handed and gently bumping his dick against the front panel, sweet-talking the equipment in gentle Spanish. Whenever not on the line, he can be located by listening for the squeals of outrage from the staff—Juan pinning a waiter up against the ice machine and molesting him for some presumed slight. This does not do good things for front-of-the-house morale. It does wonders for Juan.

James is an old man. Thirty-two and divorced, father of two. He has a master's degree in something brainy that he'd never managed to translate into a straight job, and a drinking problem. The problem is, he doesn't know when to stop, or can't, or won't. He started working nights on the theory that nights are when the bars are open and, if he was working, he wouldn't be at them. Worked great until he started finding bars that opened at 7:00 a.m. Now he works shift and a half whenever he can (doing a full night, then a cooking stretch from eight in the morning to eleven to help out the breakfast crew) and drinks only on the job. This is his idea of self-improvement. Maybe it works. He seems happy all the time even though I believe he's currently living in his car.

Freddy is a junkie. Hero is a hero. Freddy shoots smack and knocks off every day at 5:00 a.m. to rocket crosstown in his beat-ass, fifth-hand Civic to get to his second job, making bagels at a bakery in the city. Hero is tall, blond, young, good-looking, with blue eyes and a Vanilla Ice flattop like a landing pad for really bad ideas.

Freddy looks like he belongs here—he is most assuredly One of Us. Hero looks like he ought to be wearing deck shoes and crewing a regatta schooner. No one has ever figured out how he ended up here, but he did. The dick-in-the-omelet thing? That was Hero's idea. The beers out in the Dumpster corral? He started that, too. And he's fucked every waitress on the floor—will often discuss the relative merits, skills and pet peeves of each, pointing them out as they walk by the pass.

"Fat but kinky. Ready to go anytime, anywhere."

"That one? Likes it in the ass."

"That one made me wear two rubbers."

"What, is she new?"

Hero is my buddy, my backup—as tall and fair-haired as I am short and squirrelly. He comes to work sometimes straight from the strip clubs, wearing sweatpants and slip-on Vans; stripping down to boxers in the middle of the kitchen and changing into his gear. He'd been in the Iraq war—the first one—but doesn't talk about it except that his language is peppered somewhat more heavily with military jargon than is the rest of ours.

And he has moves—serious moves. Eggs is the toughest station. Straight hit, start to finish, no breaks. It takes the most delicate hand, the most patience, concentration like a Zen master's. Eggs on bar rush is like trying to build a house of cards in the middle of a street fight. It's all elbows, yelling, blood and ruckus, but you break one yolk and it blows your whole rhythm. Timing is what matters. And Hero doesn't have a brain, just a cock and thirty kitchen timers in his head. Once, he'd popped off the line in the middle of a fierce rush—no explanation, his eggs all lined up, swimming in a slick of fifty-fifty oil on the shimmering flattop, cooking away. Less than five minutes later, he came back—swaggering, dipshit grin on his face—and picked up exactly where he'd left off, flipping eggs, plating eggs. He didn't lose a single order. He'd read the slide, checked the upcoming fires, estimated the time it would take the other stations to assemble, picked his moment, and ducked out into the parking lot for a blow job from a girlfriend he'd spotted in the mob waiting at the door.

And then there's me, in charge of this motley army, top dog for as long as I can hold on—until I burn out, flake out, lose my shit or die. Starting at ten o'clock every night, I am God of the box, the brain-damaged Lord Commander of a kingdom fifty feet by five and made entirely of stainless steel, industrial tile, knives, sweat and fire. I am the wheelman, King of the Galley, and Christ save the peasants.

NO ONE IS HIRED AS WHEELMAN. You have to earn it. It's a hereditary title here, passed down from man to man within the galley family. I inherited it from Jimmy, who'd freaked out one night, hit a waitress, and was subsequently beaten stupid by all of us in the kitchen,* his former praetorian guard. Jimmy had inherited the post from Kyle, who just didn't show up one night and was never heard from again.

When I got the wheel,† I was literally knighted on the spot—a whip-quick consensus decision made by the crew. I'd been doing eggs (though I was a real good egg man, Hero is still better), and suddenly

---

*There are many ways to offend a cook and inspire him to violence. We are, as a rule, a passionate and fiery people prone to the expeditious use of fists to settle our disputes. Mostly it's done in high spirits and good humor. I've been punched by more good friends than I can count and rarely held a grudge. But if there's one thing you do not want to do in front of a cook, it's hit a waitress. For that, we'll just fucking kill you.

†The words *wheel* and *wheelman* both refer to the old-fashioned contraption still seen in some original diner kitchens: the spinning wheel mounted in the center of the pass from which servers would hang their handwritten checks. Flo would pin a dupe to the wheel on her side of the pass, the wheel would be spun until the order was facing Mel, then Mel—the wheelman—would pull the check off the wheel and shout out the order to his cooks working the line. With point-of-sale systems now installed in virtually every professional kitchen in America, the wheel is mostly an object lost to history. The phrase, though—like so much other great cook slang—persists.

there I was, kneeling down on the filthy mats in the middle of a crushing bar rush amid all the eggshells and trash while the ticket printer chattered away like a machine gun. James (who, by seniority, likely should've taken the position himself, but passed) touched me on both shoulders with the long, burnished wheel spatula that'd once been Jimmy's, and when I rose, I was showered with yellow shredded cheese like rose petals thrown by all the other guys on the line. We were all laughing like hyenas, cracking our bruised knuckles. I'd stepped to my new post so proudly I thought I would pop, while, behind us, Jimmy lay on the floor of the kitchen—cast out, forgotten, still screaming and bleeding into a floor drain.

That was about three weeks ago. I haven't had a night off since. But I'm twenty-two years old, juiced on the high of command, on pride at doing a tough job under demanding conditions with no rules and a mercenary army at my back, so I'm happy with that. Really, I am.

NOW IT'S TEN O'CLOCK on the button. I step onto the line, and as expected, the dinner crew drops everything and walks off without a word.

The slide is empty, the dining room quiet. I start going through the hundred small things that must be done to prepare for the first serious hit of the shift, due in around midnight. I check coolers, temps and doors. I rotate supplies, catalog all the things the dinner crew was supposed to do but didn't. I make a list in my head. They didn't strain the fryer oil. Motherfuckers. The mats are disgusting. The hot boxes are nearly empty. Deep prep looks good, but basic supplies are running short everywhere: cheeses, warmed eggs, oil, bacon, sausage, thawed burgers, lettuce, tomatoes. There's an hour's work here at least just to get things ready for the midnight rush and two hours to do it in. Cinch. Except that the line is still running and every time the printer chatters, it eats into the clock. Right now, it's just math: time remaining divided by number of arriving crew multiplied by possible amount of checks that will need to be cooked between now and zero hour. But in about an hour and forty-five minutes it's going to become much more personal as everyone starts to scramble.

I start pulling up the nonskids, folding them double so they'll fit into the big machine in the dish room. I run the machine myself— stepping away only when the printer tells me I must cook two cheeseburgers/fries, roll an omelet, heat-to-serve a hot turkey sandwich. On a flat rack, you can stack two mats, cram them in, and just get the door shut with enough clearance for the machine to run. Company policy expressly forbids the washing of floor mats in the dish machine. Last time someone mentioned this to us, we ran the company handbook through the dish machine, too.

Don't talk to me about policy. I know exactly what an industrial dish machine can and can't do. God knows I got enough practice back in the day.

ALL THE FREE REIN WE HAVE, all the shit we don't catch, all the looking-the-other-way done by the bosses—we've earned that. On our best nights, me, Hero, Freddy, James and Juan do just one thing that makes all the difference. We do the job.

But here's the trick. The job? The job's gonna fuck you up. The job's gonna wreck you. We all knew that coming in. We were warned.

"In the last six months, the average cook I've put on C-trip* has lasted less than a week. Most of them were gone after two days. A lot never made it to the end of their first shift." That's what I was told when I applied, by the restaurant's general manager, who, himself, had never worked a night shift and couldn't figure out why his turnover was so high. "So are you sure you want this?"

It was like a bad war movie.

No, it was like a *good* war movie. Like Martin Sheen in *Apocalypse Now*: *I asked for a mission and, for my sins, they gave me one.*

*Night shift.

And I don't remember exactly what I said to him. Fifteen years gone, I don't recall the specifics of our negotiation. But I know myself and I know a twenty-two-year-old me would've given only one answer to a question like that.

"Yeah," I would've told him. "Yeah, I want it. Bring it on."

THE PROBLEM WITH HIRING MERCENARIES IS THIS: As management, what you're looking for are guys who can do a tough, ugly job under bad conditions and survive long enough to make a difference. You hope for things like personal leadership, capability under fire, independence, guts. But when you get right down to it, what you're hiring are killers. People who like to kill other people. Staffing a kitchen is not a lot different. What you want are guys who can do the job. What you get are guys who *like* doing the job. And at the low end—in the quarter of the business where I was currently residing—what that's going to guarantee you is a line full of fucking lunatics, right off the bat. Guys who never rose through the ranks or never wanted to. Guys who want the job precisely because it is so punishing, because so many others have failed at it and because they want to be king of the dregs. Guys who hear "suicide mission" and say, "Sign me up, boss."

Jimmy had held on to the wheel for three months before cracking up—which wasn't a record, but it was a long time. Kyle had lasted three weeks. I think the guy before him went two days. In the time that I've been here, we've torn through countless other cooks, in a variety of positions, and whenever one went down, went AWOL, just threw in the towel and said, "Fuck this shit. I'm going home," Lucy, the night manager, has plugged up the holes in the line with the next guy whose name was flagged in the stack of applications and marked *WWN*: Will Work Nights. The average life expectancy of the Cherry, the Virgin, the FNG, is measured in days—few enough to count on one hand—and the only reason we keep 'em coming on is because we have no choice.

Full-body hard. That's the phrase we used to describe new hires who we knew would probably make it okay, join the family and take their places as regulars on the night line. And it meant just what you think it means: a guy who was a straight-up, toes-to-top boner in those last couple minutes before the rush came in; stiff as wood and just so goddamn excited to see what was coming that if you breathed on him wrong, he would've popped.

Me and the other guys now in the night brigade are the ones who stuck, the ones who loved the heat and the noise and the pure adrenaline high of doing a difficult job under impossible circumstances. We were (and are) totally hard for it. And though we all might like to think of ourselves as some kind of super-badass immortal legion of short-order night cooks, the truth is, my guys keep coming here night after night for the same simple reasons I do. We do it because we have to, because to not come—to be a no-call/no-show, chickenshit, lazy-ass, fucked-out slacker—would be letting down the team. We do it because most of us—myself included—know that this job is all we got. We're lucky. Without the work, we'd all just be mooching off friends, wives, parents. And while we might actually all be a bunch of bums, junkies and head cases, this way at least we're bums, junkies and head cases with jobs—with a reason to get up off the couch each day, put our pants on, fish our sunglasses out of the toilet and get out in the world.

We do it because, here, we're part of something. We're *expected*, which is only a big deal to people who understand what it's like not to be expected anywhere.

Kitchens are the last true American meritocracy. If you can do the job, nothing else matters. No one cares about your past or what you do on the outside. Color, creed, sexual orientation, personal tastes, politics—who cares. Can you cook? That's all anyone cares about. Can you do the work? You can be an illegal immigrant, an ex-convict, a Satanist, a Republican. You can spend your downtime smoking meth and consorting with prostitutes, plotting the overthrow of the government, eating dead babies for breakfast. Doesn't matter. Just show up on time and keep it together on the line.

Also, we do it because it's fun. Real, serious, big-time fun. There's fire and big knives and loud noises, danger everywhere, the potential for crippling injury at every turn. Every conversation that isn't about the job is about cock and pussy. Every moment that isn't spent on the line, in the weeds, under fire, is spent talking big and behaving badly.

By any rational accounting, we all should've been fired twenty times over—if not for minor infractions like drinking on the job or simple insubordination or occasionally locking a waiter or busboy in the coffin freezer, then for the much more serious stuff like shooting heroin on the job or punching people or *forgetting* that we'd locked one of the waiters in the coffin freezer for, like, twenty minutes. We should've all been thrown out and never, ever allowed to return. Most of us should've been in jail.

But that hasn't happened because no one else can do the job, and more to the point, no one else wants it.

QUARTER AFTER TEN.
I lean across the pass and tell the first waitress I see that the flat grills are down. I need to make twenty pounds of bacon in a hurry.

"Twenty minutes," I say. "Tell your friends."

The very next check that comes in? Three egg plates, hash browns and a grilled cheese—all off the griddle-tops. I tear the dupe off the machine, wad it up and throw it out into the server's trench.

"Not cooking this!" I yell to no one in particular. "Flat grills are eighty-six."

Nobody listens.

AFTER COMING BACK FROM CALIFORNIA and elsewhere, I'd gone immediately back to work. Restaurants were easier to slide back into this time, and I'd bounced around some—slopping breakfasts at a family restaurant in the suburbs, working briefly in a place where the guy next to me on the line showed up one night with a nasty running head wound and worked his station one-handed, pressing a side towel against his skull with the other so he wouldn't bleed on the Moons Over My Hammy.

I ran the kitchen at a roadhouse bar where the only thing I ever had to cook was chicken wings, the only thing I ever had to order was more chicken wings, and the entire crew consisted of me and an older Mexican dishwasher who I'd have to wake whenever the bus pans started stacking up. The guy had three jobs: construction of some sort during the day, the bar at night, and off-loading trucks at a grocery warehouse for a couple hours every day before dawn. Far as I knew, the only sleep he got was sitting in a gimp-legged chair with his head resting on a rack of cleaning supplies, drifting off to the mingled stink of bleach, rancid grease and industrial solvents. Most of the time I just did the dishes myself.

It was shitty work. But I'd needed something and, lucky for me, kitchen employment was plentiful for a boy of little morals and less expectation. And it's funny the way things work out: I'd actually ended up at this place because my last gig (the roadhouse with the sleepy Mexican) had been too boring. I'd stopped in for a cup of coffee late one night after a particularly dull stretch spent dunking chicken wings for the dozen-odd neighborhood stiffs who'd shown up to watch the owner's cousin's or brother-in-law's cover band mumble and thrash their way through the greatest hits of Southern-fried rock and started in complaining to Lucy (whom I'd actually known for years prior to working with her, from back when she was a night-shift waitress at a different all-nighter in the city and I was a customer who used to spend altogether too much time hanging out in her section with my no-account high school friends). And Lucy, in the style of an expert army recruiter or the person whose job it is to entice wayward young girls into lives of service to God, had listened sympathetically, nodding and commiserating and carefully sneaking in questions about my situation.

The next thing I knew, she was instructing me to mark the top of an application *WWN*. The general manager called me the next morning. I met with him early that afternoon. I started working that night.

About five months later, I took over the wheel. And now, three weeks after that, I'm about to have the worst night of my life.

Which is really saying something. I mean, you've been reading this stupid thing. I've had some pretty bad nights already, right?

Just wait.

FULL-BODY HARD.

Seriously. From day one. I would, in the future, experience worse hits, heavier rushes, busier restaurants and longer days. But never again would I *feel* them so viscerally, brutally, or with such destructive force as I did here.

The reason was just a simple quirk of geography. Several months earlier, a few months before I was hired, a forty-thousand-square-foot country-line-dancing joint had opened just a stagger away—across the street, across a massive parking lot—and it drew a huge and diverse crowd from across several counties. This was 1990-whatever, when line dancing, "Achy Breaky Heart," and the unabashed wearing of mullets were all indescribably, inconceivably popular. So at eight or eight-thirty, every Wednesday through Saturday night, the bar would take in thousands of urban/suburban cowboys, men in ridiculous hats, women with enormous permed hair, dudes and ranchers, young men in tight jeans, young women wearing more sequins than the cast of a Busby Berkeley revival. These were actual farm folk from the rural areas surrounding Rochester, fans of country-western pop music, and normal people who thought it stylish to pull on a snap-front western shirt and a big white cowboy hat, then dance like morons while drinking watery beers and comparing the size of their belt buckles. And at the end of each night, the bar spit all these people back out again—riled up, hot, drunk and hungry for pancakes.

And they all came to the diner, descending on our front door in a shambling rush, in a stumbling horde like Coors-drunk zombies in white Stetsons and stack-heel boots. Adding to this were the bar crowds from every other dive and strip club and neighborhood tap-shack within reasonable driving distance because we were (I think) the only place in the area open all night.

So from midnight until 5:00 a.m., in a dining room limited by law to 225 seats, we fed them all. What killed us was logistics. In a fine-dining restaurant, part of the duty of the maître d' and hosts is to seat the dining room in staggered waves: to set a new table, open a new ticket, about once every four or five minutes when the floor is fully committed and to bunch these tables into flights staggered by fifteen minutes or so. This is why, when calling for reservations at a nice restaurant, you might be told, sorry, but the house has nothing available at seven, perhaps seven-fifteen? This does not necessarily mean that someone arriving at seven would see no open tables, but that the floor was maxed-out on seatings for the seven-to-seven-fifteen time slot; that any more seatings just then would be likely to back up the kitchen and impede the quick and coordinated delivery of dinners.

There is an art to the smooth running of a floor, to the seamless flow of orders between the dining room and the kitchen, and a hundred different little tricks that a good floorman will have at his disposal for regulating the speed of service, the dispersal of customers, the turning of the floor, and the tide of orders coming into the kitchen and orders going out.

We had none of this sanity, stability or composure on our floor. What we had were two massive rushes: pre-bar at midnight and then bar at about ten minutes after last call. Both came all at once and were seated all at once, the dining room going from virtually empty at eleven forty-five to fully sat with fifty or a hundred more customers backed up at the door by twelve-fifteen. In our best hours, four of us—occasionally five of us, but most often four—would turn the dining room twice: 450 short-order meals served start to finish. And for an hour like that, we were paid, on average, eight dollars each.

With the wheelman's position came a bump to something like $9.15. A new guy started at six dollars. On my third night working, I'd watched a kid, just days past his eighteenth birthday and working his very first job, plunge both hands to the wrists in four-hundred-degree fryer oil.

He'd started work on the night crew right before me. No one had figured he was going to last, but he'd been trying. Hard. He was working with Juan on the fryer station, dunking french fries, in a panic of sweat and fear. He was way behind, so deep in the weeds he was shitting dandelions, and at some point he'd knocked something off the sheet tray that Juan kept balanced between the two big double-bay Frialators—a pair of tongs, maybe Juan's bowl of salt. On pure reflex, he'd made a two-handed grab for whatever it was, reaching right into the oil.

Juan had been the one who'd screamed.

The kid had burned himself so bad it didn't even hurt. At least for a few seconds. All business on the line stopped and we all watched him standing there, hands held up in front of his face, panting, saying quietly, almost to himself, "No. It's okay. It's not too bad. No. It's okay." Because the pain hadn't come yet, he was still hoping for that one-in-a-million stroke of luck, that miracle where you stand wide-eyed after an accident, wondering how in the hell you managed not to ruin yourself.

But his skin had melted. That's what we all thought at first. Like that Nazi guy in *Indiana Jones* who gets his face burned off by the magical Jesus lasers. It looked just like that—all white and runny— which would've been cool as hell except that, here, it was real. His hands were like claws, fingers stuck together, creamy goop like chicken fat deliquescing and rolling down his wrists. Juan crossed himself, muttering. The rest of us shuffled back away from him— stunned but unwilling to look away; reduced to a bunch of dumb, gawping children. Amazed, like seeing blood for the first time, like seeing real hurt.

It was so quiet. Until the shrieking and vomiting started. That part I barely remember. The quiet I'll never forget.

911. Ambulance. Sirens. Silver shock blankets like perfect aluminum foil, the kind I've always dreamed about being available in kitchens; a kind that can *drape*. We were still smack in the middle of our bar rush, tickets still coming in. Nothing stops the hit.

The kid was moved off the line, a third of the kitchen shut down.

We'd lost five minutes to the horror of watching and now danced like the motherfucking Bolshoi to catch up, a manager (not Lucy, someone else) pulling out the mats and sluicing in water to wash the puke off the tiles; everyone dropping salt on the floor for traction while we spun. Something almost superstitious about it now.

That same manager (the only one thinking clearly, but then, he hadn't had to see it) pulled Juan aside. Told him to drain the offending fryer. Turn it off and dump the oil. Why? Because some of the kid was probably still in it.

What made the whole thing worse (as if it could've been worse) was that the kid had been wearing gloves—those stupid, cheap rubber gloves that everyone in kitchens is supposed to wear all the time but no one ever does. The gloves were now a more or less permanent part of him. This only occurred to us later, sitting around, talking about it. It'd been the gloves that'd melted, not his hands. But then, the gloves had melted *to* his hands so who knew if that was better. We all tried to imagine what he'd do once he healed, how he would jerk off, where he would work. Freak show was the best we could come up with. He'd be the guy with the lobster hands, lurching around, scaring all the kids.

Truth is, none of us ever saw him again. We were busy. We hadn't even noticed the paramedics wheeling him out the back door. A replacement came in the next night. Didn't last. Another replaced him. Didn't last either. I don't remember anything at all about those guys—not their names, their habits, their skills. But Lobster Boy became part of the lore, a story we all got to carry forward with us, an almost guaranteed winner anytime a bunch of cooks got together and started talking about the worst kitchen injuries they'd ever seen.

Crippled for life for six bucks an hour.

TEN-THIRTY.

Freddy rolls in a couple minutes after the half hour, stands to babysit while I duck out back for my first smoke and beer of the night. Hero joins me a couple of minutes later. To announce himself, he rams his car head-on into the Dumpster corral, blocking the door, then clambers out, climbs to the hood, pokes his head over to look down on me where I stand, cigarette in one hand, bottle in the other. "Motherfucker, you better have one of those open for me."

"Take mine. I spit in it special for you."

Scrambling over, he drops crookedly into the trash midden, stands, snatches the beer out of my hand, drains away what's left. He clucks his tongue. "Oh, sweetheart. Now what will you drink?"

I flick my cigarette at him and it bounces off his chest in a shower of sparks. "You ready for tonight?"

"Friday night. We're gonna get *fuuucked* . . ."

"Hard, baby. Bent-over, broomstick fucked."

"Sandpaper. No lube."

"Not even the decency to spit on the tip."

Hero shakes his head. "So impolite." He scrounges out a cigarette from the pocket of his ridiculous multicolored leather jacket. "We're five-on?"

"Four-on."

"Five-on, darling. Check the schedule."

"Juan is gone, man. We don't even have five."

Hero shrugs. "We're five-on." He smashes the empty beer bottle against the side of one of the Dumpsters with a hollow, resounding boom and tinkle of shattered glass, looking back at me and giggling at the noise. "I'm going in. How bad is it?"

"We're okay. Freddy's on the line."

He leaps, catches the top of the stockade fence, hauls himself up and over. What he neglects to do is move his car. I can hear him laughing all the way to the back door. I have to pull myself up on the lip of the Dumpster and jump.

I unscrew his antennae and take the blades off his windshield wipers to square things, throw them in the backseat of my car. I would've pissed on his door handle, but didn't have to go. Oh, the joys of being a boy.

. . .

INSIDE, I CHECK THE SCHEDULE. Hero was right: we're five-on.

That makes no sense. We've been undermanned for a week, Juan off somewhere doing whatever it is that Juan does when he's not humping my fryers. Humping something else, I'd wager. It's been just the four of us every night, racking up overtime, ten hours or better trapped in the little steel box, getting flakier and rougher around the edges as the days pass. Four on a Sunday or Monday is fine—overstaffed, actually, with two or three cooks getting sent home shortly after 4:00 a.m. Start of the week is quiet. Relaxing. Closest thing there is to a vacation without actually, you know, taking a vacation.

Tuesday it gets busier. Wednesday, with the line dancing on, is worse. Thursday, worse again. Come Friday, we go all-hands—doubling a man on fryer/half-grill (usually Juan, doing his normal fryer work plus taking half the acreage of the slatted charcoal grill for steaks and prefires) and cutting out a man, usually Freddy, to do nothing but toast and pancakes.

With four-on, we've got room to move. To dance. With four-on, you can put a little flair in your game—hip-bumping the cooler doors closed, spinning plates down the rail to position. No one is climbing on your back, bashing past you, taking up your valuable inches on the cutting board or crowding you at the coolers. Five-on is crowded but cozy, like on one of those nature shows where they show the big knot of weasels or whatever, all sleeping together in their weasel hole. Five-on and you're in the slot. All you do is spin. Nothing more than a reach away.

I'd had no doubt that we could've done a Friday with just four-on. Was kinda looking forward to it, actually: wall-to-wall action for five or six straight hours, almost *wanting* the bad hit just to see if we could take it. It would've been something to be proud of, and guys like us don't get to be proud of much.

But without Juan, five on the schedule doesn't make any sense.

Somewhere deep in my head an alarm starts ringing. Softly. For the moment, easy to ignore.

AT TEN MINUTES TO ELEVEN, I find Lucy in the office. She's not alone.

"Hey, baby. *¿Cómo estás?*" She smiles, big and terrible.

Lucy is nominally in charge of this circus, this recurring nightmare. An ex-server, she's a five-foot-nothing Puerto Rican tornado who got conned into managing nights and took to it like magic. Oddly, being management, she is welcome in the back of the house because she can outtalk, outfight and probably outfuck any two of us degenerate pricks without even breaking a sweat. She is badass, and unquestionably on our side, unquestionably One of Us: in the same boat, in the same bad position, cut off with no hope of relief or rescue.

I ask, "Five-on, Luz? What's this shit?"

"You love me."

"No."

"You know you love me. You love me so much it *hurts*."

The guy sitting in the office with her has a fan of paperwork spread out in front of him. Taxes. ID. Company forms stamped with company logos—the same losing hand we'd all been dealt on day one. He's blinking, goggle-eyed, wearing a brand-new company polo, black pants, sneakers, twisting the brim of a brand-new company baseball cap in his hand.

I close my eyes. "This is not happening."

Lucy turns to him. "Dan, this is Jason. He's in charge. He'll tell you what you need to do." She speaks slowly, in uncomplicated sentences, the way one would to a child or someone who's just suffered some sort of traumatic event.

I talk like a man anticipating a traumatic event coming, squinching my eyes shut against seeing its swift approach. "You are not doing this to me, Lucy. Not on a Friday. Not tonight."

"Loco, you shut up now. Dan is five on the line. Use him. Put him . . ." Her voice trails off.

I open my eyes. "Yeah? Where?"

She makes a quick cutting motion with her finger, purses her lips as if to spit. "Your problem."

Petulant, I actually stamp my foot. "Lucy, it's Friday! We are going to get murdered."

She shoos Dan out of his chair. He steps past me sideways, out into the tiled reach of the kitchen, cramming the hat down sideways on his head and affecting the pose of a kid who is ready for anything—a pose I knew well once upon a time. The two of us together, we look like a before-and-after picture: him the fresh-faced newcomer in his company gear trying to look cool in the face of the unknown, me in my stained black pants, disgusting work boots, Misfits T-shirt and black bandanna covering the fuzzy wreck of a half-grown-out Mohawk, my hands covered in burns and scars, my skin gray, my eyes hung with big, dark bags looking like . . . something else.

"Go," Lucy says. "I've got paperwork." She means me, but Dan thinks he's still being spoken to so he starts walking toward the line. I turn to call him back, and when I do, Lucy pushes the office door closed with her foot. I say bad things to the closed door, which would look ridiculous to anyone who hadn't seen what came before. Probably it looks ridiculous anyway.

I yell to Dan, "Where do you think you're going?"

Dan shrugs. "Dunno."

Dan points. "Up there?"

"No." I say. "No, you're not. You ever cook anywhere before?"

Dan says he has worked at the Wendy's down the road. Three months.

"Wendy's? You serious?"

Dan nods.

"Wendy's."

Dan nods.

"Turn your fucking hat around straight."

Dan turns his fucking hat around straight.

I see James stroll in through the back door with one hand stuck down the front of his greasy chef pants and a graying T-shirt with a picture of crossed AK-47s on the front. He's smiling. He's always smiling. As far as problem drinkers go, James is as gentle as mashed potatoes. I wave him over.

"You have a new friend," James says, nodding to Dan.

"James, this is Wendy. Wendy? James."

"Dan," says Dan. He giggles and I want very much to punch him.

"Morning, Wendy," says James, then to me, just a raised eyebrow.

"Wendy is our fifth man tonight, James. Isn't that fantastic?"

James's other eyebrow starts racing the first, the two of them making a slow-motion dash for his receding hairline. "Smashing," he says. "Just *smashing* is what that is."

"He used to work at Wendy's."

"Really."

I nod. "Wendy's."

"A fortuitous development." James has read a lot of books. He likes big words. "That makes him an expert then, doesn't it?"

"Take him up and show him around, huh?"

"Are you going to yell at the door some more?"

"Just do it. Please?"

"Pleasure."

James drops an arm over Dan's shoulder and starts force-marching him toward the line. "Oh, Wendy, what a night we're going to have. We will gird our loins and sharpen our knives and have ourselves a great adventure . . ."

BACK IN THE OFFICE.

"I never said it was a good idea," Luz tells me. "Juan is not coming back. You ever want a night off, we need another guy."

"What happened to Juan?"

She shakes her head, curly hair swirling over her collar. "Drop it. He's just not coming back."

When she wants to, Lucy can cook alongside the best of us. She always wears a hairnet, just in case. This makes her look like a school lunch lady, or like someone who is carefully trying to grow a second head, hair first.

"Fine, but Wendy's? Seriously?"

"Believe it or not, Jason? He's the best we had." She hands me her cigarette and I take a seething drag. Usually, a fifth man will be some day/breakfast cook with his nuts up, someone who thinks it would be cool to be on the pirate ship. Freddy had been a breakfast cook. Kyle, too, I think. Sometimes it's a friend of a friend, sometimes a total stranger like I was. But it's never a rookie. Never someone totally green. It's going to screw us up with him getting in the way, asking questions, breathing our air. Only so much air on that line during a hit. Not enough to share.

"Why tonight?"

"Why not tonight? He was available tonight, so he's here. Have him make toast. Split out James and Freddy on the grill and have him drop bread all night. It's fine. It's better than nothing, isn't it?"

"No."

"It's not worse than nothing, *papi*. If he lasts the weekend, I can probably sell him down to day crew on Monday and trade for a fryer cook."

From outside the tiny office I hear Hero's voice: "Galley is eighty-six. No checks. None."

I bounce up, already imagining the worst. "We're gonna get killed."

"We were already going to get killed. Just go deal with it."

ELEVEN P.M. Sixty minutes before the first rush.

On the line, they're lighting everything. Fryers are being super-heated, burners roaring. The four front flattops and the two in the back—the cake grills—are being cleared and wiped clean of oil. Sheet pans are being laid over the grills, double-stacked, and even the ancient gas four-burner is being coaxed to life. Usually it remains covered with a thick, custom-fitted plastic cutting board, used for storage, as a shelf on the already overcrowded line. There's nothing on the menu we can't do on the grills, in the fryers, in the two nukers bracketed to the wall above the cold table. It's faster not to use burners.

Only now, the cover is popped and all four rings are blazing merrily away, bleeding flames across the grated top because the gaskets are worn and the gas lines leaky.

"Why are we eighty-six?"

I get icy, pissed-off stares; quiet wrath. Nothing. I'm going to kill Lucy. I figure this is all Wendy's fault somehow; you don't just bring someone new into the family without asking.

"Look, guys. If this is about *him*"—pointing—"I had nothing to do with it. I just—"

Freddy kicks the front of one of the fryers. "It's Friday, dude. What the fuck?"

"I know, Freddy. That's what I told Lucy."

"This isn't about him," James says.

"Dude, fish. *Fish!*" Freddy is shouting now. "It's fucking Friday. Where's all the fucking fish?"

I stand stunned. And then I fold as if punched, right up around the impact point of the sudden realization of what I'd forgotten. I close my eyes. Brace my elbows on my knees. Pinch the bridge of my nose between my fingers. Try not to scream. Shit, shit, shit . . .

Behind me, James is muttering, talking to himself. Freddy's still yelling. Hero, laughing, slapping the board with his spatula. "You suck, wheel!"

It's Friday night. And this being Friday night in upstate New York (all full of Catholics—Irish Catholics and Italian Catholics and Polish Catholics, Catholics who've come here from everywhere that Catholics have fled)—that means fish fry. Fish dinners with fries and a monkey dish of milky-sweet coleslaw, fish sandwiches going the same way, both battered and dumped in a fryer sequestered just for this foul, noxious, evil duty. Not just a tradition, an edict. God's law. Friday fish fry.

How had I forgotten to check on the fucking fish? Favorite trick of the dinner crew: not pulling the tubs of cheap, rock-hard haddock fillets out of the coffin freezer in the back for their slow thaw. In a water bath they take two hours or more. Dumped out on a prep table and allowed to collect bacteria, even longer. The fish would've been on special all night, written up on the board by the front door, put on a menu insert, programmed into the servers' POS system: SPEC FRY or SPEC SANDY. They'd probably served two hundred fish dinners earlier, would've gambled on how few cases to pull to leave us maximally screwed.

From my wounded hunker, I ask Freddy, "How many fillets we have?"

"Six, man. And they all stink."

I try to think. We'll only do half as many orders tonight—it technically being Saturday for most of the shift—but I can't have the fish pulled from the menu. Friday fucking fish fry is pure heaven on any restaurant's books—a fast mover with low food cost, high menu price and customers commanded by God to eat it or else they'll go to hell. I blame the Pope, the dinner shift, the management, everyone. But the last, best curses I save for myself.

Then I stand up straight. I look around at my guys, at Wendy. Briefly, I wonder if there's still some way I can blame this on him.

"All right. Wheel sucks. I forgot to check the fish. My fault."

Mutiny in the eyes of the crew.

"But we know what to do," I continue. "We can do this. Freddy, whatever fish is in the coolers, bury it. James, set the pans. Hero, get the hose. Freddy, on me when you're done. Wendy, on James." I step up to the pass, lean across the gleaming, hot aluminum, ducking my head under the glowing heat lamps, looking for Lucy. I call her over, tell her where we're at. "How's the floor?"

The floor is mercifully empty, servers rolling silver, slicing lemons, preening, staring dumbly at the walls—whatever servers do when there are no customers to pester. I tell Lucy to stall any new tables that come in as long as possible, then we break.

THERE ARE TWO WAYS TO DO A FISH FRY at a short-order restaurant.

The first is to slow-thaw a bunch of haddock fillets in a forty-two-degree prep cooler or under cold tap water in a clean sink. Once thawed, the fillets then need to be individually inspected; trimmed, if necessary, of excess skin or blood-dark belly meat left attached by the fishmonger; laid out on clean paper towels and stacked three deep in a clean, dry fish tub. The tubs are then stacked Lincoln Log–style in an upright ready cooler or lowboy. As soon as an order comes in, a single fillet is delicately lifted from its bedding and the company of its friends, dusted with flour and gently, lovingly dredged through a pan of room-temp beer batter made sweet and strong with buttermilk and a good stout. The gummy fish must then be thinned by running it between the index and middle fingers—surplus batter scraped back into the pan—and only after all this can the jacketed haddock be placed carefully into a hot fryer using a swirling motion: introducing it to the heat slowly to keep the fillet from curling as the batter tightens and to keep the batter itself from just bubbling away. There's a motion to it. A grace. Work one Friday night on fryer station in Catholic country and you will never forget it.

A couple minutes in the oil and voilà: perfect fried haddock, golden brown and puffy, religiously satisfactory and ready to be plated alongside crisp french fries and cold coleslaw. That's the way to do it right.

Then there's the way we do it in a hurry (the way we do it tonight):

1. Collect from the freezer the eighty pounds of frozen haddock fillets that the dinner crew neglected to pull. The fish is already separated into ten-pound consignments—each batch a solid block of chunky gray ice inside a stiff-sided but flimsy plastic box. The boxes are heavy, slippery, annoyingly hard to handle. They'll take the skin right off your hands if your hands aren't bone-dry. When the crew is hurrying, the odds of a broken toe from a dropped box go up dramatically. Doesn't happen tonight, though.

2. Take those boxes out the back door, pull off the locking lids, set them up inside empty bread racks braced at an angle against the back wall, and let Hero open up with the power sprayer we use for

cleaning the floors and the grease out of the hood vents. With the hose screwed into the hot water tap and the sprayer turned against ice, it might as well be a flamethrower.

3. Power-wash the shit out of the fish tubs until the steam stops and the ice starts to crumble, stopping periodically to set back up the racks that have been pushed over or to retrieve the icy fish bricks that have slipped from their boxes and gone skittering off into the gravel. During these interludes, the chances of the sprayer "getting away from" Hero and "accidentally" soaking either Freddy or me are 100 percent. Tonight, Hero gets Freddy while Freddy is lighting a cigarette, his timing perfect, catching him just as he bends to cup the flame of his lighter against the wind. Freddy jumps, sputters, charges and takes a running swing at Hero. This just gets him another shot with the hose. The two of them need to be separated briefly. I shove Hero aside, tell Freddy to go back inside, and he does, shaking water out of his long, ratty blond hair.

4. Bring the partially thawed cases into the prep kitchen, dump them out on the tables, and split the disintegrating fish-cicles lengthwise into twenty portions, preserving as many whole fillets as possible. Place each chunk of fish ice into a long, shallow metal baking pan called a hotel.

5. Walk twenty laden hotel pans onto the line where James (with Wendy's bewildered assistance) will have set up deep bains* on every available hot surface, each filled with a few inches of (hopefully already boiling) water.

6. Set hotel pans on top of bains, making twenty scratch double boilers, and cover hotels with plastic wrap, now making twenty jerry-rigged pressure cookers.

7. Wait. Smoke cigarettes. Bicker angrily with crew. Freddy is off in his corner by the fryers (standing post for the absent Juan), muttering under his breath and staring death rays at Hero. Hero just keeps laughing. This is going to come to a head soon, but not yet.

---

*A bain, or bain-marie, being any vessel capable of both holding water and having another pan set on top of it or into it.

8. After ten minutes or so, pull the plastic wrap off the hotels, and what you have is eighty pounds (give or take) of surface-poached, center-frozen, limp gray haddock fillets and a god-awful stink. To get rid of the stink faster, pop the filters out of the ventilation hood and just let that baby roar. Hero does this, climbing up between the grills and pulling the greasy filters out of their tracks. The suction immediately snuffs the flames on the four-burner. This is going to come back to haunt us, too. But not yet.

9. Because they are now half-cooked, the fillets will flake to pieces at the least prompting. Look at one wrong and it's likely to dissolve into fish mush and ice. Owing to this physical instability, they can no longer take the pressure of being dredged in batter so must be casseroled. In assembly-line fashion, bring in a new set of hotels. Layer each one with batter, ease in as many fillets as it can hold using a long spatula, then cover with more batter. Stack the pans back in the freezer for a few minutes to firm up the batter and shock the fillets, then remove to the ready cooler. As orders come in, shovel fillets gracelessly into the oil. Fry long and hard. Carefully remove to plate for service.

10. Pray to whatever god might be listening that no one catches you.

Oddly, the fish actually tastes pretty good this way.

Well, maybe not *good*, but less bad than you'd think. Flaky and slightly oily outside, mid-rare in the middle. In texture it's not unlike a poached fillet of sole, and in flavor only as bad as frozen haddock ever is—which is pretty bad even under the best circumstances.

The real problem is, going into the oil cold (and often still frozen in the center), the fillets will drop the temperature of the fryer oil precipitously. This screws with the fry cook's timing, and when cooking for drunks—especially *lots* of drunks—the fry cook's timing is of paramount importance to the synchronization of the rest of the kitchen. It also makes a terrible mess, pisses off the dishwashers, breaks about a dozen different health codes.

And it's just wrong.

You probably think that wouldn't matter to a bunch of guys like us. But it does. It matters a lot. If you've ever worked in a kitchen, you understand what I'm talking about. You know that little catch you get in your chest when you're doing something you know is wrong. And if you haven't worked in a kitchen, you'll just have to take my word for it. All the bullshit, the punching, the posturing, the macho crap; all the bad behavior and criminal impulses; all the hard talk and pleasure-seeking and shameless conduct—that's all true. That's The Life, the atmosphere in which so much food is created every day. But it's also true that we want to be *good*.

Not good people. Not good citizens. Not good in any general way. A lot of us (and I'm talking about all cooks here, not just the four guys standing with me on this line) prefer the opposite of good so long as we can get away with it.

But we want to be good at what we do because being good at what we do is what saves us—balancing out all the rest, at least in our minds, at least in *my* mind. Someday, when the heat comes down, when they finally slap on the leg irons and the Hannibal Lecter mask and lead me off to come-what-may, I want my guys to be able to say, "He was a good cook. Sure, he was a reprobate, a degenerate animal. Always broke. Always borrowing money. He was a foulmouthed, bad-tempered, cross-eyed, snaggletoothed, brain-damaged, tail-chasing fuckup and a total wreck of a human being. But man, Sheehan could really cook."

That would be enough, I think. Mitigation—that's all I'm after. And I'm not alone in that. I've known chefs who'd scream and curse and throw pans and torture cooks for any little slight. I've known guys who went to jail for stealing food stamps from old ladies, for sticking up convenience stores; guys who would work any angle, screw their friends over for a buck, behave in ways that are just unimaginably bad. But I've seen these same knuckleheads quit good jobs rather than do wrong by the food. I've watched them take pride in the perfect placement of scallops in a pan, in cutting a microscopic *brunoise,* in standing up under fire on a Friday night with a bunch of other like-minded bastards, throat-cutters and fuckups without blowing it for the team.

Cooking can be a miserable gig sometimes. Gouge-out-your-own-eyeballs awful. But when you sign on to a kitchen crew, what you're doing at the simplest level is indenturing yourself to the service of others. You're feeding people, providing for one of their basic needs, and that is—all else aside—a noble thing. And I have long held to the conviction that at every station, behind every burner, in all the professional kitchens in the world, is a guy who wants to walk out the door at the end of the night, into whatever personal hell or weirdness is waiting for him, knowing that, if nothing else, he did one thing real well.

But tonight, we have done wrong and are duly ashamed. Still, that's how you set up eighty pounds of fish fast—freezer to line in just a little over twenty minutes. It's a nice trick. Jesus is satisfied. The Pope is satisfied. Management will be satisfied. All our masters are pleased. Everyone is still pulling sheets and bains off their stations, yelling for the dishwashers, when I holler out to Lucy, "Luz! Galley up! Bring it on."

The printer starts chattering immediately.

THIRTY-FIVE MINUTES TILL MIDNIGHT.

"James, grill. Hero on eggs. Freddy, fryer/half-grill. Yes?"

Everyone nods. Wendy is standing in the doorway, out of traffic, staring down at his shoes, his hands folded in front of him.

"Salads?" Hero asks. "Cold garni?"

James says he'll take them. The cold table is closest to the grill station anyway. "What about cakes?"

"I'll pop the half-flat behind me and put up cakes," I say, inclining my head toward Wendy. "FNG on toast. He can drop cakes for me when I can't. He'll learn fast."

"Really?" James asks.

I look up. "Wendy, you a fast learner?"

"Yes."

"You ever eaten a pancake before?"

He looks confused, as if this is some kind of trick question or double entendre.

"A pancake, dumb-ass. Round thing? Syrup on top?"

"Yes."

I nod to James. "He'll figure it out."

Hero says, "He better."

James shakes his head. "I have very little faith in the youth of this country."

"He will," I say, ending this particularly fruitless discussion. "Okay, we covered?"

Assent from the troops.

"Good. Load heavy. We can't be running off every five minutes for supplies. Get your shit squared away. We're thirty minutes out, so . . . Yeah. Let's have some fun."

Everyone rolls out. My forces are arranged, supplies being laid in. After the fish debacle, things have smoothed out. A little.

ELEVEN-THIRTY.

"It's a toaster, Wendy. Bread goes in here. Toast comes out the other end."

I show him, laying two slices of white down on the little grated conveyor belt that will take it between the heating elements, spit it out browned into the chute on the other side. He nods, fascinated, like it's some kind of magic. I show him the box by his station where all the open, bagged loaves are kept, the racks outside the door with their shelves full of fresh bread, arranged by type: white, wheat, rye, sourdough, Texas, bags of bagels, hamburger buns, boxes of English muffins. It's a lot of bread, but then it's heavy breakfast business in the middle of the night. Almost everything goes out with toast on the side.

I explain, "White and sour go through once, wheat and whiskey twice. Texas goes to the grill—that's me—because it's too thick to go through the machine. Unless it's a French toast order. That goes to Hero next to me. Bagels go through twice, EMs once. EM, 'English muffin,' got it?"

Wendy bobs his head. Sweat is running down the sides of his face, soaking his collar. The sweat is making his eyebrows shine. It's not even hot yet.

"Really?" I ask.

"No. What's 'whiskey'?"

"Rye bread."

"Why?"

"Just is."

"Okay, what's 'Texas'?"

"Big place. Lots of cows."

" . . ."

"That's a joke. Texas toast. Thick-cut white. Big like Texas."

"Okay."

"Look, this is easy. One order of toast is two slices. Put 'em in, take 'em out, butter, slice, and stack 'em here. On toast plates. Unless an order is dry. Then there's no butter. Flag those somehow on the plates so you remember which is which. You've got three toasters and plenty of room. I'll call everything to you, so just listen and you'll do fine. Like if I say, 'One white, two wheat—one dry—one whiskey down; two Texas my hand, one Texas for French, bagel dark,' what do I need?"

Wendy stares at me blankly. "I have no idea what you just said to me, man."

TWENTY MINUTES.

Cook's cockney: OE, sunny, po/no po. Waiting, dragging, on a wait, on the fly; to the board, to the grill, to the rail, *on* the rail, my hand—my *hand*, motherfucker, right fucking now!—then whiskey down, cakes down (fast math in the head: if a short stack is three pancakes, a full stack five, and side cakes are three half-sized pancakes, then how many cakes does 'flying cakes . . . six tall, six short, four sides of three, two tall chocolate, all to the rail,' equal?*), fries down, tables up and orders up and fire orders. All-day, bennies, French, sizzlers, call me half, call me steady, gimme two, gimme ten, out for ammo, out for smoke, out for good. A thousand ways to say "Fuck you," running from pissed off to downright tender. A thousand ways to call for help. There's slang for every item on the menu, every special order, every kind of plate (wheel plate, big round, monkey dish, soufflé, side); sometimes doubled-up and tripled-up slang for one thing, jargon that only makes sense if you were there on the night the term was born and are able to track its permutations across days and weeks. Like, we cook the occasional order of awful, mealy potato pancakes here. They were *po cakes* in the wheel vernacular; became *ho cakes* one night after being ordered by a particularly skankish, drunk woman in the dining room; became a *ho stack* just because James thought it was funnier and because potato pancakes only came in one size so there was less chance of confusing it with a standard cake order; then became a *haystack* because that's kind of what potato pancakes look like when cooked: a haystack.

"Double haystack: bacon/well bacon, going apple, jizz." Two orders of potato pancakes, both with three strips of bacon, second order well-done, the first with applesauce on the side, the second with sour cream. Anything white, any sauce, anything that comes out of a squeeze bottle, can be referred to as jizz. Really, it's like poetry sometimes. Fucking lyrical.

After ten minutes, I've given up trying to teach Wendy to recognize called orders. It's like trying to teach Spanish to a rock. We've settled on a faintly mathematical par system: "At all times, have waiting six orders of white, four wheat, four sour, two rye, and two toasted English muffins. Keep half this grill full of pancakes. The rest, we'll cook to order, à la minute, until you catch on. If I ask for some-

---

*Seventy, total. Forty-eight regular-sized, twelve small, ten regular-sized and studded with chocolate chips.

thing and it's not there, I will kill you. No one will ever find your body. Got it?"

Wendy bobs his head.

I slap him on the shoulder. "You're gonna do fine."

Craning across the pass to check the door, I see that we're still in the clear. I check my watch.

"Breaks!" I shout. "Rotate out. Make it fast."

James slides up next to Wendy. "You smoke, little boy?"

Wendy says no.

James shrugs. "You should learn." Then he slides away.

FIFTEEN MINUTES.

I pounded a beer and half a cigarette in three minutes, but my hands won't stop shaking. After blowing it with the fish, I'm triple-checking everything, all the long-haul stores: line butter, grill oil, bags of frozen fries stacked like sandbags on cardboard on the floor next to Freddy. Bread. Cake batter in five-gallon buckets. Fish batter in deep six-pans that we don't even need now that the fish has been fucked up.

I duck out the back door for another couple drags and look up into the sky, trying to read some kind of portent in the stars, the position of the moon. Cooks—at least most of those I've known—are highly superstitious creatures. We are animists, brooding deists who see a cunning and malevolent intelligence in almost everything. We believe there are plots against us, conspiracies hashed out between the potatoes and management, and that fate always has worse in store. We have charms, rituals against fell destiny. Lucky pans, lucky boots, a favorite knife or spoon. Certain songs on the galley radio mean the world. AC/DC has always meant bad things for me. I believe I can calm eggs just by speaking to them in gentle tones. I sing some-times to my ingredients. My favorite spatula—the one I inherited from Jimmy—bestows on me special powers.

On the line, I believe that there's life in almost everything. I know that almost everything is out to get me.

• • •

EIGHT MINUTES.

Hero is standing just outside the line, leaning against the tiled corner, sucking on a Marlboro Light. James is laughing. I can hear him before I can see him. Wendy has a nervous, snuffling grin. And Freddy is dancing.

Freddy is doing the running man in front of his fryers—reaching out, touching the handles of his fryer baskets, popping up into the air, spinning, patting his hands down the length of the cutting board, touching his knife, a door handle, dropping into a squat, bouncing up again. Pantomime of panic, of adrenaline jitters, and he's panting, "Okay . . . We got . . . Okay . . . Now this . . . Right here . . . Okay . . ." He stops, freezes, looks up, bellows, "RADIO!" then gets right back at it.

Hero cracks up. James loses it. Wendy giggles, and even I can't help laughing, though it's me Freddy's making fun of. It's his impression of me on my first night on the line, working fryers for the night brigade, and it's a good one.

"You should be swearing more, Freddy," I say, then turn to Wendy. "He's right, though. I looked just like that."

"Dude, we thought you were gonna *die*." Freddy is catching his breath. "You were trying to cook everything yourself. The whole line. We just stood back. And 'Radio'? That just kills me."

James explains, "His first night, Jason was banging the fryers so hard he knocked the radio off the shelf, right into the oil."

"Fried the fucking radio," Hero adds.

James. "Do the voice again, Freddy,"

"Funniest thing." Freddy laughs. "The way you stopped. *'Ray-dee-ooooh* . . .'" He howls it, drawing it out mournfully. It's like that scene in the movies where the cop loses his partner or the soldier his best buddy—wailing the name to heaven. Everyone laughs. I laugh. James has tears.

Radio: now code for a double load of fries, both baskets full and down. It's a panic call, works for almost anything. *Radio toast* means just cook it till I tell you to stop. *Radio browns. Radio cakes.* The splash from the oil almost blinded me that night. It missed my right eye by half an inch, blistered my face. I still have the scar. Funny shit.

I guess you had to be there.

MIDNIGHT, MORE OR LESS.

These things don't happen on the dot. They happen when they happen. We're standing around, joking, catching a ticket here and there—the printer clacking, pausing, waiting, clacking again. Probing attacks. The enemy feeling out our defenses. But then we all go quiet, straining to hear, to sense the rush descending like a high-pressure system sweeping in. You learn to feel it in your bones: one minute nothing, the next you just know it's time.

James says, "Here they come."

"ORDERING . . . Country-fried steak going OE mash. James: double, no *triple.* Triple halfs going middy-well, middy-well, well. Drop three fries, please. Three burger setups to the board. Wendy: three burger rolls to the board. Adding fries going gravy. Hero: I need OEs, two on two—that's three all-day. Browns three times, going bacon/cakes, bacon/cakes, white toast. Two sides of three."

"CF, four fries, thank you."

"Three OE, browns, two bacon. Thank you."

"Mid, mid, well halves. Setups. Thank you."

"Adding on: browns-times-four, Hero. Wendy: two white, two wheat. Scramble times two, OE—that's four all-day—sunny. Split, split, two links. Cakes: two tall. That's two tall, two sides of three all-day, Wendy."

"Two scramble, four OE, sunny. Seven browns. Meats holding eggs, thank you."

"Hold up, Hero. Five OE. Six. *Six* OE all-day. Freddy, I need two more fries, both going fish so two fish dinners fries. Adding on, Wendy: white, side of three."

"Six all-day, CF, two fish."

"James?"

"Wheel. Talk to me."

"You are solo on those burgers-going-fries, fries-gravy. Brick 'em. Sell it on go."

"Bricks down."

"Wendy?"

"Yeah."

"Wendy, say *wheel.*"

"Wheel."

"I need four white, two wheat, two full stacks, three sides of three, three hamburger buns to James. Take your time. Get it right."

Breathe. I'm rolling two omelets myself. Watching six orders of hash browns—now eight orders of hash browns—cooking in a puddle of oil on the grill. I'm poking these first couple orders into the slide, pushing them down to make room for new ones, watching the server's trench, and chewing—working my jaw, feeling the muscles clench and unclench—flexing my fingers, bouncing on my toes. Antsy.

"Floor!" I shout out into the trench. "Come on. Keep 'em coming."

In answer, *clack clack clack clack* from the printer, the spooling paper curling toward my grill. Such a sweet sound when you want it. When you're expecting it and keyed up and hard for it. When you *need* it to let off the pressure of waiting for it to come anyway. The greatest sound in the world sometimes. Also the worst. Definition of a love/hate relationship, this way I feel about the printer. Like the bass drum in a parade, I can feel it tapping and clattering in my chest and belly, tickling that sweet spot between lungs and guts. I want to climb up onto the pass and hump the printer. Love it right up. Sometimes I hear the fucking thing in my sleep.

"Going down . . ."

Hero: "That's what she said!"

"Going down . . . Wendy: Texas for french. Side of three. Hero, OM going links. That's it."

Freddy: "Wheel, fries coming up. CFS in the window. Waiting on . . . ?"

"OE/mash. Say again: OE/*mash*, please. That's a single. Hero?"

"Put it up, fryers."

Freddy puts a leathery, up-from-frozen chicken-fried steak on a plate, big blob of up-from-powder mash from the steam table, naps both with peppery white gravy, then sends it skidding down the hot aluminum of the pass shelf. Hero catches it without looking up, slides a perfect binary set of over-easy eggs onto the empty third of the plate, and pushes it to the top of the pass.

"Eggs say sell me!"

"Sold," I bark, pull the dupe off the slide, check the server name. "Mary, pickup!" I slap down the check and I'm feeling good. That's one. Only a couple thousand left to go.

James: "Fryer. Burgers. Po me. Wendy, I need burger rolls, little buddy. Like right now."

Freddy's pulling fries. I turn and see Wendy standing still, eyes banging around in his skull. I reach out, touch him in the middle of the chest. Just touch him. He jerks as if I'd stabbed him with a hot fork.

"Hey, Wendy. Relax. Breathe. We're okay. Your man needs burger rolls. I need toasts and cakes."

Hero yells, "Wendy, Texas for french."

"Hang in," I continue. "Just listen. Do what you're told. You'll be cool."

"I need a knife," he says quietly, in a small voice. I look down at his board. Afraid to ask where anything was, he'd been spreading butter with his fingers.

"Eggs in the window!"

"Fries waiting for plates!"

"Jesus . . . ," I say.

THINGS ARE LIMPING ALONG. James and I are sharing the weight of helping Wendy do his job, holding his hand, walking him, time after time, back up out of the weeds. It's not impossible. On a busy line, everything is about time. Time is broken down into discrete intervals and repetition. How long does it take you to reach for an egg? Crack an egg? Whisk an egg and spread it across the shimmering steel of a flat-top grill? You time those, put them and their required motions together in series: that's a unit. The assembly of ingredients atop this skin of egg is another. Rolling the omelet, folding it using only the blade of the spatula, and lifting it onto the plate? A unit. Put those three units together, you have an omelet. Somewhere in there is always ten seconds to call a check, search the rail for an AWOL plate, help Wendy make toast. The thing you give up is the time you might've taken to rest, to take a breath, to collect yourself. Ten seconds at a time.

Clack clack clack.

"Ordering . . . steak/eggs, steak/eggs, motherfucker . . . Meat loaf going dinner salad, please, James. Short stack blue, two sides of three. Dammit. James again: club sandy going fries, please. Freddy, help James. Those steaks are mid-rare, middy. Hero: eggs are scrambled. Side bagel, dry. Side bacon."

Clack clack clack.

"Adding on . . ."

Freddy: "Wheel, selling fingers/fries, cheese sticks, fingers/mash, fish times four."

Me: "Hero?"

"Two minutes."

"Eggs and browns sell me, buddy. Poachers, four over."

"Two minutes."

Freddy: "Fryer dragging eggs, dude. Come on."

Hero scowls, lagging.

Me: "I'm selling the check, Hero. Plates are one, two, three, four, five-up—right in front of you." To the trench, shouting: "Floor! I need Summer, Mary, Blond Mary, right now. Orders up!" To the line: "Adding on . . . Easy layup. Two quarter cheese, both mid-rare, both fries, setups to the board. Freddy, that is . . . That's twelve fries all-day."

"Wheel. Twelve, thank you. Fryer is six up, six down. Waiting meat and *eggs!*" Freddy bounces a frozen french fry off Hero's head.

"Fuck you, Freddy. Wheel, overs up, poachers up, browns up and down. Sell it." Hero reaches over and shoves Freddy. Freddy just laughs.

And then comes the explosion—a huge, chuffing *whoof* from behind me, sappers inside the wire. I feel scorching heat and smell burning hair. Someone is screeching. I hear cursing like I've never heard before. I spin around, see flames. Somebody hits me from behind.

"Man," Hero shouts, "you're on fire." He hits me again.

It was just my hair—rat-tail of my grown-out Mohawk, lit like a candlewick. Wendy has retreated, shaking, all the way to Freddy's end and looks ready to leap into his arms.

"Extinguisher!" I yell. James is already running for it, shoving Hero and me out of the way. I lose my balance and put my hand palm-down on the flattop. Don't even feel it. There's fire on the back line, scorch marks on the plastic. We've got about ten seconds before the ANSUL system goes off—the automatic fire-suppression equipment under the hood that will fill the entire line with chemical smoke and foam. "What the fuck happened?"

"Four-burner!" Hero yells, pointing. He shoves past me. One of the toasters is on fire. I grab it, tear it out of the wall and hurl it back into the kitchen through the open door. Hero slams both fists down on the edge of the cutting board covering the gas four-top, pops it out of its place and drops it to the floor—partially melted. When it comes free, flames leap in a huge mushroom cloud, then collapse into a minor inferno on the stovetop.

"Extinguisher for fuck's sake! James!"

There's a god-awful banging coming from the kitchen. Hero is trying to kick the melted, smoking cutting board clear.

Hero: "Gas is on!"

Me. "What?"

"Gas!"

He runs his hand along the tops of the dials that control the gas to the burners, yelps, kicks a massive dent in the front of the antique four-top. The fire dies down but doesn't go out. With its leaky lines and bad seals I wonder what it would take for the entire thing to go up like a bomb. I lift a bucket of sanitizer water from the end of the cold table and dump it over the top of the stove, dousing the remaining flames. Smell of hot bleach. Smoke. Everyone freezes, all eyes on the gleaming silver nozzles of the ANSULs.

We wait for it.

And wait.

James comes around the corner at a run, hits the soapy bleach water splashed onto the floor, and goes out lateral like in a Benny Hill sketch—feet out from under him, hanging in the air. Then he goes down on his ass. Make it better? The extinguisher lands right on his stomach, knocking the wind out of him. Could've been funnier only if it'd hit him in the nuts. Then went off.

Clack clack clack clack.

"Okay, someone tell me what the fuck just happened?"

Clack clack clack clack.

Here's what happened: No one had shut off the gas to the four-burner after thawing the fish. When we'd popped the filters out of the ventilation hood to get the poached-fish stink out of the line, the resultant suction had snuffed the flames and pilots. With the fires out, no one had thought to check to see that the gas was actually shut off—which it wasn't. All four valves were turned to full-on, and since the numbers had long ago worn off the dials themselves (two of which were missing anyway, leaving just metal stumps like on a broken car radio), no one had noticed. I don't know the math—what volume of flammable gas was being pumped out every minute for a couple of hours—but later that night, after business is done and we are talking about it, rehashing the whole scene and laughing so hard we cry, I feel as though we had gotten lucky. Most of the gas, I assume, had been sucked up into the hood. Some of it apparently hadn't. Add a spark (probably from Wendy's toasters), and *boom*—one very localized Hiroshima. A giant column of flame that probably just missed blowing the roof off the building, seeing as the ventilation ducts were likely full of gas as well.

So we're down one toaster, one cutting board and one haircut. The back of my neck is red and burned, the calluses on my palm seared. (It smells like barbecue, just so you know.) Hero burned his own hand pretty good on the two dials. (I crank down the two stumps with a pair of tongs.) James bruised his ass and can't stop laughing. Wendy, though unhurt, is completely traumatized.

I ask James what took so long with the extinguisher.

It was locked, he tells me; the latch that connected it to the wall bracket closed with a little gold padlock like one a teenage girl would have on her diary. He'd tried to pry it loose with a soup ladle and, when that didn't work, had bashed it off with the baker's gram scale: the heaviest thing close at hand.

"Locked?" I say, outraged. "They can't lock a fucking fire extinguisher! What if—"

James reminds me of a couple months ago when we'd thought it would be funny to surprise one of the FNGs with a shot from the extinguisher while he was outside smoking. This had turned (as these things will) into a fire-extinguisher fight. After that, management had locked up the firefighting equipment. And James is right. I guess I'm not that surprised.

"That was a good night," I say.

"Damn good night."

"We should do that again."

"Maybe later, huh?"

Clack clack clack clack.

WE'RE BEHIND NOW, and coming up on the bar. It's actually been a pretty light hit so far, all things considered. A warm-up. Undercard for the main event, complete with fireworks. We scramble to catch up, each of us in the slot, working with mechanical precision—crack, shake, flip, turn, crack, turn, flip. Everything is right where I reach, my hands falling unerringly on target. Orders are all coming up at the same time. It's magic time. Checks are being sold seemingly the minute they come out of the printer, as fast as I can yank them off the slide. For a blessed few minutes we hit that groove where nothing outside our little box of steel and fire exists, where the entire universe is reduced down to the moves that we all (even Wendy) know by heart: flip, turn, reach, crack, reach, turn, flip.

"I need Blond Mary, Summer, Wally, Slim. Sold, sold, sold and sold."

Slapping dupes down onto the hot metal of the pass, pinning them under plates. A refire on a steak buries James temporarily, screws up his rhythm on the grill, but he recovers fast, dancing out of the weeds.

"Wheel, refire medium. Sold!"

"Mary, Mary, Slim. Orders up, you fuckers. Sold and sold."

We're cooking so fast that we're running out of room on the pass. Plates are getting stacked on top of plates.

"Floor! Goddammit, I need servers. I need pickups."

I see a waiter go skulking by: Slim, the fat kid. "You!" I point, hoping to pin him to the floor with my magical wheelman superpowers. "Don't walk away from me, motherfucker. Go get your friends. Checks up!"

Slim shrugs, stammers and backs around the corner.

Hero plates four egg orders: bang, bang, bang, bang. He leans in close to me. "Call in the runners, man. We can clear this."

I look across the dupes on the slide, check the three in my hand, the clock, the condition of my troops. I do some quick math in my head. Hero is right. A couple of runners who can get all this food out of the pass and onto people's tables might be enough to put us ahead of the curve. I see a patch of daylight and run for it.

"Two minutes," I tell Hero. "I'm calling them in. Pass the word."

Hero tells Freddy. I tell James, tell Wendy to put everything he has on plates, like, now. "My hand, Wendy. Everything." Then to the line: "Fire it all. Let's dig out. Go."

Everyone puts their heads down, quickly memorizing everything they have on the board. I take a deep breath, clear my head and start re-calling everything on the slide, factoring in the new orders in my hand. Before I'm even halfway through, James and

Hero and Freddy start calling back to me—repeating everything I say out loud in their own order, their own slang, which helps everyone remember, helps them focus when they're mapping twenty burgers onto the grill, forty orders of pancakes, two dozen egg orders, whatever.

"Blow 'em out," I finish. "Wheel down for two."

I sprint off the line, collect two busboys and two dishwashers who have to strip out of their disposable plastic aprons. These are my runners. I herd them ahead of me out into the trench and start loading them down with trays, sending them out in two squads of two to deliver food to waiting tables—anything I can lay hands on, clearing my pass for more food coming.

The instant the servers see runners on the floor, they freak out and come at a sprint. My using runners means that they are not waiting on their tables. Their tips go down. They get inundated with sudden requests for bottles of ketchup, straws, refills on water or coffee—all the things that the runners don't carry with them. Management gets complaints from angry customers who were ignored by "that little brown feller with the dirty fingernails" or cursed at in Spanish for requesting napkins, a spoon. This all makes the servers' jobs harder for a few minutes, means they bring home a few less dollars at the end of the night.

But ask me how much I care about the servers' tips right now. Go ahead. *Ask* me.

TWO A.M. Ten minutes till the bar rush arrives.

The whole dining room is fed. The rail is clear. We're dug out and back on top, catching our breath. That's when Freddy decides to slug Hero.

Sucker punch, actually. Hero's back is turned. And it isn't hard and Freddy is laughing—just joking, really, payback for the hose thing earlier—but Hero takes it all wrong, spins around and lays Freddy out; hitting him with a solid, straight-arm punch in the chest. Hero has been having a bad night. He's just in no mood.

A fight on the line is dangerous. There are lots of knives, boiling oil, long, pointed forks, any number of things that would make excellent clubs or cudgels. It's some seriously medieval shit. You could kill a guy with a ten-inch chef's knife, easy; cave in someone's skull with one of the heavy pig-iron weights we use for bricking well-done burgers and steaks.

But Freddy chooses none of these things. He hits Hero with a fish.

More accurately, with a handful of fish, a big wad of it clawed up out of one of the pans full of poached haddock and batter. He struggles to his feet and crams it right in Hero's face.

Blinded, Hero flails. The fish pan gets knocked to the floor. The two of them grab each other and they both go down. Somehow, Freddy ends up on top, smearing chunky fish and batter into Hero's hair, humping his back, moaning at him, "Oh, yeah. You like that, don't you? You *looove* the fishies, don't you?"

It's like hockey. No one is so dumb that they're going to get between two guys fighting in such cramped quarters until they hit the ground. Hero is still flailing, trying to get his hands on Freddy, but James steps in and grabs Freddy by the hair and collar. I plant my boot in the middle of Hero's back and kick him down. Separated, both of them bounce to their feet, covered in fish chunks, batter, whatever disgusting detritus had stuck to them while they were on the floor. They look like trash golems, panting monsters brought to life out of the fetid crap left over at the end of a hard rush.

James stands between them, holding out his hands like a traffic cop. "Stop!" he yells. "You're scaring Wendy."

I've got my hands on Hero's shoulders, but he shakes loose of me. I'm wearing some of his fish on my T-shirt. Freddy's bent over now, massaging his chest where Hero hit him. Both of them are giggling.

"Go get cleaned up," I tell them. "And no hitting. Be nice."

Hero gouges some fish out of his eyes and wipes his hands on my shirt in passing, making sure to get plenty down my collar. Freddy locks James in a big bear hug. They head for the back door, leaving sticky footprints on the red tile kitchen floor.

Clack clack clack clack.

I tear the ticket free. Ten-top. Just sat. "Here they come again," I mutter, then shout back over my shoulder, "Make it fast, guys! We got tables incoming!"

Wendy is staring at the check over my shoulder, puzzling over the computer-printed hieroglyphs.

"What do you want?" I ask.

"Just looking," he says. "Is it always like this?"

I hang the check, look at the mess of the fryer station, the fish batter smeared everywhere, the torn french-fry bags, eggshells that missed the trash, dropped toast, greasy handprints, crumbs and sausage links and burger rolls ground into the nonskid mats. Looking out across the pass toward the hostess stand, I can see parties starting to back up again at the door. In the bathroom, I can hear Hero and Freddy having a water fight.

"Yeah," I say. "Pretty much, it is."

THE NEXT THREE HOURS WERE A SCREAMING, stinking, crushing nightmare that none of us thought was ever going to end. The tables, they just kept coming. And coming. And *coming*. We couldn't get them off the floor fast enough to chew through the bottleneck at the door, couldn't fight our way far enough ahead that we could ride the wave of a turn—the lull between seatings where the busboys are frantically clearing tables and the servers taking drink orders. It was just a solid wall of tickets on the slide, a fat stack of them in my hand; panic calls for fries and toast and cakes and burgers and fish and eggs and eggs and eggs: fill the grills, empty them, fill them right back up again.

In the baking warmth, the fish started cooking on us. Hero was the worst off because no matter what he did, he couldn't scrub the batter out of his hair. He worked the rest of the night wearing a crown of gummy fish batter, a decomposing meat helmet cooking in the heat rising up off the egg grill.

Around four in the morning, I started slipping, forgetting my place in the tangled skein of checks and holds and fire orders, the whole line of them blurring out into senselessness. And maybe that could've been forgiven under the circumstances. I mean, I'd been lit on fire. There'd been the fish, the fight. This was my twenty-second consecutive night shift.

But those are all just excuses—rationales for collapse. And even if they were pretty good ones, they didn't help. You did the job until you couldn't do it anymore, until you died in the traces like a sled dog in a Jack London story—proud to have held up as long as you did, happy to have gone down fighting and among friends. That's the deal you make with yourself. That's the deal we all make together, every night.

I started slamming Texas speedballs to keep my head together: two strong coffees with a beer chaser, darting off the line every time the grills loaded up, putting holds on checks and running out for the Dumpster corral to pound a longneck and half a cigarette, rotating Hero, James and Freddy out like relay runners, slapping them on the back, giving them two minutes of quiet and darkness.

When I ran, Hero would spell me on wheel, grinding out tables as fast as he could, assembling checks from spare parts and plates left on the pass, robbing two tables to sell one. When he ducked out, I flipped eggs—sliding smoothly into his spot, my focus narrowing, cracking and flipping and plating as fast as I was able. But he was doing more of a favor for me than I was for him. All I was doing was standing in his place, splinting a temporary break in the line. He was watching my back, bracing me up, covering for me in my weakness without saying a word. He had every right to call me out of my post, saying, "You're fucked. Step off." But he didn't.

"You're my friend," he said. "Let's get this night done."

And he was wearing the fish hat, ferchrissakes. He smelled like death and the ocean. He was in way worse shape than I was. But he was still in there, still swinging, trying to keep me on my feet and the line together. I loved the fucker for that.

THE LAST TABLE CLEARED the pass just after five.

"Trip-waffle—fruit, fruit, dry. OE going bacon, side of three. Order up! Rail is clear. Line is down."

We all filed out, through the kitchen, into the back hallway where the morning bread and dry-goods order was already coming in. We curled up on the flour sacks, sprawled on milk crates and empty bread racks. With Lucy joining us, we lay in a pile like corpses, heads on each other's shoulders, stinking feet up on knees, chain-smoking and scrubbing ice water into our faces, joking weakly, crunching handfuls of ibuprofen in anticipation of the pain that would come when the adrenaline wore off. The night was already passing into memory, becoming part of the lore of the house. Remember that time the kitchen exploded . . . ? Remember the fish fight . . . ? Remember Wendy . . . ?

Wendy. We never saw him again after that first night. That's probably no surprise. There are easier ways to make six bucks an hour.

But the rest of us? Eventually we peeled ourselves off the floor. We scrubbed down the line, bricked our grills, cooked a few early-riser tickets while we stocked up for the breakfast shift (a far less odious collection of fellow travelers than were the dinner crew) and hauled our trash. By 8:00 a.m., we were headed out to our cars. The sun was up. It was Saturday morning. In just a few hours, we were all due back to do it over again.

SOMEONE HAD SCRAWLED FUCK U across the windshield of my car in fish batter. It had dried in the morning sun to a hard crust. I climbed in, lit a cigarette, turned on the engine and hit the wipers.

Someone had removed my wiper blades.

Hero roared up next to me in his car, gave me the finger and punched it out of the parking lot, laughing the whole way.

I drove home, squinting through the smeared batter, trying not to fall asleep. When I woke up, I told myself, I would take Hero's wiper blades out of the backseat, screw them onto my own car's wiper arms. When I woke up, I would clean the windshield. When I woke up, maybe I would talk to Sam, take a shower, have something to eat, dress last night's wounds. When I woke up, I would pretend, for a couple of hours, I had something on my mind other than fryers, fish, egg plates, numbers and the countdown toward midnight when the next rush would come.

LA MÉTHODE

lost the wheel shortly after. I don't remember how long I hung on, exactly. Maybe another month. Probably less. But when I did finally go down, I did it in *style*: in a storm of curses, finger-pointing recriminations and whining, too drunk even to stand at my post, too burned out to care, tired beyond what I thought to be my capacity for exhaustion. By the end, I wasn't even calling checks anymore, just random combinations of menu items—frantic transmissions from my frontal lobes, garbled requests for fries, cakes, sandwiches, anything. Shouting them out of some panicked, lizard-brain reflex, calling them because *something* needed to be called, and just hoping that I would somehow hit that magic sequence of orders that would fix everything, lift me out of the hole I'd gotten myself into.

All I needed was five minutes. "Just gimme five minutes. Five minutes is all I need. I'll be fine." But I needed so much more than that. When neither Hero or James could talk me down off the post, someone went for Lucy. I was already heading slowly for the floor by the time she got there.

Luz walked me out the back door. I apologized the whole way—between explosions of incoherent fury—and she just nodded her head. "You're done, baby. You're done." As was my habit, I blamed everyone I could think of—my guys for conspiring against me, the management, the customers who would just not stop coming.

Outside, she sat me down against the back wall and left me there. Like trash. A piece of ruined equipment. At that point, it felt okay to stop fighting. I'd done as well as I could for as long as I could, had eventually failed as every machine eventually must. For the past couple weeks, I'd been dreaming about work every day while I slept. Nothing weird, just work. I would do my time on the line, come home, crawl into bed, close my eyes, then do another full dream-shift in my sleep, waking tired and sore a few hours later to go and do it again for real. It'd been so long since I'd seen a night without work that the dark felt strange, the quiet foreign.

From where I sat, I could hear cars coming and going from the parking lot. I could see their lights. Orders were still streaming through my head. Lists of things that needed doing, stock levels that were running low inside. It was a busy night, but not a killer, and if I felt bad about anything just then, it was only leaving my guys a man down and missing out on all the fun. I fell asleep sitting by the back door, waking only once to stagger over behind the Dumpsters and throw up. Once my head was clear enough to drive, I went home and slept for two straight days.

James took my place at the wheel. As fads are wont to do, country line dancing quickly faded in popularity. The bar across the street briefly became a teen nightclub, I think. Or something like that. The county probably uses it to store snowplows today.

In any event, things were never really the same. I feel fortunate now that I'd been there for the good times. I know that I was lucky to have been witness to (and a willing participant in) the madness that went on there, to have learned the kind of things I learned— the tricks, the moves, the style. I was tough now. I had no fear. I'd earned my stripes in the box, and the scars I walked away with were enough to prove my worth to anyone. Some people feel blessed to have been in the stands when the Red Sox won the Series or on the floor of the New York Stock Exchange when the tech bubble burst. Some people think that the best, most important days of their lives were the ones they spent at war. Me? I'm just glad I was cooking when "Achy Breaky" was huge. When silly hats and big belt buckles were all the rage.

• • •

HERE'S ONE OF THE GREAT THINGS about working in restaurants: in the annals of career-ending food-service freak-outs and high-speed kitchen meltdowns, my little tantrum barely even moved the needle. In the real world, you show up at the office one day in a shitfaced lather, waving a knife around and accusing your coworkers of a clandestine conspiracy against you, it's going to be a problem. Stick with the act long enough and it's probably going to land you on the evening news.

But when hanging out with chefs, I don't even tell that story anymore. It's just not worth it. In a high-stress, high-pressure business like the restaurant industry, heavily populated as it is by egotistical perfectionists, knife-wielding manic-depressives, short-timers with often highly dubious histories and unstable sensualists of every stripe, jobs get quit and careers get tarnished all the time. When sitting around with the lifers telling tales of crews deserted and positions abandoned, it's really assault-or-better to open. Being shown the door in the middle of a drunken snit? That's not even enough to cover the ante.

According to legend, when a young Bobby Flay burned out on the Manhattan restaurant scene, he had a friend get him a job as a clerk on the American Stock Exchange. When I tried to find my path out of the industry, I got a job working the night shift at a porn store thanks to a friend in Rochester whose dad managed a chain of them. I guess what they say is right: it's all about who you know. Anyway, at least I was comfortable with the hours.

After a couple months, when I soured on selling cheerleader-gang-bang videos to skulking old men and inflatable sheep to drunken frat boys, I ended up delivering magazines (normal ones) door-to-door. That lasted roughly two weeks. Right up until my car— a fifth-hand Dodge Aspen with a bad carburetor and no radio, bought for three hundred bucks to replace the Caprice Classic that'd taken me all the way to California and back and to work at the diner every night—died from the stress and shame of being used to haul hundreds of pounds of *Ladies' Home Journals* around the neighborhood.

IN THE END, I always found my way back to the kitchens. Year after year and city after city, restaurant after restaurant after restaurant. Nowhere else in the world did I feel in control of my life. Nowhere else did I feel so strong.

Plus, I honestly did love the food. I found it completely fascinating—the power of artichokes, the history of salt, beef's marbled topography and the secret language of shallots dancing in the pan. I studied a lot on my own time, reading books, experimenting in the cool and quiet of Monday night, pre-hit, or mornings when the kitchen was still gentle and everyone was trying to work mindlessly through their hangovers. At home, I watched PBS cooking shows, devoured cooking magazines for the pictures and for the writing of people who seemed even more fascinated by tuna, by saffron, by salt, than I was.

I even read a couple cookbooks, though found no help there. The cooking described in nearly any commercially available cookbook has about as much in common with the cooking done in professional kitchens as I do with Julia Child. Cooking times? Measuring cups? Five hours of prep time for a dinner for two? You must be kidding. Cookbooks (with a few, rare exceptions)* are porno for kitchen hobbyists and well-meaning amateurs. In my world, when recipes existed at all, they read like brilliant little haiku, like hieroglyphics—an alien tongue far removed from any natural language, pretty gibberish to all but those on the inside of the cult that produced it. *Pull chix. Pound chix. Roll chix. Brown chix. Hold.* That was one of

---

*These being books like Harold McGee's *On Food and Cooking*, some stuff by Patricia Wells, Payard, Pépin and Julia Child, sauce-stained and ragged English translations of *Larousse Gastronomique* or even the original French, some of the Dornenburg-Page books (for inspiration), a surprising amount of old Betty Crocker cookbooks broken at the spine to whatever recipe gave the chef the most trouble or the most joy, and *The French Laundry Cookbook*, which was probably one of the first gastroporn cookbooks written *for* chefs.

my favorites—prep instructions for making chicken roulade, written out on a cocktail napkin and hung above the station of a part-time banquet prep cook at a hotel kitchen in Rochester. Not too long ago, I spent a day with a good friend in his kitchen in Denver. He's a brilliant cook, a young chef who came up the same way I did. Sitting with him at the bar in the morning, he showed me the plates he was going to be working up for the night's tasting menu by pulling a wrinkled sheaf of papers from his pocket, smoothing them against the rail, and tapping them with a capped Sharpie marker. One plate per page, and on each page not a single word of direction, not a breath of ingredient lists or cooking times—just a sketch showing plating, a scattering of letters and numbers, cryptic reminders to himself scrawled in the margins: *grape cav, whipped bals, nitro, olive dust, clean office.* This would be what he and his crew would be working from that night, what they would use as their prep list, their map for navigating the night's service. Even after years off the hot line myself, I still understood the language, the cant of the professional. Had my buddy dropped dead from a heart attack right there on the floor ten minutes before the first seating, I would've been able to step in and help. A little, anyway. I wouldn't have been completely lost.

SO EVEN IF SOMETIMES (oftentimes . . .) I would find the industry maddening, owners foolish, customers intolerable, and The Life a crippling bad influence on any attempt I made at becoming a decent, good and reasonable man, there was always the food—at the center of my every day at work.

For years, food would be my first concern in the morning, walking into quiet kitchens, the chilling cold of walk-ins, to sniff garlic, tug the skins of chickens, run my fingers across mushrooms in their cases to feel for dampness and earth. It would be the last thing I thought of at night. In my twenties, I was still learning, still gathering knowledge and skills and lore. But today, I could write you a book about barbecue, a novel of fish (because so much fish knowledge is specious at best). The dubious stories of French chefs dispatched to the far corners of the globe in cuisine's dark ages, like missionaries of cassoulet and *sauce gribiche*, tickle my inner geek the way uncertain histories always have. The legend of baklava?* I love that, have thought long and hard and have determined that were the choice given to me—apple of knowledge or peace and honeyed walnuts—I would've been perfectly content wandering the Garden with my ding-dong hanging out and eating baklava forever.

In the galley, on the line, even in the worst backroom and basement prep kitchens, I was being paid to play with knives and fire, to spend pretty much every waking hour surrounded by the one thing I found most interesting in all the world. I've gotten to know a lot of cooks and chefs since then. And among them, the story is almost always the same: they got into the industry for the money, for the ready access to cheap and powerful chemicals and the opportunity to sleep with athletic and morally challenged waitresses, but they stayed for the food. I was no different. Even when I was broke and exhausted, hungover, beat-up or hurt, even when I was slopping buffet breakfasts for hotel guests or standing up in my white jacket, toque and black button-caps carving steamship rounds for wedding receptions, I knew I was lucky. As I'd once done at Ferrara's, every time I went back to the industry, at the beginning of every new job, I made the same promise: *This time*, I would tell myself, *this time I'm not going to fuck it up.*

I FUCKED IT UP. Every time. I fucked it up until there wasn't any up left to fuck. My first time handling black truffles (not the big, beautiful, fist-size monsters only ever seen in gastroporn cookbooks or TV money shots, but small, serviceable ones about the size of a withered knuckle), I was told by the chef to be careful. This was in Buffalo, working under a sous-chef in a kitchen laid out like a factory floor.

---

*The way the story goes, baklava was what Adam and Eve were fed in the Garden of Eden—honey and nuts—and that an imperfect knowledge of it was what they brought out into the world with them when they left.

"Slice," he said, holding my wrist, bringing his big hand down like a karate chop onto my palm. "Then chop. Not rough, not fine. Just *between*, yes? Then here"—pointing to the giant mixing bowl in which I was making wild-mushroom stuffing—"then there," pointing to the big, recalcitrant baker's oven.

"Yeah, chef."

"You must watch," he said, jabbing a fat, mauled fingertip at his own eye, then the oven.

"Yeah, chef."

"Watch."

And that's the part I screwed up. I ducked out for a smoke and to wash what I then thought was the horrible, earthy, sour-sweat stink of truffles off my fingers. Meanwhile, the truffled stuffing burned. Just a little, but enough to ruin it completely. And the chef didn't yell. He didn't throw the pan against the wall in a rage. He called me over, made me scrape it all into the trash myself with a spoon while he (and everyone else in the kitchen) watched.

Then he had me make it again.

"Watch," he said, and this time I was afraid to blink.

I broke sauces. I broke equipment. In a tiny, cramped galley where I worked as a saucier and sauté cook, I broke my hand (again) in a knockdown scuffle on the garde-manger station trying to punch a station cook who'd stolen my chive sticks—little lengths of chive, brilliant green and used for garnish. The smart move would've been to simply cut more chive sticks, but this was a matter of principle. The guy had stolen from my *mise en place*. Unforgivable—like fucking my wife or taking my knife. But when I went to hit him, I missed, punched the door handle on his cooler, worked the rest of the night with my pinkie taped to my ring finger and in a fog of ibuprofen and cooking vodka.

I'd come from the low end of the culinary world, both personally and professionally. I'd never eaten coq au vin, pâté or crème brûlée growing up, and I'd certainly never cooked these things. But I picked up cuisines the way some people do languages: by immersion and repetition, beginning with a few basic phrases and building a workable

lexicon around them. After the diner, after my final attempt at walking away from the restaurant industry and then coming back to it
like a recalcitrant lover who'd gone hound-dogging but come back
home again when the guilt became unmanageable, I'd accepted that
kitchens were where I was happiest and that cooking was just something I had a knack for. Not the art of it necessarily. That came, but it
was never my strong suit. I learned early that I was a soldier—not just
the kind of guy who could *survive* the pressure, the heat, the killing
stress, but one who thrived on it. I came to love the long hits, the
machine-gun chatter of the ticket machine spitting out orders, the
throbbing surge of panic adrenaline when the rush came in—first
seating, Saturday night—and the screaming, the curses, the flames.

True, I also adored the odd lull, ducking out into some stinking alley or dark loading dock for half a cigarette sucked down while my
station was cool and the garde-manger man was getting murdered. I
loved the beginning of the day and the calm of a house not yet awake
and the end of the night when all was said and done. Slammed,
buried, *dans la merde* on a Friday night, nothing more was expected
of me than to find my way out again, to perform with perfect machine
precision and faultless replication—to sing out loud in the only language that truly mattered.

The worse things got in the kitchen, the quieter things got in my
head, until the act of slicing a single bulb of garlic, the quartering of a
tomato, the precise placement of a halibut fillet in a smoking-hot pan,
could expand and balloon outward to fill my entire universe.

AT HOME, Sam and I would eat cold omelets, cold steaks, lukewarm
pastas barely reheated in our one pan over an electric element in the
weird light of 2:00 a.m.—everything brought in from my kitchens,
eaten in bed, on the fragile cusp of exhaustion. Sex on rumpled
sheets, sleepy and disjointed, our bones knocking together when we
were skinny and poor; her kisses tasting of Canadian beer and dope
tar, mine of cigarettes, low-grade dread and, only later, Moët, truffles,
foie gras. I took after the guys I worked beside. I was smoking three

packs of cigarettes a day. I was either explosively keyed up or asleep. I would fight over anything. I couldn't get through a sentence without using the word *fuck* seven or eight times, as a verb, an adjective, an adverb, a reflexive noun, a personal pronoun—sometimes all of them at once: "That fucking fucked-up motherfucking little fucker."

Early on, when my world was back-to-back weekend doubles, riding the fryers, cooking for drunks and calling orders to galleys full of junkies, dropouts and mercenaries, I thought things might be different in the fine-dining world.

I found that they weren't. Not even a little. And that suited me just fine.

I'd had six or seven or maybe eight different restaurant jobs by the time I was twenty-three. By twenty-five or twenty-six, it was maybe double that—some of which I would admit to, some of which I wouldn't. The time I'd spent in hash houses and diners, checkered-tablecloth neighborhood Italian joints and terrible, awful, troughlike buffets made me a precious commodity to a certain type of boss. In busy houses and established kitchens, speed was always more important than smarts, stamina infinitely more priceless than a canonical knowledge of Escoffier. The prevailing wisdom at the time (a view that has fallen ridiculously out of favor these days, and you can taste the effect) was that skills could be polished and recipes taught, but chops you gotta earn. I was surprised to find that no one cared what I knew or didn't know about scalding, braising or emulsification. All anyone wanted to hear about were my hours (which is to say how much money my former places of employment rang up during their prime seatings), my covers (how many individual people my kitchens and crews could feed in a night), and my cost (how much I expected to be paid for lending my muscle to the team).

Hours, counts and covers—those numbers were easy. I knew them inside out and backward because they were akin to bragging rights: three turns of an eighty-seat dining room inside a five-hour dinner service, plus bar and patio, was a cinch. At twelve to fifteen bucks a head? Call it a grand, even—though I could easily lie and bump that up to a grand and a half with no one getting suspicious.

And as for how much I was worth? That varied wildly from year to year, place to place, whether I was being put on the books legally or paid out of the register at the end of the week. But the paychecks always came down to the same hard juxtaposition: being both more than enough and not even close to enough. You put in a hundred hours a week, that doesn't leave a lot of time for spending money. You pay your bills when you remember, you buy a little weed and a lot of beers. After a couple months, you start feeling rich because there's a fat wad of cash or stack of IOUs scrawled out on waitress dupes. But then you do something stupid. You get pissed at the chef, grow bored with the menu, get to hate the mix tape that the *grillardin* plays all night, every night, on the skeevy galley radio, and you walk out. All of a sudden, the money just *goes*, because now it's Saturday night and you don't have a kitchen, a double shift, sixteen hours on the firing line, to keep you out of trouble. You have to pay for food rather than eating free in the kitchen. All of the little scams dry up, the network of favors owed. At the bar, you're in civvies, not whites, so no one's buying you drinks. You have to pay full price for your drugs. You don't have the structure, the rigor of the work, so you're sleeping till noon, staying out all night, buying things. And before you know it, you're a month back on the electric bill, bouncing rent checks and wondering whether that little bistro down the street might be in need of a warm body on the line.

I would work anywhere, and did. I would leave Rochester and go to Buffalo following the promise of work, leave Buffalo for Florida, leave Florida for Rochester (again), then New Mexico, Colorado, elsewhere. I worked for dumb, rich knuckleheads who would open French restaurants, then frantically front-load the menus with cheeseburgers and pastas when three days went by without anyone ordering the warm leek soup or duck or *salade composée*; who would pay five hundred bucks a pop for custom-made sconces in the dining room, then think they were getting a bargain by paying their illegal-immigrant dishwashers a buck under minimum. And I worked for dedicated craftsmen, for owners who staffed their above-the-line posts with real talent, for chefs who ran their brigades like the small, private armies that they were and understood just by looking at me, my journeyman knife kit, my overcrowded résumé, that I was there as an apprentice—there to learn all I could, work as hard as I could, then move on.

Those French and German and Alsatian expats that I worked with and for, the Russian émigrés, Swiss hotel-school graduates, strange, pale, broad-faced men who could've just as easily been cast as the sweating gunrunners or expert forgers in a Graham Greene novel—they understood what *apprentice* really meant because, for the most part, they'd come up as apprentices, too.

Apprentice meant "slave," or worse. It meant the guy who had to do everything he was told, without question, for little pay and with maximum abuse. Thus did I scrub out grease traps, polish hood vents and stay in the kitchen after closing to scour the backsplashes. I babysat stocks and demis like they were sick children, staying up with them all night, worrying over them. I boned out chickens and ducks, pulled the pin bones from black bass and red snapper, brushed (never washed) the dirt from cases of mushrooms and reduced thousands of damp, verdant bunches of flat-leaf parsley to small piles of chopped parsley that were then used to top innumerable bowls of mussels in garlic-shot beurre blanc and innumerable plates of sole meunière, to make buckets of persillade. I pulled a million stems from a million leaves of spinach and bitter field greens by hand. Why? Because stems taste terrible, have a nasty, woody texture, and look inelegant in a composed salad. I go out to eat now and get a salad full of stems pulled straight from the bag of spring mix mesclun by some nose-picking dipshit of a garde-manger man and it drives me crazy, because I can remember, back in the day, sitting bowed over the prep sink for hours like a brain-dead hump, picking stems until my fingers turned green, knowing that if I missed just one and the chef saw it, he'd probably send me out into the alley to stem the leaves off a fucking tree.

I learned a million tricks over the years. A million and one. I learned to never give up, to never fail, to never, ever admit that I was beat. I learned that there is always another way to do a thing: if you've tried everything you know and nothing is working, try something else. I learned that, above all else, what matters is putting dinner on the table. It makes no difference how you do it. It makes no difference what you, personally, had to go through. No one cares about your struggles, your sweat, your long hours or what final, last-minute miracle you pulled. Just put dinner on the table. And once dinner is on the table? Walk away. If you've done your best, if you've truly done all you can, then there is nothing more you can do. There's always tomorrow for doing better.

At the Left Bank in Buffalo, Matt—one of the cooks, a station chef—explained to me everything there is to say about the business of professional cooking. He summed it up in two sentences: "We cook the food," he told me. "And then we go home."

AS I BOUNCED FROM NICER RESTAURANT to nicer restaurant, I rose quickly: prep crew, then pantry (which I loved), and garde-manger (which I didn't), and finally back onto the hot line. Born Italian in this business, I would find myself being raised French, earning my stripes and my scars as part of a proper brigade. I flourished within the brutal strictures of the old Frog brigade system, with its militaristic hierarchy and promise of rewards for distinguished service. It was a universe that made sense to me—small and rigidly defined, with the chef as God, his sous or chef de cuisine as prophet and translator of God's sometimes incomprehensible orders, and the rest of us as his quaking, dope-smoking acolytes with our dirty élan and miserable esprit de corps, as closed and weird and zealous and insular as any secret society.

At the time, being a chef or a cook was a straight blue-collar gig. We worked like plumbers or carpenters or masons would, doing the job because the job itself was noble enough. It was a craft, not an art, not a path to anything else. In the days before the Food Network, before cooks got to sit down in their cheap suits and borrowed shoes to rap with Matt and Katie on the *Today* show, parents didn't brag about their kids going to work in kitchens. They lied and said Junior was waiting to hear back from Harvard or angling for a job with the city collecting trash—just doing a little cooking until his father could get him a union card.

These days, too many kids go off to cooking school and then take on their first professional gigs expecting to be called Chef right out of the gate. They act sometimes as though actual *cooking* is beneath them, as if this kitchen work were just something they have to do until their first cookbook deal comes through. But at least among the guys I came up with, chef was Chef—was the end that justified everything that came before and the ultimate goal of all the struggling it took to get there. And there was something decent in that, an order and tradition that was comforting even in a cook's worst moments. Chef got to be Chef because he'd once been a dishwasher—a *plongeur*—like you; a pasty-faced, quivering prep monkey stuck for fourteen hours in some squalid hell, scaling and gutting a quarter ton of sturgeon like you; a stoned pantry cook saddled with the unlovely responsibility of turning Saturday night's leftovers and whatever over-the-hill produce could be salvaged from the trashed walk-in into frittatas or puttanesca or some nightmare "fisherman's stew" for the Sunday special just like you; a sharp, vicious station chef like you; a hard-eyed veteran sous like you. Chef had *earned* his post, so if he screamed at you for trussing the duck crookedly or slapped a fistful of cold liver in your face because the pâté didn't quite meet with his impossible (and never quite articulated) standards, that was okay because the universe was an orderly place. The same thing had been done to him once, and the promise was that someday you'd do the same thing to some other junior *rôtisseur* or *poissonarde* in turn.

Abuse and terror and awe and strong drink were what made the world go round in the cramped, hot, despotic and nepotistic microcosm that I called home, and I loved it because, seriously, without that, how else was anybody going to learn to truss the fucking ducks?

THE REST OF MY LIFE I lived like any other college dropout in a rust-belt town. First in Rochester, then Buffalo, Sam and I had a series of awful studio apartments and converted second-floor walk-ups with orange shag carpeting and fake wood paneling with peeling veneer. The places were nearly as empty with us living there as they had been when they were vacant, and at times—strange, castaway nights while between jobs or suffering from insomnia or the spins—I would find myself in a room I barely recognized. Knocking around, alone in the daylight while Sam worked, I would pace the length of these small apartments, counting down the minutes until I was due back at work because without the kitchen I had nothing to do and nowhere to go.

There were notebooks and old take-out containers, piles of dirty T-shirts, newspapers that were weeks old, empty beer bottles, broken chairs, a half dozen ashtrays overflowing with cigarettes and the roach ends of joints; once, a Christmas tree stayed up until August—until it was completely naked of needles and a terrible hazard in a home with two smokers. None of our kitchen or bathroom sink faucets ran smoothly because the little filters had been pulled out to serve as screens for bowls. I suppose, at the time, I saw this as monkish austerity suffered in service to my particular dedication to kitchens and to cooking.

But that was bullshit. Our futon, sleeping bags, milk-crate dresser, twelve-inch black-and-white TV—all of that was kept just because we had nothing else, because I was working a hundred hours a week or more, which doesn't allow a lot of time for shopping. I kept my savings in an envelope stuck under the TV, a mix of cash and IOUs and checks, some of them dated back two months, often getting cashed just ahead of their ninety-day expirations. I owned two pairs of pants that weren't chef pants, two button shirts that weren't restaurant-issue, and one pair of shoes that weren't my work boots.

Kitchens—or anyway, the ones I've known—tend to come as an all-inclusive package deal to those lucky enough to have made a career of cooking dinner for strangers. Along with a paycheck, you get friends, a family, a posse to roll with—automatic, the instant you pull on the whites. You get connections, dealers, girls, booze, opportunity, heartbreak, angles, options, ulcers, scars. A life, complete and real. Kitchens give you a history (even if it's a borrowed one—the history of the last twenty guys who held down your post), a past, a future, however moment-to-moment it might be, a present and a place to belong in it, which is probably the most important thing of all.

It's right there, laid out in abundance, yours to swim around in and get weird with. And for someone like me who had, outside the kitchen, almost none of this—was tabula rasa, brainless, useless, lost, unable sometimes to find my own pants or have a conversation that didn't devolve into some jinky, gutter-mouth prattle about covers, pussy and garlic—this instant sense of community and shared experience was a life preserver. Kitchens were my map and compass, *La Méthode* like a constitution outlining the basic tenets of my republic of one. By the time I was twenty-five, if there was anything to me beyond that which was defined by a white canvas jacket, a perfectly roasted capon, the pure sex of a knife slipping through ripe melon, I knew the rest of it was all just a wound.

PREP AND PANTRY

When Sam and I first moved to Buffalo, I worked at the original Pano's on Elmwood—a twenty-six-seat short-order all-night diner that had been open close to forever. It held down a tiny piece of real estate at walking distance from the university and about three hundred different bars and was infamous across several generations of Buffalonians as a great place for souvlaki or to get your teeth kicked out. No lie, come 3:00 a.m. the lines would stretch out the door and down the block. I worked with two waitresses and one dishwasher: that's it. It was a one-man kitchen placed right behind the counter, open to the entire dining room. I worked close enough to the people at the counter that they could reach out and grab me, and often they did. It was crazy. I loved it. It was such a killer, man-alone, *Lord Jim* trip that I would have done it for free.

When Pano's moved, giving up its old location in favor of a newer, larger, infinitely more plastic one just a few doors down, I quit. In the new digs, there was a proper kitchen and crew, gleaming prep areas, an expansive floor. It was just no fun anymore, and I don't think I lasted even a week before walking out.

For the money, I took on a job at the Clare, a big Irish bar and restaurant attached to a hotel in North Buffalo, just a week before St. Patrick's Day. The owners, in an attempt to staff up in advance of the coming booze-and-blarney shitstorm, were hiring aggressively, offering big money* for experienced guys and decent money for any ambulatory knucklehead or shoemaker who could grip a knife in his claw.

On Saturday morning, I got plugged into the prep line, helping to clean, trim, steam and slice a literal ton of corned-beef briskets. Hustled along by the chef and his sous (two total lifers, as close as lovers, both organizational wizards and master shortcutters totally spaced out on the volume and long hours), I was stuck next to a knife-crazy girl cook and career prep specialist who—for at least our first six hours together—completely schooled me when it came to pure, raw volume of production and the particulars of the St. Paddy's Day feast.

It took us three days, working twelve-to-fourteen-hour shifts, to get through the tractor-trailer load of corned beef that'd been delivered to the Clare's back door. I will never forget the smell (a meaty, soupy, almost sweaty stink rising off the mountains of fat and scrap that accumulated on the prep table) or the feel, the particular *weight*, of the slick, pink, finished briskets as we tossed them, one by one, into storage tubs. Because of the amount of knife work involved in the trimming and slicing, I developed blisters through my calluses, broke them, rubbed the skin raw, and developed even thicker calluses along the ridge of my index finger and the fat pad at the top of my palm. I remembered being told once, at Pano's, *by* Pano, the owner, that I held my knife like some kinda queer—so delicately, so tenderly, while I sliced tomatoes and butchered heads of lettuce. And I'd looked at him like he was an idiot. I held my knife correctly, like a professional, because that was the way Ange had held his all those years ago, and I'd tried to copy Ange in my first, tentative stabs at cutting.

"And this," Pano had said, pawing through the garbage can set at the end of my table, pulling up the tops of a few tomatoes that I'd cut off and discarded because the rippled flesh near the top of a tomato

---

*Probably twelve or thirteen bucks an hour, which, for a line cook, was about as big as it got then upstate.

where the stem grows is sour and tough. "If I was your mother, would you be wasting my tomatoes like this? Go do something else now. I'll find someone who knows how to use a knife."

Among low-rent cooks and those for whom prep consists of little more than stocking a cold table or mangling a few vegetables, the knife grip is like a fist around the handle, constantly punching downward toward the table or cutting board. For professionals, though, it *is* delicate—a loose hold on the handle, thumb slightly extended, index finger either extended along the forte of the blade or curled just a little. It is balanced, allows one to feel the bite of tip and edge, makes maximum use of the knife's own weight. It is the knife fighter's grip, the killer's grip. And after fourteen, forty, four hundred hours, your hand will freeze in that position, your muscles will remember it and never, ever forget.

I also got good with the diamond steel at the Clare and learned to appreciate, on a highly personal level, the art of knife sharpening; developing an almost obsessive tick about wiping my knife on my apron, both sides, then tidying the edge with the steel a dozen or a hundred times a night. Like folding my side towels in a certain way or purposefully melting the flanks of a speed-pourer with my cigarette lighter (a trick I learned from Hero) until I could dent the plastic to the contour of my hand so that I could get a better hold on it when I was rushed, distracted, sweating or under fire, this was a habit that hung with me until I left the kitchens for good.

When the brisket was done—when the last of it was cleaned, steamed, sliced and banked away in the cavernous walk-ins, sitting in a thick brine/marinade made from bay leaves and peppercorns and a large portion of the briskets' own fat—I got moved. One whole day, I did nothing but peel carrots and cut them, *bâtonnet*. I got lucky in that I'd dodged the foul job of prepping the cabbage (by a long reach, the smelliest and most monotonous of the tasks, so therefore handed off to the lowest of the low men on the food chain), then got lucky again in riding a wave of sudden fuck-you resignations straight onto the service line. The chef and sous-chef were both busy coordinating all the prep work and massive geometry problem of storage and shipping. We were using cooler space at a variety of restaurants, and all that product had to be kept track of, figured into the rotation, picked up and delivered. Because of this, I received a battlefield brevet to saucier, claiming a turf of six burners and a flattop.

Wednesday passed in a blur. I had about an hour to look over the menu and figure out how to cook everything on my station before the orders started coming in. Whiskey béchamel, mixed veg (which came off the burners, from out of one huge sauté pan kept over low heat and constantly refreshed with produce), stout gravy for the bangers and mash, a creamy dill sauce, really good lamb stew simmering in a massive stockpot, and some kind of awful cheese sauce to go on top of the "Killarney Chicken" (or whatever it was called), which was nothing more than the cheap cheddar base of an insipid American mac-and-cheese. It was easy enough.

Thursday the floor manager broke his arm—or rather, got his arm broken by a brainless server going out through the in door between kitchen and floor. I stood there in my spot on the line and watched him crumple, the door hitting him just right to shatter the point of his elbow. He was a big guy, rotund but solidly built along the same body lines as a former college pulling guard—heavy but able to move fast over short distances. He went down like a cow hit with a brick, making these adorable little mewling noises, his lips pursed like he was air-kissing an invisible girlfriend.

The chef got the floorman back on his feet, poured the first drink down his neck, told him everything was going to be okay even though he didn't have enough range of motion left to spank the monkey. The guy barely missed a table being sat—washing a fistful of aspirin down with a couple more shots and getting right back to it, keeping his arm folded tight against his belly the rest of the night, looking like Napoléon minus the jacket and silly hat. His hand swelled up and turned purplish. A doctor (friend of the house, a regular at the bar) was rustled up during a break between seatings and took a look at the floorman.

"You need to be at a hospital," said the doc.

"I've got a full dining room," the floorman replied, "I need to be *here.*" And that was that. The doc went home, fetched a sling and some painkillers, brought them back. The floorman never stopped working.

This being Buffalo, it didn't matter what day St. Paddy's actually was. The party went on for a week, nonstop, but on Friday (it being Friday in upstate New York, again), we added a fish fry to the short holiday menu. I got shifted off saucier/sauté and stationed in front of a fryer, surrounded by fish tubs and batter in five-gallon buckets that I would thin periodically throughout the night with bottles of porter poured right in, thinning my own blood the same way and at about twice the rate as I did the batter. With the weekend, the bottles of liquor and other sundry chemicals had been brought up from the locker room (where, in locker number nine, there'd been a bucket full of iced Labatt Blues kept cold for all comers and a bottle of Jameson Irish in number thirteen) and right onto the line. We kept a pour-top of gin and sour mix in the speed rack above the sauté station, and anytime anyone pulled open the freezer door, the entire kitchen filled with the sweet, thick smell of pot smoke.

While setting up the last of the dinner prep, I pulled a sheet tray full of something out of one of the stacked convection ovens. Someone else was coming through the narrow alley between the ovens and the prep table. He went low, I raised the pan up high, accidentally laying the edges of it flat against the insides of both of my forearms. The burns didn't hurt a bit, which was how I knew they were bad—that and the crisp little edges running around the clean, smooth, shiny white lines where the hot metal had actually made contact. Knowing I'd be spending the whole night sunk up to my elbows in bloody fish water, scooping out raw fillets for battering, I put gauze pads from the medical kit over both burns, taped them in place, then wrapped my forearms in plastic wrap. At the time, this had seemed like a wise solution. Now, whenever I get a tan, you can still see the scars real nice.

When St. Paddy's week was over, the chef and his sous collected a bonus based on the amount of business the kitchen had done. It was a small piece (maybe 2 or 3 percent) but that still translated to a fairly huge chunk of change considering the line was firing constantly, three meals a day, from about six in the morning till about two in the morning, and the floor never saw a minute when it wasn't backed up by a turn or more for seven straight days. As soon as they had that money in hand, both were gone. I should have seen it coming. They were on vacation, ostensibly, but I don't know if they ever came back.

Suddenly, I was left in nominal control of the kitchen, responsible for the dinner shift: prep monkey to chef de cuisine in seven days. Not a bad run, except that I hated it—hated every goddamn minute because, for one, I had no real idea how to command an entire kitchen,* and for two, everyone else had quit almost as soon as the chef and sous were out the door.

I was left with a kid so dumb he could fuck up water and an ex-marine who was just nuts—prone to paranoid fantasies and sudden, unexplained absences from the line; who brought a .45-caliber pistol with him to work every night and kept it tucked into the back waistband of his gigantic, size XXL Chefwear pants. He was always pulling up his T-shirt to show me the bullet holes in his hairy back, saying that he'd already done *his* work and needed to take a break now. The only good thing about this arrangement was that the restaurant did hardly any business at all in the few days after St. Paddy's, and I didn't have to do any serious ordering because we were still working through the massive back stock of basic provisions brought in for the holiday.

When I tried to quit, one of the owners offered me a 100 percent raise to stay on—bumping me from around ten an hour to something in the neighborhood of twenty. I agreed grudgingly. That night, the ex-marine pulled his pistol and threatened to shoot one of the steam tables. I stayed late to clean, finished scrubbing down, then sat in the chef's office and wrote a letter detailing all the reasons why I couldn't

---

*I could cook, sure. I could've cooked the Clare's menu standing on my head. I even had some experience with running a crew. But executing a menu and riding herd on a bunch of line cooks is a very different thing from running an entire kitchen. There was ordering to be done, schedules to be written, three meals a day to be coordinated and stocked for, and massive amounts of management and oversight, none of which I'd ever had to concern myself with before.

stay—beginning with the boredom of cooking week-old leftovers for geriatric Hibernians and ending with my very real fear that, sooner or later, my grillman was going to put a fucking bullet in me. By the time I was done, no one else was left in the house for me to quit to, so I spiked my resignation to the cutting board with one of the house knives, packed my kit, and left without looking back.

I've rarely been so happy about leaving a job. My fervent hope was that the owners—in a fit of panic—would be forced to call either the chef or his sous back from whatever weird debauchery they'd sunk themselves into and that one of those bastards could spend the next 360 nights slopping out lamb stew and Killarney Chicken to the good people of Buffalo because I had neither the patience nor the desire.

Finding work was fun. I took a job in a fusion restaurant that opened in a former hair salon and closed almost before the smell of rancid fryer grease had supplanted the stink of burnt hair. I got a job once based almost entirely on my ability to quote from that scene in *Goodfellas* where they're all sitting around, making dinner in prison, and Paulie is slicing the garlic with a razor. Another because I claimed (lying though my teeth) to have just returned from living in France. I wrote an event menu based on my imaginary time there—roasted capon stuffed with lemons and thyme, mussels, *frites* with coarse mustard, pavé of salmon dripping with beurre blanc, and *blanquette de veau*, most of which I didn't know how to prepare—inspired by the gas lamps, cobbled streets, burbling rivers and warm, cozy cafés of a town I'd never seen. I worked a line that operated only with portable butane burners, as a pizza delivery driver (briefly), and as a station chef under the command of an exec I never once met or even saw in the restaurant, but who had assembled a menu that read like it'd been pinched from some psychotic CIA foreign-service lawn fete—all melon balls and prosciutto in simple syrup, oysters Rockefeller, crepes, thin slabs of foie gras on toast points with grilled apple slices and frenched lamb chops wearing those absurd little paper hats.

. . .

BY THE TIME I'D BEEN IN BUFFALO TWO YEARS, I would just run into guys out at the bars, walk into a place for dinner and end up talking with the chef or the owner. I would be pumped for information and gossip in the kitchens or on the loading docks of restaurants all over the city. The inner workings of standing crews would be explained to me over ice-cold bottles of Tsingtao beer and dim sum at the smoky back tables of Asian restaurants frequented by the chefs.

There was always work, always a kitchen with a hole that needed filling, always a chef who was unknowingly on the outs and an owner who wanted a guy in place, ready to step up and take command. I know that when people talk of great American food towns, no one ever thinks of places like Buffalo—of the small, less than cosmopolitan cities scattered throughout the United States. Even today, to the serious, coastal foodie it's all about New York, San Francisco, Los Angeles. But this is a ridiculous conceit because the United States has been experiencing a massive migration of chefs since sometime in the 1980s, a diaspora of talent that had even by the mid-nineties, spread the children of Manhattan's greatest chefs far and wide. Yes, at one time a chef working in Los Angeles would've had to import his pastry department, probably his sous-chef, maybe a station chef or two, simply because there weren't enough talented, out-of-work mercenaries in the city to staff up the number of new restaurants opening there. This hypothetical L.A. chef would've had to do this much like the great restaurants of midcentury Manhattan had to bring in their talent from France by the boatload.

But with each generation, with each run of apprentices, commis cooks and cutthroat line-dogs willing to do anything to move up, the dispersion continued. From Paris to New York, from New York to L.A. and San Francisco, then to Chicago, Miami, Dallas, Atlanta and Seattle. True, Manhattan has an enormous concentration of excellent restaurants run by the kind of celebrity chefs who get noticed in airports and asked for their autographs when pumping gas. Below them is a deep reservoir of above-the-line chefs with résumés that read like galley porno (a year at Le Cirque, garde-manger at Daniel, a *stage* with Eric Ripert at Le Bernardin . . .), and below them, a massive army of cooks just looking for their shot at the bigs, enough bodies to staff a thousand restaurants.

And while this is precisely the sort of petri dish required for the growth of a scene like New York's, it also drives the dispersion of talent because, in an environment like that, a chef has to work ten times as hard to get himself noticed, has to pay ten times as much for his space, has to battle like a pit fighter to get the best guys on his line and the best product in his coolers. Get knocked around enough in the big city and all of a sudden Elsewhere starts looking pretty damn attractive. In the eighties, Elsewhere was California. When things started getting crowded in California, Elsewhere became everywhere—anywhere that some people grew food and some people ate food and some people thought it an attractive notion to spend lots of money for *really good* food.

Working as a chef is a tough gig no matter the area code, but things are just a little bit easier in places like Buffalo. Like Pittsburgh. Like Denver, for that matter, where I will end up when all this storytelling is done. That the best of the best will naturally gravitate toward the hot, dense centers of the culinary universe is, to a certain extent, true. But some who, having gone away and tested themselves against the best, will always come home again or go further and plant their flags on street corners that no one in the big cities has ever heard of. Who in the food world knew of Yountville before Thomas Keller opened the French Laundry there?

These prodigal chefs will open restaurants that might, in Manhattan, have been dismissed as just another neighborhood bistro, just another gastropub, cooking delicate little slips of foie gras with onion jam in cities where they are the only restaurant serving such a thing rather than just one of two dozen. They will make their own blood sausages, hang their own *bresaola* in secret in the basements of their restaurants and haunt the farmers' markets looking for the best ramps, the best heirloom tomatoes, the best of whatever their particular foodshed has to offer. They will cook for their community, for their neighbors, because that was what *all* chefs once did before it became de rigueur for a chef to cook for himself first, for his career, his brand. I know great chefs now who cook just blocks away from the streets where they grew up, who never saw any need to leave the neighborhood. There was a time when, if you were serious about food or cooking or cuisine, you absolutely had to make a run at one of the big scenes or else spend your life flipping burgers, maybe sweating over steamship classics (beef Wellington and steak Diane and artichokes French) in the one place in your hometown where everyone went for their wedding receptions. That's not the case any longer. Not when one of the best sushi bars in the country is in Denver, Colorado, when you can get Vietnamese *pho* in Albuquerque, perfect Moroccan *bastilla* in Conshohocken and fish cooked by one of Jean-Louis Palladin's ex-*poissonardes* in Rochester.

In Buffalo,* in the years I spent there, there were perhaps half a

---

*In *The United States of Arugula*, David Kamp tells a simple, throwaway story that, to my mind, establishes Buffalo, New York, not Manhattan, as the American city where the French-American culinary revolution truly began, linking the 1939 World's Fair, the repealing of the Volstead Act, the Nazi occupation of Paris, and Buffalo all together into the moment that American cuisine was born. How is this possible? Simple. See, in 1939, the United States was just beginning to recover from the deleterious effects that the Volstead Act (better known as Prohibition, enacted in 1919, repealed in 1933) had had on the nascent fine-dining restaurant scene—which was in those years, limited primarily to the big industrial cities of the Northeast. This was also the year that the World's Fair came to NYC (Queens, actually), and as a part of the festivities France set up the French Pavilion and, within it, the Restaurant Français—essentially denuding some of that country's best restaurants of second-rank kitchen staff (sous-chefs and such) to staff just one foreign outpost that, in the course of its two-year run, served over one hundred thousand visitors $1.60 plates of coq au vin de Bordeaux and $5.50 bottles of 1929 Cheval Blanc.

Enter the Nazis. In June 1940, Hitler and his armies took Paris and the French promptly surrendered, leaving everything in the hands of the Vichy puppet government. In the United States, though, the World's Fair had not yet come to an end, and all those French cooks and chefs (including Henri Soulé, Pierre Franey, and Jean Drouant, to name just a few) were still laboring away in Queens for the rapidly diminishing crowds of fairgoers. When the fair did finally wrap up in 1941, they were screwed. They couldn't go home (didn't really want to go home, I'd guess), but neither were they legally allowed to stay.

That is, until the U.S. government decided that, owing to the situation in France, all French refugees would be allowed to get permanent American work visas and stay in the States provided they had jobs lined up here and were willing to ritually reenter the United States—which is exactly what all the Restaurant Français staff did in the middle of 1941, traveling across the border into Ontario and reentering the United States by walking across the Peace Bridge into . . . where else? Buffalo, New York.

dozen French restaurants. I worked at (or for) half of them. There were Italian restaurants, both high-class and low. There were fantastic greasy-spoon Greek diners, open all night, and sushi restaurants and Thai restaurants and more Italian restaurants and Polish restaurants and so many Irish bars that I could probably have stayed drunk a year without ever setting foot in the same place twice. Because of the universities, there were Lebanese and Korean restaurants, places for falafel and buck-a-slice pizza served late to the kind of people who'd be out looking for buck-a-slice pizza at four in the morning. There were a few great chefs, many great cooks still making their bones, and masses of terrible, dumb owners (and a few good ones), which is exactly what a scene needs in its formative decades so that the money keeps flowing, the spaces keep coming open as restaurants fail and the bankruptcy auctions keep the professionals in cheap, barely used ranges, sets of copper pots, and economical dining room furnishings.

I started running kitchens, and did it in the only style I knew—the way I'd been taught. I yelled and threw things, cursed with nearly equal facility in French, English and Spanish. I worked eighteen-hour days and hundred-hour weeks; slept on the flour sacks in restaurant basements when I slept at all; got stoned with my crews on the dock when the shift was done, drank like a fish, blew needle-thin rails of cheap (read *someone else's*) coke off the stainless steel prep tables in the baker's station, and generally behaved like some kind of two-bit, small-town rock star with powerful delusions of grandeur—a roadhouse roof-shaker who could maybe fill the house on a Friday night provided the bar was pulling dollar drafts, but who nonetheless thought he was Mick fucking Jagger.

Still, from this point on out, in any above-the-line post I made money for my owners. Sometimes lots of money. Occasionally hand-over-fist kind of money. And I did it only because I remembered every trick I'd ever been taught, every dodge, every gimmick. My owners or execs saw it as ruthlessness, but it wasn't that at all. It was only *rightness*. I never threw anything away if I could help it. I kept minimal stock in my coolers, preferring to make everything fresh whenever it could be made that way because it was cheaper and better. Commercial stock or chemical demi? Why would I pay for that when my kitchen produced vegetable scraps and bones in such profusion? Hollandaise sauce made from powder? Man, that's not even food.

My specials (cribbed over the years from dozens of different chefs and filed away in my head as rainy-day knowledge, saved against eventual need) moved like there was crack in them. Focaccia pizzas with duck and fig paste,* or with port-wine reduction and sausage;† a lobster tail tortured into verticality and mounted atop a ring-molded chop salad‡ or a salad of butter lettuce *aux lardons* dressed in a walnut vinaigrette à la Jeremiah Tower; poached scallops, sliced, fanned and served cold on a half shell with a citrus *gastrique*;§ penne and grilled shrimp in a vodka-spiked *arrabiata* and fired in the salamander, flatiron steaks in whiskey béchamel,‖ tournedos of beef "Rossini," which were, now that I know better, really nothing more than mini-Wellingtons sans pastry, and pork loin with an apple compote that was my secret weapon—essentially a recipe for cinnamon applesauce with the blending step removed. I was a sucker for salesmen—always falling for their pitches and attempts at unloading their trash or treasure on my dock. But I never bought anything I didn't have a use for. Or better, two uses. Or twelve.

Because I hated the idea of wasting a body to expedite orders between line and service, I set up my crews to expo their own plates in the way I'd been taught: grouping them by fire order on the pass, ranking apps right, entrées left, with servers trained to wipe plates and garnish exactly the way I (or my exec) wanted. This way, I could

---

*Borrowed from an article I'd read once on Ed LaDou, crown prince of the California gourmet-pizza revolution and Wolfgang Puck's first chef at Spago.

†Barely remembered from when my mom and dad would throw the occasional cocktail party at the house and serve this unbelievably delicious port-wine jelly sauce with chunks of Hickory Farms beef stick speared on toothpicks. I would always eat the leftovers the next day.

‡Stolen, more or less completely, from Alfred Portale's menu at Gotham.

§Which, now that I think about it, was probably inspired by that hotel restaurant meal in New York when I was a kid.

‖Not really stolen because it's a classic preparation, but taken straight from my experiences at the Clare and a killer bestseller everywhere I used it.

stand my shift at sauté, still call orders, still see every plate that left the kitchen, and do something more constructive than act as a traffic cop for plates of hanger steak and crème brûlée.

I was thrown out of a food-service bar one night for climbing up on a table, dropping my chef pants and wiggling my cornstarch-dusted tackle at a room full of fellow travelers still in their bloody, grease-stained uniform whites and checks. I did it just to get the attention of a busy cocktail waitress who I thought was deliberately neglecting my table. And in a show of the kind of absolute solidarity I expected of my crews (and for which kitchen crews in general are legendary), my boys climbed up right beside me and did the same, presenting to all and sundry a dozen nuts and six bare wangs. Threats were made. The police were called. We climbed down rather than face a night in the drunk tank. Most of us were due back in the kitchen in just a few hours anyway.

When my guys and me showed up at the same bar again the next night, we were met with rousing applause from the assembled crowd and pelted with dozens of pairs of underwear. It was one of the proudest moments of my life.

On another night, I slipped while brutalizing a frozen hunk of U10 prawns my prep guy had forgotten to thaw and put an eight-inch Wüsthof cleanly through my left hand, between the second and third knuckles, feeling the cold blade tick against bone as it went. In full view of half my crew, I coolly drew it out, wrapped the hand in a side towel secured with a boxer's wrap of duct tape, and worked a full Friday night on the sauté station one-handed.

I didn't work *well*, mind you, but I worked. "One hand is better than no hands," I kept saying. "And I'll be damned if I'm gonna let you motherfuckers have all this fun without me."

Two weeks after that, my grillman and butcher beveled the tip of a finger—taking it off at an angle about halfway down the nail and leaving it hanging there on the cutting board, connected only by a little tag of skin. He took three shots of cooking vodka, had a busboy drive him to the emergency room to get the thing sewn back on, and was back—totally bent on painkillers and chalky from loss of blood—for the second dinner seating.

"Nine fingers is better than none," he said when I tried to send him home, and though he was as useless on the grill that night as I'd been on sauté two weeks ago, that wasn't the point. He was there. He was on his feet and still swinging when the last table cleared out. That was a pretty good night, too.

When I shoved a produce supplier in the alley behind one restaurant and threatened to knock him out because the man had brought me a flat of mushy strawberries too close to the start of Friday service for them to be sent back, my price went up and my reputation skyrocketed. That such a thing would've gotten me arrested, fired, or at least forced to sit through some aggression-sensitivity seminar had I been working in any other field was why I loved my job, why—even when I doubted my own wisdom or the sanity of those surrounding me, when nights blew up or friends went down, when I would come home drunk, bloody and done in after a double shift where absolutely everything had gone wrong, so tired that I would miss my subway stop or find myself talking to people who weren't there—I still knew, deep down, that there was no other place for me.

COMING UP, I'd learned a lot of useful things. I knew how to shell five pounds of garlic cloves in two minutes, how to jerry-rig the plumbing on a dish machine, resuscitate a broken béarnaise, turn some chicken breasts and jugged Italian dressing into a buffet entrée for fifty on the fly, and stop an arterial bleed from a knife wound. I knew to swallow a shot of olive oil before a night of serious wine drinking to cushion the blow of grape juice slugged down on an empty stomach, and who to call at noon on a Saturday when the owner wasn't around if I needed money to cover a C.O.D. meat order and was willing to part with, say, one of his convection ovens, cheap. I could make the best whiskey cream sauce you ever tasted *and* get you a decent six-inch Japanese *usuba* knife for four bucks.

But even as early as Buffalo, I was also learning to be a perfectionist, a control freak, an obsessive. Looking back, if I was a good mimic of cuisine, I was an even better mimic of people, and since my bosses (the good ones, anyway) were all absolutely committed, uncompromising workaholic pedants, so, too, was I.

Here's the thing about perfectionists, though. There only gets to be one who actually succeeds at it, one guy for whom it all works out. The rest must all necessarily break at some point and shatter themselves against their own ridiculous expectations. And while it sometimes seems today that so many of the new young chefs coming out of the culinary schools take success (if not excellence) as their birthright, I and most of the cooks I knew back in the day took driven excellence and the inevitability of collapse as ours.

We'd all seen chefs blow up, burn out, go crazy and end up in jail, in Mexico, running the line at Applebee's, or worse. We cherished these stories, collected them like baseball cards, traded them like lore. We'd seen promising careers end, known guys who'd just flat lost their shit one night and never recovered. It was the pressure that did it. The grind: same menu, night after night after night. It was the proximity—four or six or ten men jammed into a space often not much larger than a prison cell, baking in the heat, listening to the incessant clacking of the ticket printer. It was the difficult conditions, the crazy requests from owners, from customers, from your absentee, cokehead exec phoning it into the kitchen from the golf course, changing the menu at four forty-five on a Friday night, and the hundred small frustrations a day. For us, this was just the way that chefs' stories all ended: in the shit or selling used cars.

Today, I can think back to those years and almost convince myself that it wasn't true—that the pressure was less serious, the drive to succeed less severe, that it wasn't the way I'm remembering it at all. I can tell my stories with a wink and a nod as if to say, "Didn't we all *think* we were such badasses back then? Isn't it cute the way we behaved?"

But, secretly, I know that this is false. I know how I felt, how my guys felt, my crews. I know how seriously we took everything, how crushed we could be by one plate sent back, by one table lost in the melee. And I know that while the restaurant industry in general and kitchen life in particular is well-known for attracting people of libertine tastes, with sketchy backgrounds and slightly bent moral compasses, people who could not—or *should* not—mix regularly with the civilian population, I also know that a lot of these people had found kitchens as a sort of last resort and, once acclimated, found that they loved the work as much as the hedonistic freedoms it engendered: that they loved *La Vida* with its late nights and weird characters, powerful chemicals and crazy pressure, but loved, too, the brainless calm of slicing mushrooms, the skillful juggling of pans on the hot line, the look of a flawless *quadrillage.*

To fail in the work, then, became tantamount to failing for good—failing at the only thing, in some cases, they'd ever been really good at. That was why a good cook shows up for work when he's sick, when he's hungover, when he's still drunk, if he has to. That's why cooks work through pain and humiliation and loss, why insult only makes them work harder, why they would die before letting down the team.

In that environment, success becomes the end of the night, perfection the thousand small moves it took to get there, each done as well as it can be done. I can't hear the Pogues song "South Australia" anymore without thinking of a small bistro in Buffalo where that was the first song on the tape we'd slide into the galley radio when it came time to break down and clean the kitchen. We only played it on good nights, ones where we could look back proudly on what we'd accomplished. It means nothing to me, even today, but a job well done. And I can't eat mozzarella sticks without remembering a place in Florida where the owners made me put them on the bar menu because I'd screwed up the food costs so badly that we needed something that cost a nickel and brought in $6.95 just to get back within hollering distance of the black. Ten years gone and I'm still ashamed of that.

While I did not always epitomize this striving toward success and pride and precision, I did so much of the time and lived surrounded by better men than me. While I might not always have been the best cook I could be, I did really try. And now, when I get asked occasionally why I act so proud to have worked in places like Buffalo, Tampa, Albuquerque and elsewhere, why I never took my shot at the Big Leagues, why I never made the chef's pilgrimage to France, I laugh. I waffle, hem and haw. I have a rote response, the perfect sound bite. When asked, I say that when I was a cook, I never had the time, and once I became a writer, I didn't have the money. That always gets a giggle.

What I should say, though, is the truth. That when I was cooking, I was happy just to have work. New York? Paris? Come on . . . I was a blue-collar kid from upstate, lucky enough that I wasn't riding the back of a garbage truck or punching a clock at Kodak. For me, the City might just as well have been a foreign country, and Paris, the moon. I had bills, rent to pay. Most days, if I looked forward to the future at all, it was only as far as the next turn, the next table, the next plate.

And as to why I never reached for anything greater or tried for anything better? Motherfucker, there *was* nothing better. I was a cook. And for me, that was enough.

AND THANK CHRIST that kitchens don't just respect this driven, dedicated, perfectionist mind-set, but encourage it, foster and cultivate this sense of absolute right and wrong, best and all-fucking-else. In my twenties, I liked the absolutism. I liked the thought that I was truly sacrificing for something greater than myself. Like that night at the diner, I liked the thought that something might go down that would hurt me, that would challenge me, that might—*might*—finally put me down for good. In a dark and little-examined corner of my mind, I probably liked the abuses when they came my way, too. Truss the ducks, stem the greens, watch the demi all night long. A lobster sauce will be made *this* way, not *that* way. A roulade will be *folded*, not fucking rolled. What are you, lazy? Stupid? Are your hands broke, you motherfucking little shit? How many times do I have to show you? Now do it again. And again. And again.

I never worked in a great restaurant, under a chef whose name anyone outside his own family would recognize, in a place that was loved by anyone outside the neighborhood, the town, or the city where it was located. I don't know a single chef who wouldn't have liked, at some point in his coming-up, to have run off to France and cooked with Bocuse, to have spent a year (or two, maybe three . . .) learning to make pasta in Porretta, real Neapolitan pizza in Campania or at the foot of Vesuvius, to have built a time machine and seen Vatel fall on his sword. Some cooks do that.* Most don't. Most chefs don't end up sautéing foie gras for superstars, arranging Ducasse's pantry, lugging vats of calcium chloride for Ferrán Adrià. They wake up in the morning, brush their teeth, have a cup of coffee and go off every day to feed their friends and neighbors. They do the best they can wherever they are, and, like me, if they look forward to anything, it is only the next hit, the next day off.

There are exceptions, of course. All those celebrity chefs? They all had to come from somewhere. Some of them even came from ac- tual kitchens in actual restaurants—were guys just like me, except smarter, more talented, more ambitious, better-looking, generally taller. They somehow saw their way clear to leave the rest of us be- hind, making the soup.

The rest of us *imagine* what it might be like to work in a great restaurant, with a name chef. I imagined it a lot—the humidity- controlled coolers, gleaming Jade ranges, clean and clinical stations scrubbed down every night by an invisible army of night porters, and cases of stiff, cotton-wrapped French pears that my food-cost num- bers would never allow me to purchase. Usually, I imagined it while trying to juggle ten pans on six burners while some gin-blossomed, geriatric motherfucker with a ladle in his hand screamed at my back and threatened me in damp, spitty German, or while squatting on an overturned plastic milk crate in some stinking alley, squinting against the cigarette smoke trailing into my eyes while I tried to gimmick a

*Not the time-machine thing, but you know what I mean.

recalcitrant gas ring into working one more night by fiddling around in its guts with the point of a utility knife. Sometimes it was in the sweet quiet of sudden and unexpected unemployment, sometimes while waking, hungover, on the floor.

And there were days I could almost wake up next to Sam early in the morning, look out the window of whatever crumbling bolt-hole apartment we were buried in, across the backs of churches and row houses, through the forests of rusted TV antennae, and see the chromium Gernsback spire of the Chrysler Building on the horizon, looming there like an unanswered challenge. My dad once told me that no one ever really regrets the chances they take, only the ones they don't. For a minute, I would kinda wish I'd listened to him.

Then I'd get up, brush my teeth, have a cup of coffee and go to work.

AT A PLACE I'LL CALL LA CITÉ, I found a strange kind of release as a full-time commissary prep cook. Here was a gig where I was still cooking, but no longer cooking specifically for people. I was cooking only for a prep sheet, for par lists sent in by the three or four different quick-serve French sandwich shops and bakeries the owners held: fifty gallons of winter-squash soup, thickened with warm whipping cream, brightened with a touch of turmeric; six cases of stemmed portobello mushroom caps to be salted, seared—softened in butter over high heat—and eventually eaten like steak. There was cheese to be cut down and portioned from whole wheels, plastic tubs of Provençal shaved-carrot salad to be made, taken from a recipe that was identical to the kind of shaved-carrot salad (with a little wine, a little vinegar, some shallot, a touch of crushed lavender and mint) I'd done elsewhere, identical to the shaved-carrot salads I imagined Provençal farm wives making from the last of the season's take from the garden.

Here was a professional kitchen that was *all* kitchen. There was no rush, no hit, no line, no ticket printer, no chef standing over my shoulder, sweating port all over me and cursing me for the way I rotated my pans. Here, there was quiet. Here, there was calm. Here, there was a great chef called Bird, who worked cleanly, gently and with a restraint that I found remarkable.

I was bored out of my mind after about fifteen minutes.

Luckily, I came into the job right about the time the owners were looking at opening their first real restaurant—a place with its own kitchen, a proper dining room, a real menu. They were poaching kitchen talent from all over the city, grabbing guys from places where I'd worked previously, from places where I someday wanted to work, moving in with all the subtlety of Michael Corleone going after the heads of the five families.

They already had a crazy Russian baker to do all the batch work, supplying wonderful, beautiful, impossibly flavorful bread; a guy they allowed to work by himself through the night on the production line just to keep him out of contact with the rest of the employees for as many hours as possible. When alone, he was able to focus, to create, to translate the simple instructions left for him through the mess of sour neurons and hamburger that passed for his brain and come up with the proper weights in dough to be run through the conveyor ovens: four hundred *boules*, two hundred baguettes, two hundred *bâtards*, fifty loaves of black rye. Being alone didn't stop him from talking. He spent his nights arguing with himself, the machinery, the mop bucket in the corner, and legions of imaginary enemies; telling the walls stories of his dissident's existence in Odessa before glasnost came and fucked up all his fun.

After the baker came a mob of mercenary dishwashers and cleaners, busboys, servers, managers for both floor and bar, service captains. They had Bird as an executive chef, but he'd made it plain from the start that he wanted nothing at all to do with day-to-day ops at any restaurant. He was happy doing what he was doing, he said. A reasonable schedule (ten or eleven hours a day, six days a week), a dependable paycheck—these things meant a lot to him. Also, he knew better than anyone about the intimacy of prep. He knew that he would still be handling a lot of the stock for the new restaurant first, before anyone else got their grubby hands on it, and could therefore have a significant influence over the final product of the new kitchen without having to be anywhere near it.

What the owners needed was a chef de cuisine. I volunteered for the job. When it appeared to me that they weren't taking me seriously (I was, after all, just a prep cook on their books), I volunteered louder. About two weeks before the new kitchen was scheduled for its test run—a series of friends-and-family dinners—they brought in Matty, a line cook and station chef poached from one of the city's better French restaurants; a white jacket they'd probably had their collective eye on for a long time.

Matty was their guy. That much was obvious. And though they were saying that he'd only been brought on to help with the ramp-up to opening, everyone knew that Matty was it: just twenty-five years old and about to get his stripes.

I wanted to hate him. Instead, we became fast friends in that way that feels inevitable, like succumbing to unseen gravities.

We could've been brothers if not for the fact that I already had a brother, if not for the fact that he was tall and dirty-blond, wild-haired, and goateed like some kind of rockabilly front man, loud, boisterous, cheerful under almost any circumstance no matter how foul, an inveterate optimist. He was my complete and total opposite, but we were exactly the same in those ways that mattered. We were both cooks. And that was enough.

Matty lived just a few blocks away from the new restaurant in a big, old run-down house with a rotating gang of other industry brats—anywhere from three to a dozen depending on the season and how close it was to rent day. For him, home was just where he kept his other shoes, a couple T-shirts, some beer. I was living in a crosstown apartment with Sam. For me, home was where I kept my girlfriend. For both of us, our real home was our house—the restaurant, the kitchen—because that was where we always were. If we'd had hats, the kitchen is where we would've hung them.

He'd started cooking young; so had I. He hadn't ever learned to do much else other than play guitar and sing a little. I hadn't learned to do anything else at all. Now, we were both coming to the end of our apprentice years. We'd worked for some of the same bosses, suffered the same abuses. I was faster with a knife than he was. He worked finer and cleaner. He had a thing for meats, for grill and oven work, for soups. I loved sauces, sides, garniture and sauté. We both wore our galley tans, pale skin, scars, bruise-dark circles under our eyes and near constant hangovers like badges of rank and honor. Neither of us had seen the sun much in, oh, say, the last six or seven years.

We both had the same strange love/hate relationship with the French: the hard-earned knowledge that the damned Frogs, for all their myriad failings of temper, perspicacity, abstention and taste in everything from movies to cigarettes to music, were just better than everyone else, ever, when it came to food. They'd spent centuries studying and stealing from every cuisine in the world, finding the best ways to cook everything that walked, hopped, crawled, slithered or grew anywhere, and (this is the important part) *writing it all down.* They had The Canon, and it was irrefutable.

For Matty, this was problematic. He saw it as limiting—strangling, really—and tended to fight philosophically against it even while holding his knife the way he'd been taught by the French and cutting a *brunoise* the way he'd been taught by the French and dipping his pinkie in a sauce, judging it against the perfect French version in his head. His tastes ranged more broadly, his acceptance of cuisines was more ecumenical, and he chafed at the tyranny of supposed French rightness. For him, if a plate needed color, there was always the option of a *mojo*, a salsa, a chutney, and he was certainly more qualified to carry the title of chef than I was because he had his own ideas, his own prep strategies, ideas for specials that weren't all lifted from *Larousse.*

Again, I was the opposite. For me, The Canon was liberating. I'd hardly been to church since my First Communion. I didn't have a religion to call my own or a God with whom I was on speaking terms. But I did have *la Cuisine.* I had demi-glace and cassoulet, the holy trinity of a well-cut mirepoix, and the magical transubstantiation of sauces done *montées au sang*; the unconditional lucidity of right and wrong. And most of the time—*most* of the time—that was enough for me.

So when we saw the first draft of the menu for the new restaurant and saw how thoroughly Froggish it was, we were thrilled—him secretly, me openly. It was a beautiful board, like poetry, like history told in verse because it wasn't just French but French *colonial*, which we thought was a stroke of genius, even if only because we'd never seen it done anywhere before. French colonial was truth told in food; was the record of food's travels on the back of politics, war and national expansion. Thus, ours would be a French menu that allowed for excursions into Vietnamese and Southeast Asian cuisines—not as fusions but as whole plates given their own places of honor on our list. There would be hints of North Africa, touches of the Caribbean. If one could imagine a French chef packing up his kit one day back in, say, the early 1950s and traveling for years to every corner of the world where a French flag flew, ours would be the menu he came back with. There was *pho* on the menu; there was *tagine*, couscous and jasmine rice alongside *steak-frites*, simple roasted half-chickens with sauce *moutarde*, and *salade composée*—classics, every one.

As an ass-covering measure, the owners had given over some menu space to the influence of barely recognizable Northern Italian modernism—to inventive pastas, focaccia pizzas, a full spread of crostini with bitter black-olive tapenade; to lemony *skordalia* and paper-thin veils of San Daniele prosciutto that we cut ourselves in the basement on an ancient rotary slicer. And yet, the stamp of Frenchness was all over that single-page, handwritten sheet that Matty and I were given about a week before the opening. Penne in a white wine and Gorgonzola béchamel with potatoes? An Italian would sooner cut his own throat than mix starches like that. The pizzas were called pizzas only because no one could think of anything French to call them. They were to be mounted on an Italian bread (the round focaccia loaves split into a top and a bottom, brushed with oil, and given a pass across the charcoal grill before being covered, topped and slipped into the oven), but then dressed with port-wine reductions, with smashed figs, duck, rabbit, compound cream sauces jacked with so much butter I'd have to force and roux them just to incorporate it all.

Matty and I had helped test the recipes and arrange the load-out for the new galley. We'd made coolers full of tapenade and *skordalia* and clarified stock and demi. But neither Matty nor I had been offered the kitchen. With three days to go before the first friends-and-family, no big dog had been chosen, no boss. And for that matter, no crew.

We'd heard troubling rumors that the owners themselves had decided to cook for the first few shifts—a sure recipe for disaster, though something I would've paid good money to see. It's not that the owners weren't food people. A couple of them were. One of them had been a career cook, a chef-owner of well-respected country-French restaurants. Another was a food designer and default wine expert by dint of having the money to travel all over the world buying up cases of grape juice. Another was a high-line restaurant brat, a young hipster who'd never cooked but thought he knew everything about kitchens because he'd watched that movie *Big Night* a couple times.* The three of them trying to cook through a busy service would've been like a Three Stooges movie, only with real blood.

One afternoon, Matty and I stepped out back for a cigarette to hash things out for ourselves. Matty knew that the owners had probably brought him on with every intention of having him run the new kitchen, but—once having gotten him extracted from his former gig—had simply forgotten about their plans for him. The work was getting done, the coolers were getting full, and as so often happens in this business, he'd likely only been interesting to them so long as he was something they wanted. Once they had him, he was set aside in favor of other, more pressing concerns.

---

*There would actually come a night later when, at the apex of some sort of penny-pinching fit, this guy would come bursting into our kitchen at the end of a long night waving the linen bill in our faces. "Look at this," he'd say to Matty and me. "Look how many aprons and chef coats you guys go through in a week! You know, I was watching *Big Night* a couple days ago, and in that kitchen? Those guys never got a spot on their aprons. Why can't you do that?" Matty and I would look at each other, each of us daring the other not to laugh, not to even *smile*.

He was fine with that. He was a soldier. If they expected him to run the kitchen, he'd run the kitchen. As for me, I just wanted to be involved. I'd fallen in love with the menu. My hands had already become accustomed to the unique prep required for it. The two of us had already taken a couple tours through the new kitchen, had drunk a few beers at the new bar, so in my head (and then on paper) I'd diagrammed where everything would need to go in the coolers, what everyone would need for their *mise en place*, how many cooks would be required, how the menu would break down across the stations. This was one of my strong suits: strategy, the disposition of forces and supplies, the tactics of fighting off a dinner rush with the fewest friendly casualties. I told Matty that I knew I could be useful. More, that I could be *good*. Most important, I just didn't want to lose my shot.

Matty knew what I could do. And he knew we got along well together—a necessary consideration when you're talking about a situation where two guys are essentially going to be spending every waking moment (and a good number of sleeping moments) together for the next six months, minimum.

The way I remember it, we decided that we would be partners. The kitchen would have no chef, per se, but two c-de-c's, each handling the jobs they did best. During service, he would work the grill half of the line, I would stand sauté/saucier. We would share calling tickets. Prep and setup would be my thing, cleanup and shutdown his. Further, no one in our kitchen would be addressed as "Chef," and we would even go so far as to not wear the solid black pants that, in the French brigade system, denote an executive position. We wouldn't even wear the heavy white chef coats. We'd double-order cheap white dishwasher's jackets and checkered line-cook pants and just wear those.

Why would this matter? Because it matters. Because tradition matters, because rank and uniforms and image matter. Because we'd both spent much of our careers looking up to the guys in the buttoned-up white Bragard jackets, the black pants, and because kitchen work tends to give rise to certain idiosyncratically abstemious personality traits. A lot of us put on the hair shirt, become ascetic, believe with total conviction that only unqualified dedication can save us, purify us, grant us the power to do all the things we want. In many ways, setting out to become a career cook and eventual chef is not unlike going to seminary or becoming a monk. Both demand a total commitment beyond the realm of normal human capacity. Both have, at their core, a blind worship of long-dead saints and faith in powers beyond common comprehension. Both are full of magic and superstition, peasant hoodoo, damnation, ritual and sacrifice. And in most cases, neither offers any tangible reward. We decided to wear dish jackets because, in our minds, only chefs should wear chef jackets; because, in our minds, the uniform really meant something. You don't dress a cat up like Patton and give him command of an infantry division. If you put on a policeman's uniform and start handing out appearance tickets to assholes on the highway, eventually a real cop is going to come along and throw your ass in jail. In our minds, a dish jacket (short-sleeved, snap-front, made of the cheapest polyester) would place us, in terms of uniform, at the lowest rank in the kitchen and keep us humble in the face of cuisine.

We stopped short of refusing to wear pants, but just barely.

SO THAT WAS OUR PLAN. Now, there were only two things left for Matty and me to do. First, we had to run it by Bird because Bird was the real deal—an actual chef and, more to the point, *our* actual chef. After that, we'd go to the owners.

When we asked Bird to step outside for a quick word, he cut us off before we could make our pitch.

"How many times am I going to have to say this to everyone?" he said, hands massaging the kinks in his back, eyes flashing with real anger. "I don't want the new kitchen. I want to stay here. And you know what? After you guys get up and running, I'm taking a long vacation somewhere where there's no phones. If you two want to go, go. I think you should go. I think you both need this. It's time."

"Well, we're going to go talk to the owners now then."

"No," Bird said, crossing his arms over his chest. "Don't do that."

THE WHITE COAT

leven minutes," Matty says, checking the steel-bodied German dive watch clipped through the top buttonhole of his chef's coat.*

Bird's advice had been exactly right. Matty and I had done just what he'd said we should that day: cleaning up our stations in the industrial kitchen for the last time, packing away our stuff, piling into Matty's car with a load of supplies that needed to be delivered, driving over to the new kitchen and just not leaving. We'd moved in, taken our spots on the line, and that was that.

"Total?" I ask from the other end of the line, turning to make a bare-handed grab out of the salamander, counting *one-one-thousand-two* in my head as I set a searing hot platter on the stovetop rail. Me, shaking my hand out of habit—not in pain, because I know I could've held the thing through three-one-thousand before the calluses on my hand, as thick now as bomber-jacket leather, began to burn. "Total, or since the last time we checked?"

"Total," says Matty.

Me, nodding: "Give it a couple more minutes."

We're making risotto—our experiment being carried out in the middle of a busy dinner service, bubbling merrily away in its pot as we

*I know we *said* we wouldn't wear chef's coats, but that doesn't mean we didn't. The things are handy—heavy canvas, pockets in all the right places—and they just look cool. We actually each kept two: one for working in and then another, hung out of harm's way, kept perfectly white and clean, which we would shrug into if ever circumstances required us to walk the room during service.

spin finished plates down the pass, fighting to get ahead of the printer. So rigorously French-trained, so up-from-nothing hash-slingers, neither of us had ever made risotto before. Never been asked to.

Like truffles, like rubbery slabs of handmade *glace de viande* and the powerful Black Sea salt we'd been taught to covet like the dust of diamonds, we understand that risotto is something special, something deserving of respect, but have no idea why. Thus, we have come to it almost reverentially, and not without a measure of fear—poking, cringing, sniffing, tasting, curious and cautious both.

Still, it's going onto the menu as a special soon, on orders from one of the owners, a whim. *We need a rice dish, maybe a risotto . . .*

So okay, now all we have to do is figure out how to cook it. Now. Tonight. Right this minute.

"How long now?" My head is in the oven, fingertips running over the wrinkling skins of chickens going through their first par-cooking, feeling the way the flesh is puckering, crumpling around the joints.

"Thirteen minutes."

"Okay."

Ours is a sense-heavy kitchen. We have no spike thermometers, no portion scales, no measuring cups. Matty's watch is the only timer allowed on the line. But we're pretty finely tuned instruments ourselves, and we know that things are done when they look done, are right when they smell right—that oil is hot enough when it takes on a vaguely popcorny aroma, that a thick steak is medium-going-medium-well when it has the same spring as the fat knob of muscle between the thumb and first finger. So now, we converge on the pot like dogs, leading with our noses, bending over the rice, sinking our faces into the steam.

We'd toasted the rice in our best olive oil, left it to simmer in a pot of stock, allowed it to cook down until it was almost dry. There are no recipes here, only instinct. All of our amounts were guesses, measurements based on other rice we'd dealt with, other cooking methods, lore, rumor, half-remembered cooking shows on PBS. Now the arborio rice is creamy, pale gold. Gorgeous, I'm thinking. Until we taste it.

Matty makes a face. "Not right. Just not right."

I concur. The swinging doors swing, each flutter of them marked by a wave of noise from the dining room, a waft of air. Plates go out. Plates come back. Out of the corner of my eye I can see one of the Mexican dishwashers scraping a mostly uneaten entrée into the trash, trying to block my view with his body because I take that very personally. *¿Qué es esto? ¿Motherfucker, porqué no comer?*

"What now?" Matty asks.

"Stock," I say, and Matty goes for the chicken stock, adding it to the pot one saucier's ladle at a time. And we watch, transfixed, as the grains plump, greedily drinking up the hot liquid. I stir—lifting and gently folding the sticky grains from the bottom of the pot into the top, treating the stuff like a meringue, like an egg-fluffed mousse in imminent danger of collapse. Amazed, we watch the risotto come together, tasting it a grain at a time, plucking them out and laying them on our tongues while, behind us, the printer chews through paper—spools of it curling, tumbling off the pass.

We ignore it. This is magic. We're children watching the man in the shiny suit make the milk disappear from a tube of newspaper, pull a rabbit out of his shit-smelling top hat. The simple tricks are always the best the first time you see them.

First time seeing porn. First time laying a speedometer down past a hundred. First time your child falls asleep in your arms. First time making a woman come, you feel like Superman (or Superwoman, depending). I remember thinking I deserved a Nobel Prize or something. If only I could've remembered how I'd done it . . .

First time getting plastered on serious wine. Mine was accidental, a bottle of boutique South African red. Several bottles, in fact, shared among Matty and me and the kitchen crew. We thought we were drinking up the dregs of the tasting that'd gone on that night—getting rid of the swill that regularly got passed off on the rubes, the yuppie bait we used to get the gold-card crowd through the doors on a Monday night. Come to find, we'd actually gotten into a case that our wine buyer had brought back special from a purchasing trip: a couple hundred bucks per bottle, intended for a party she had scheduled for the following weekend.

And we drank them all. When they were gone, we drank whatever else we could get our hands on. A party erupted when some of the other crews from the surrounding restaurants saw that our lights were still on, heard the Pogues rattling the plate glass, saw us all smoking cigarettes and slumping around the bar. I remember the first couple glasses and thinking to myself, "Wow . . . This is . . . Just wow." Speechless, which, for me, is really saying something.

Heavy and smooth and purple-black, spicy like fresh-ground pepper, fruity like Amarena cherries steeped in sherry. After putting down the equivalent of a bottle, it wasn't even like being drunk, it was like being high. And then we all went into the alley and got high, so it was like being *double* high. And then we drank some more and turned the radio up and I attempted to cook some snackies for that portion of the crowd that was still maintaining verticality and accidentally lit myself on fire—flames from one of the burners climbing the pilled cables of the sweater I'd thrown on over my T-shirt like water running in reverse.

To put myself out, I fell down. Once I'd fallen down, there was just no way I was getting back up. I napped for a time on the floor of the line, and when I woke up, I saw Matty and the hostess from one of the restaurants down the street. He had her lifted up onto the cutting board in front of one of the cold tables, her skirt hiked up around her waist, his head between her knees. I lurched to my feet angrily—not offended by what they were doing or that they were doing it essentially right above my head, but that they were doing it on my station, on *my* cutting board. Matty stood up. The girl bounced down to her feet, giggling—cute in a hammered-cheerleader kind of way. I was in no mood. Scowling, I popped my board up off of its pegs, tucked it under my arm, and went to sleep in front of the garde-manger station. I kept the cutting board with me just in case. I'd like to say it smelled like her, but honestly I just don't recall.

FIRST TIME GETTING A MUSSEL RIGHT: standing in my broken-soled work boots, black bandanna tied around my head in place of a toque, misfit

whites, filthy checks, bad teeth, bruised knuckles—a fucking mess
with tears in my eyes and my mouth hanging slack. How many mussels had I cooked? A thousand? Ten thousand? Twenty? I'd never
once done it right. I'd *tasted* them done right, sure. I'd had them done
right for me by other cooks, other chefs, so I knew what right tasted
like. I'd been chasing right for so long I couldn't even count the time.

Such a simple thing, *moules et frites*. Even more classic (among
cooks, anyway) than *steak-frites*, than *soupe l'oignon*, than cassoulet
(which has as many different recipes as there are chefs working) or
coq au vin. *Moules et frites* may as well be the definition of all that
is perfect and beautiful about French brasserie cuisine—a three-
ingredient sauce (white wine, butter, shallots), a squeeze of lemon,
an animal that is alive until the minute it is thrown into the cooking
liquid; killed by the double fistful for every order. Get it wrong and it's
still pretty good, but get it right and it's an epiphany.

And now, here, I finally get it—capturing a flavor, a depth, and a
balance I'd only ever tasted before coming from someone else's hand.
The smell of it done right is enough to unlock my knees, a drop of
sauce licked off the tip of my pinkie rewires whole neighborhoods of
my brain. Actually reaching into the bowl and eating one of the mussels? Pure sex, a beurre-blanc lightning strike right in the savage-
animal pleasure center, like growing a second, tiny lemon tongue.

Those who go in for Zen archery have a spiel about how the man
who draws the bow a hundred times knows a little something about
drawing a bow, how the man who draws the bow a thousand times
knows a little something about loosing an arrow, and how the man
who is fortunate enough to have drawn the bow ten thousand times
no longer has to concern himself with either the bow or the arrow because he's the one who knows a little something about bull's-eyes.
Every arrow the lucky man fires will inexorably find its mark, so he
no longer even needs the bow or the arrow because the bull's-eye is a
foregone conclusion.

I always thought that was such total crap.

Not so much after my thing with the mussel, though. All it took
was 9,999 tries. But for me, every mussel after number ten thousand

was a foregone conclusion. I was now the guy who knew a little something about bull's-eyes, and until I got there, I hadn't even realized how hard I was trying.

Standing in front of my stove tasting number ten thousand? Those were tears of relief.

FIRST TIME IN COMMAND. First time cooking for other chefs—for guys who would come in specifically to eat the food that Matty and I were making, the ultimate compliment from one's peers.

First time cooking escargot. Those fuckers explode sometimes. No one had told me that. And when they pop, the garlicky snail goo goes unerringly for the eyes and genitals like a final vengeance.

First time knowing true calm and competency and sweetness in the kitchen. I've told so many hard, mean stories here already, described so many brutal moments or cruel or funny or ridiculous ones. But most nights on the line were none of these things. They were just nights at work. And I think that anyone who finds himself finally in a place where he truly belongs must, at some point, also look up and recognize the long train of quiet, occasionally beautiful hours that have led him to that place. The first time I was able to glance back and see my own boxcars of time stacked up behind me was at La Cité, on one of those countless, interchangeable, unmemorable nights when nothing was exploding, nothing was terrible, nothing was collapsing, and everything just was. And there was nothing more to it than looking up and knowing that I was living in a best moment—one that I would probably not specifically remember because of its softness and cool, but would recall forever as a feeling of fragile, almost painful rightness.

LA CITÉ HAD GONE LIVE on a Friday night. The wait at the door was three hours. We'd stayed open and served two hours past closing time just to get everyone fed. It was, needless to say, a smashing success.

And after that? A blur. I can remember only moments.

I remember the smell of Ivan the Russian's fresh bread in the morning, waking to it on occasion after sleeping in the basement or just coming in from out of the cold for the start of morning prep and being enveloped in the nutty, soft, sweet scent of hundreds of boules, all sitting on the racks, most destined to become bread crumbs or crostini or whatever because this was still Buffalo, after all, not Paris, and people here bought their bread at the grocery store.

I remember the night I nipped off the tip of my finger while slicing shallots. The injury was not as memorable as peeing the pool of blood that bloomed like a rose in a nature documentary, seeing a small piece of myself severed and set free, cut adrift on the expanse of my cutting board. Not so memorable as the feeling brought on by my bright idea that dipping the offended digit in a bowl of high-octane cooking vodka would sterilize it. The pain—so swift and awesome—knocked me out cold.

I remember Amy, one of the waitresses, running down the stairs into the basement where I was slicing prosciutto, pounding down the steps, frantic, scratching madly at her crotch. Amy didn't see me, didn't even hear the clattering, whirring old rotary slicer running, until she'd itched for a good ten seconds. Then she looked up and dissolved into laughter.

"I just shaved," she said. "It itches like hell."

"I can only imagine," I said.

"Want to see?"

I remember the way the kitchen was arranged—in the round, European-style. There was the service door, then the dishwasher to the right, my station to the immediate left. Our pass was a shelf that rose from the middle of the kitchen: grill, broiler, six-top and four-top ranges, ovens and fryer on one side, everything cold on the other. At the end of the pass, nearest the door, was a small, rickety, stainless steel prep table that, during service, became the expo station.

Heat lamps hung over the center pass. On the first night of actual service Matty and I broke them beyond all hope of repair. Heat lamps were a crutch. If we were doing our job well, they would never be required. We were right. We started accidentally dropping any plate that wasn't white. A couple months in, Matty stole all of the lovely little salt and pepper shakers from the tables in the dining room, tossed them into a garbage bag and threw them away. If we were doing our job right, no one would need salt and pepper. He was right about that, too, even if the servers, the owners and the customers didn't see it his way.

I remember the night Andy, our garde-manger man, showed up bent out of his head on opium, claiming he'd eaten it (accidentally) on a salad in the park.

"Who eats salad from a stranger in the park?" we asked. The answer: Andy did. We tried to send him home. He wouldn't go, insisting that he was fine to stand his station. For the rest of the night, we'd call an order for a simple salad and would be handed a pepper mill. We'd ask for rillettes, for a double-garden-on-the-side, and Andy would look across the pass with his eyes blown out, staring into some distant O-space, and start fiddling. We'd get half heads of lettuce dressed in *skordalia*, white plates doodled with sauce, completely imaginary salads: one plate, set with a fork and a squeeze bottle. Andy was inventing dadaist cuisine on the spot, and for a while we were having so much fun waiting to see what he'd come up with next that we forgot that someone needed to back him up and actually do the job.

That task fell to Al, our emergency-backup, all-hope-is-lost dishwasher and prep guy. He was a friend of Matty's, lived (sometimes) in the house with him, was supposed to be going to school to be a dentist. No matter when Matty put in the call, Al would show up. He was absolutely dependable in that way, even if his condition upon arrival was always a cause for wild speculation. He was a regular abuser of strong chemicals—heroin, mostly—but in the psychoactive hierarchy of kitchen work, a functioning junkie was preferable to a onetime opium eater.

When Al arrived, Andy was out in the alley having a conversation with the chain-link fence.

"What's up with him?" Al asked.

Al was talking to the dish machine, but at least he was inside.

. . .

OUT ONE NIGHT DRINKING at Faherty's down the street with the guys. It's two in the morning, maybe three. The whole place is full of white jackets, some still in uniform, sauce- and blood-spattered. There's waitresses and hostesses, food-service groupies. The music is numbingly loud, the smoke thick as weather systems. We're upstairs, shooting pool—team cutthroat against the crew from one of the other restaurants downtown, knocking the balls around for money, beers and pride.

And I'm drunk. Just completely hammered. When my turn at the table comes up, I grab the cue, set myself without thinking, and make an impossible jump-shot over the eight—sinking a ball that I could never have done sober, that I've never been able to do since.

The ball drops. My guys go wild. I throw the cue onto the floor, point at the cooks from the other house, say, "That's just to prove that we're better than you at *everything*."

I stride off then, headed for the bar to claim my drink on the other guys' tab, and promptly fall down the stairs.

This is not the same night I show my junk to the cocktail waitress. This is not the same night Matty's girlfriend left him and we commandeered the jukebox to play nothing but his favorite songs until closing time, having to fight off a rush of enraged line cooks the fifth or tenth time a particular Crosby, Stills, Nash & Young tune came around. This was just another night, but they may as well all be the same night—one long last call, one night that never ended.

I REMEMBER MY BIRTHDAY: number twenty-three or twenty-four. I'd spent most of the night working in a funk, pissed off, throwing pans and snapping at anyone who came near me. I hadn't told anyone my birthday was coming; I didn't care if they knew.

But Sam . . . I'd gotten it in my head that Sam had forgotten my birthday, and it bothered me. I hadn't actually seen her in a few days. She was working as a management troubleshooter for a chain of mom-

and-pop health-food shops, going from store to store and explaining to the hippies how to merchandise the wheat germ, artfully front the tiny bottles of calendula oil and ayurvedic dandruff treatments. She worked a more or less normal schedule, from sometime in the morning until sometime in the evening. Then she'd go out with her friends, my friends, people from work—like a regular grown-up.

I was working from about nine in the morning until one in the morning on an ordinary day—one that didn't require me to be in earlier (in which case I'd sleep at the restaurant or at Matty's place) or stay later (in which case I'd also just sleep at the restaurant or at Matty's place or on the floor wherever I collapsed). When work was done, I'd go out for a few drinks to chase those I'd already put down while cleaning, the others I'd been knocking back all day while working, the little bit of weed in the alley to cut the jitters, the pills I'd been swallowing and gallons of coffee. At the bar, I could unwind, relax. It was better than going home, because at home I'd only be up, pacing the living room, chain-smoking, trying to work off all the leftover adrenaline from the shift, worrying about all the things that needed to be done for tomorrow.

So I'd come home (maybe) at four in the morning, five, six— usually before the sun was up, though I was often racing it. I'd collapse into bed. Sometimes Sam would be there. Sometimes not. She'd taken to sleeping over at friends' places. Needless to say, the cat box was not getting cleaned. Dishes were not being done.

But on my birthday? It seemed cruel to me for her to have just forgotten—like something out of a John Hughes movie with me as Molly Ringwald. I worked the night in a lather of frustration, getting angrier and angrier, until finally I decided to talk it through with my guys. Every one of them assured me that she was banging someone else, revenge-fucking for all the nights I'd been away. They'd shrug. *It happens, bro. What're ya gonna do?* Not exactly the comfort I was looking for.

Toward the end of the shift, with just a few tables left in the dining room, one of the waitresses came back and said that someone was at the bar to see me. This was not rare. Friends, owners, fellow travelers—people knew where to find me when they needed me because my orbit was small: kitchen to bar to bar to bar to bed to kitchen. I pulled on my clean jacket, tucked my hair up neatly under the black bandanna I wore, dropped my dirty apron on the board and stepped out onto the floor.

Sam was there with a cake, candles, the whole nine. Smiling.

My best friend, David,* was there with her. Smiling. One hand resting on her shoulder.

They both shouted, "Happy birthday!" There was applause. Sam kissed me. I loved her fiercely in that moment, all my doubt and fury draining away like water down a hole. I hugged her, opened my eyes, saw David standing there, watching.

All my doubts except one.

SOME TIME AFTERWARD, I asked Sam to marry me. Thinking it an excellent excuse for a party, she said sure, why not? We were still a collective mess, but it seemed like the right thing to do after all the years of being messed up we'd already put behind us. Together, we told our parents. And though obviously not overjoyed at the idea, neither did any of them scream, faint or start laying odds on our inevitable failure right there at the table. We took this as an overwhelming endorsement of our nuptials and threw a party for our engagement, where everyone got drunk and hit someone, then set a date about a year off for the actual wedding.

Here I was, the kid who'd snuck the copies of *Gourmet* under his bed, the angry little punk, the half-assed junkie, college dropout, loser. Here was the sum of all those scrubbed, pink and manic faces staring out, frozen, from the Wheel O' Jay—an equation that, when

---

*I didn't have many friends outside the industry, but I had a couple—people I'd known since I was a kid, civilians I'd gotten to know later. David was one of these. We'd known each other since grade school, had been in Boy Scouts together, school together, and even spent a night in lockup together. We'd even lived together for a short time in Buffalo, and when work had me staying away from home for longer and longer hours, I was happy that David and Sam got along so well. That my best friend was there to look out for her when I couldn't be.

seen in the mirror some mornings, almost made sense to me. I'd done okay, I thought. Now I had the girl, the job, the white jacket and a bank account. Matty and I had been running the kitchen at La Cité for about a year. I was a good cook working in a healthy, happy house with a crew I loved like brothers. Everything was working out. Right up until the moment it all came to an end.

Without our consent, without our involvement, without even our *knowledge*, the owners had hired a chef. Chef-with-a-capital-*C*. A boss. Matty and I hadn't heard anything about the chef until the afternoon he showed up in the house, wanting to get a look at his new kitchen and crew. It was as though, in the absence of any executive decision having been made about the operation of the kitchen a year ago, the owners had been happy enough to let Matty and me play around simply because we were the ones who'd shown up. Thankful that the choice had been forestalled, they could sit back, take their time, let us make our mud pies and gumdrop soup, pat us on the head and tell us how *smart* we were, then shuffle us out the door and bring their own guy in when the time was right. History would start again with him, invalidating everything we'd already done.

The new chef was tall, chiseled and pretty with too many perfect white movie-star teeth stuck like pickets in his jaw. He arrived wearing his cooking school whites, black exec pants, jaunty blue neckerchief and a probe thermometer in his shoulder pocket. All around him hung an aura of yellow-duckling newness so soft and bewildered that it seemed like a corruption when juxtaposed beside the slick, skeevy, shiny, damp disorder of a working kitchen. He looked like he was dressed for an audition, like he'd seen a chef once in a movie and had gone out and bought all the necessary parts of the costume. *Tonight, the part of Chef will be played by . . .*

His dark hair was perfectly combed. The creases in his pants looked like he'd ironed them across the blade of a razor. His hands were as soft and pink as powdered marzipan. I had him pegged as some kind of visiting galley dignitary, friend of the owners. Worse, a consultant. I disliked him instantly, but still, I set aside my knife, dragged my palms across the thighs of the ancient pair of grease-stained check pants I was wearing, and went to introduce myself because that was the polite thing to do. All evidence to the contrary, this business truly runs on the politeness of presumed competency and tribal belonging. Chef was chef, still and all, and he was wearing the white coat.

I was dressed for work in a dishwasher's jacket open over a sweaty green T-shirt with CHARLIE DON'T SURF screened across the front in big white letters. My pants were held up with a hotel belt—a stretched band of plastic wrap tied with a bow. My pockets were stuffed with cigarettes, the neck of my T-shirt festooned with Sharpie markers. I looked like the poor country cousin of this big-city swell, yet it never occurred to me to read anything into that. I was a chef in everything but name myself. So was Matty. We were veterans now, pros. We were in charge here (or so we thought), and technically this new man's superior. I stepped up and put out a hand.

The new chef gave me a thousand-watt smile, a hit-and-run glance and a knuckle-cracker handshake in return. He said to call him Chef.

Behind me, Matty was straining stock, perched on an overturned milk crate and babying the vital liquid through oversize coffee filters shoved into a china cap. He bit his lip, looked away and didn't say a word. I laughed it off. I had to. We were an hour and change from the start of the first seating when the guy walked in, and my crew (not one of whom had ever called me Chef) was busy. We had two full turns on the books, plus walk-in traffic, plus the late theater rush we'd get an hour before closing (mostly apps, garde-manger work, desserts), then the trickle of bar orders that would walk in while we were trying to break down and clean. It wasn't a crusher, but we were anticipating a busy night so everyone was sandbagging—the crew (which had swelled somewhat since opening night) laying in backups for their stations, then backups for their backups, filling fish tubs with ice, arranging their *mise en place* just how they liked it, squirreling away stashes of side towels, cooking wine in speed bottles, change-out trays. They were centurions preparing for battle; old hands going about their business with a practiced efficiency that might look to an outsider, a civilian, like ease but was really just the habit of long experience.

I was doing the same, so I smiled, laughed, said, "Good to meet you, Chef," or something equally noncommittal, gave him a final questioning once-over—noticing that his goofy-ass clogs, too, were brand-new and spotless—then returned to my cutting board in front of the four-burner mini and fell right back into the pleasant, mindless trance of prep, forgetting all about the chef until I heard the long string of Spanish curses erupt behind me, coming from Diego, our champion prep-runner and occasional pantry cook.

I turned around again. Now I was getting pissed because prep time was quiet time in the kitchen. Jazz on the galley radio. Not much talking. It was time for communing with one's ingredients, grooving on the staccato *tap tap tap* of knife blades on the board, the sexy feel of a sharp knife sliding through mushroom flesh, the licorice and pepper smell of chiffonade basil on the fingertips. Distractions annoyed me. Further, they cost minutes that we would all have to make up elsewhere with rushing and shortcuts, which I hated.

On the other side of the kitchen's center island, I saw Diego standing with his knife out, and the schoolboy chef in his immaculate whites with his pretty hands held up like he was being mugged.

In deference to the white coat, to hierarchy and tradition so in-grained in me that it was almost subconscious, I asked the schoolboy, and not Diego, what was wrong.

The new chef said he didn't know. I don't think he spoke Spanish.

THE HISTORY OF MODERN AMERICAN COOKERY is the history of American immigration. As has often been said, if one day in this nation every working Mexican line cook, Indian porter, Ecuadorian dishwasher, Cuban busboy, Costa Rican saucier and Russian night baker, legal or no, decided not to come into work, the entire industry would come to a screeching, immediate halt. Everyone would have to stay home and eat cold Dinty Moore out of the can, because the blacks, the browns, the yellows, and all the cappuccino-colored people who'd come from all those funny-shaped countries on the unpopular parts of the map form the backbone of the restaurant world. You know who fills the majority of posts behind the bar at sushi restaurants in the United States today? Mexicans. You know who makes that delicious bread at the little neighborhood French bakery you go to on weekends? Some Frog-trained Cubano hard boy who earned his chops in Miami, in New Orleans, in Atlanta, before working his way north looking for better money and more stable employment.

Consequently, a chef who can't speak Spanish* is not much of a chef because he is unable to speak to a large portion of his staff in the language with which they are most comfortable.

Most conversations in any galley are held in a mishmash patois of English, Spanish, French and lyrical, heavily inflected pop referentialism as dense and fluid as cockney rhyming slang, with each kitchen and each crew developing their own uniquely obscene linguistic cocktail over time. One needn't be fluent (Christ knows I never was), but a chef with no Spanish at all is the equivalent of an orchestra conductor who has never heard a violin before.

I CHECKED MATTY'S WATCH, which was sitting on the rail between our two stations, and saw that we now had just *fifty fucking minutes* before the start of service. Confounded, I turned to Diego and asked him (in Spanish) what'd happened and why he was about to commit premeditated murder at the garde-manger station.

"Motherfucker tried to touch me," Diego said, not lowering his knife.

Fixing my attention back again on the new chef, I asked, "You tried to touch him?"

"His hand," the schoolboy stammered.

"And why were you trying to hold my man's hand, exactly? Do you love him? Are you going to ask him out on a date?"

---

*And increasingly, these days, a little Russian, a little Vietnamese, a little Hindi—everything helps. French is still a good fallback. Most Latinos working high-end kitchen gigs learn gutter French before they learn passable English anyhow.

"No!" said the chef, his face twisting into a mask of equal parts revulsion and fixated horror. He'd no doubt been through some cooking school's crash course in butchering and breakdown. He knew precisely what that thin-backed, eight-inch Global that Diego was holding could do to a chunk of soft meat.

"Just back up off my guys, Classroom," I said. "And, Diego, remember our rule? No stabbing."

The schoolboy stepped away. Diego shrugged and went back to turning big piles of ugly, lumpy, useless vegetables into beautiful little piles of mirepoix. And that, I figured, was that. I took a breath, cleared my head and addressed myself once more to dicing stiff, cold red-skin potatoes.

Prep angry and your food will feel it. Prep bitter and that sour taste will be conveyed to each plate you cook. Work with love, with a calm head and a full heart, and the food will know. It will behave for you. Everything you touch will taste better.*

But Mr. Bigshot? He couldn't leave it alone.

"It was his knife," said the new chef, walking around the island to my side of the line. "He wasn't holding it *correctly*. To make an *even chop*, I mean. And in *my* kitchen, knife skills are *very* important. He should know how to do it *right*."

I looked up. The new chef stood straight as a ladle, his arms folded, looking down at me across the ledges of his cheekbones. Across from him, Diego was cupping a fistful of sweaty nuts through his Chefwear and telling the schoolboy to suck his dick. In Spanish, of course: *Chupe mi piñon, Jefe. And don't spare the tongue.* All eyes were on me, everyone waiting for me to take this bed-wetting dick-faced *pinche güero* cocksucking dipshit *bonito* motherfucker's head clean off for his offenses against the dignity of the family and the calm of the house.

Why it was my job, I don't know. But I was the one standing there.

"Who in the fuck did you say you were again?"

"I'm your new chef."

*And when all else fails, try singing.

"New *cook*, you mean."

"No. Chef."

I DIDN'T NEED TO SAY ANYTHING. I didn't need to do a thing. I felt sure this guy wouldn't last sixty minutes in a real kitchen. Not thirty. He was about to not last ten. The first night under fire would break him like a two-bit punk, and his one night in our kitchen would just become another funny story for the rest of us—the lifers, the mercenaries and serious professionals among whom I'd hoped and intended to spend the rest of my working days. Something we'd talk about at the bar, a tale told over and over, passed around until it became old and soft and faded, until this "Chef" became like a face on a trading card: something we all owned.

And I tried to do that. I really did. With forty minutes left, I tried to get us back in gear.

"Look," I said. "Whoever you are, you're in the way. You want something to do? Make rice, okay? Four hotels, steam-table prep." In my view, I was being gracious—ridiculously, archingly, obsequiously courteous to this nobody interloper jerk-off who was taking up my time and fucking up my routine. Fully within my rights under the schoolyard rules that governed the bully sociology of any kitchen to throw this new guy out on his ass or give him a poke in the nose for talking shit about one of the family (for talking at all, truth be told), I had instead offered him a warm handshake, a hot bath and a blow job from my sister. I was giving him my time, my consideration, my respect.

"No, that's all right," said the new chef, shrugging, waving a hand dismissively. "You all just keep on with what you're doing. I'm not ready to cook tonight. I just stopped in to see how my cooks look while they're working."

I just stood there, dumbfounded at this strange creature standing before me, talking gibberish, smiling like he owned the place. No doubt he thought he was doing well. Potential stabbing aside, he probably thought he was making friends.

My favorite dishwasher broke the silence, yelling, "The fuck you got that costume on for then?" over the grumble of the dish machine. Matty laughed like a donkey and almost spilled the stock.

"Five minutes," I said. "Everyone. Smoke break."

They filed out into the back alley without a word. I walked out in the other direction with Matty following, out through the swinging doors and into the dining room, where one of the owners sat, at the bar, balancing the previous night's receipts in the company of a half-drunk bottle of wine. I lit a cigarette, stood waiting to be acknowledged, and, when that didn't happen, said quite plainly, "You can't hire this guy. Just *can't*," adding that if he'd already been formally hired, he must be terminated immediately—preferably with a shovel to the back of the head, though simply showing him the door and making sure he went through it would be enough, provided it happened, like, now.

"We don't need him. We don't want him. And he's going to fuck everything up anyway," I said. "I don't know what you're doing, but please, God, just get rid of that stupid, pussy bastard before he jinxes the whole fucking place."

And the owner (a good guy, a *food* guy and former cook himself who Matty had known for years and I'd known of, at least, since my first days in Buffalo) only shook his head. He didn't even look up at us.

"Can't," he said, and as we stood there, he laid it all out for us—explaining why Matty had never been asked to be chef, why no one had been hired up until now, why, finally, we'd ever been allowed to run the kitchen in the first place. The new guy, he said, was the nephew or the cousin of one of the other partners. Related, somehow. His chefdom (as well as an ownership stake, if I remember correctly) was a foregone thing and had been for a long time. No one had wanted to tell us because we'd been doing okay. Things had been running smoothly. Everyone was happy, everyone was making money—us a little, them a lot. Had they told us, he figured we would've left right away.

"This has been coming since the day the kid signed up for chef school, Sheehan. Believe me, there's nothing I can do."

He stole a drag off my smoke and handed it back. Behind his steel-rim reading glasses, his eyes were rheumy, lit and swimming in a misery that I would remember and mistake for commiseration for a long time. He had been a cook once, a real cook. Maybe he understood.

"Him?" he said, tilting his head back toward the kitchen in wino slo-mo. "That's the future. And maybe it'll be okay. All that school, he must've learned *something*."

"Guess you're gonna find out," I said. "I'm sorry."

I walked back into the kitchen, full of misguided but stately purpose.

The crew, hearing me come banging back in through the swinging doors, poked their heads in from the alley. I collected my gear, had a brief, whispered conference with Matty down at the fryer end of the line, pulled off my apron, dropped it on the mat and walked out the back door. I didn't say anything to the new chef, even though I wish I had. I just walked out into the alley and the afternoon sun, into a future full of chefs with pretty hands, nice teeth, spotless whites and no Spanish. As happened every time I walked out of a kitchen, I felt a knot of tension the size of two balled fists suddenly unwind in my back. I felt light, unburdened. Suddenly, there wasn't anywhere in the world I needed to be.

I went the only place I knew to go when I wasn't working. I went to the bar.

I DON'T KNOW EXACTLY WHAT HAPPENED at La Cité after I left. Of course I'd like to believe that the whole place took an instant nosedive. I'd love to be able to say that my guys followed me out, throwing down their own aprons, shouting curses over their shoulders and stealing everything that wasn't nailed down on their way out the door. I wish I could say that we then all went off somewhere and started a restaurant of our own and lived happily ever after.

But no. Most of my guys, they had families, mortgages, bills to pay. And with the kitchen suddenly a man short, they were in a position to ask for massive raises, shaking the owners down until nickels fell out. That was just business. I was involved in something much more personal.

From what I understand, Matty hung in for a few days, then packed it in. I heard that the bar manager and the best server took off for Hawaii. Slowly, the family slunk away in shame. I heard rumors that the owners were forced to pick up a second address next door, knock down a wall, and throw in a gourmet pizza counter just to keep the place viable. I heard that two of the owners—the ones I liked, Vince and Maura—sold their stakes after the new chef took over, and that, later, there was a mysterious fire.

But who cared. I was gone. I could've found another job in Buffalo, another kitchen, another crew. I had a few bucks, so I could've sucked it up and tried New York, followed my Chrysler Building mirage. But I didn't. I headed south instead, because south's the way you go when you're falling.

FNG

The best thing about Florida is leaving it. You can say Disney World, Orlando, that killer whale they make do tricks for baitfish. You can say Miami Beach, art deco dreamlands of ice-cream-colored high-rises, lovely beaches, girls walking around with tits like varnished beach balls.

I say bullshit. Florida is one of those places you've either got to be born to or love so much beyond all rational reason that you're blind to what lives there, just below the delicate scrim of civilization.

Florida, that suckhole. That sink-pit of bad feelings and worse memories. Every minute I spent there, every *second*, was a torture except for the ones that weren't. The international courts have been trying for years to ban the practice of waterboarding prisoners of war. That's where you take someone who you think knows something he's not telling and simulate the sensation of drowning by strapping him to a board, lowering his head, covering his face with a wet towel and dumping water over him. From what I hear, it's a fairly efficacious way to get a fella to spill his guts. Not a nice thing to do, certainly, but effective. Florida was like that every day and most nights. Every breath was like drowning. I would've done anything, told any secret, just to get out and stay out. And eventually I did.

I went there because Florida—America's flaccid wang—is as far down as you can get without fighting the tides and floating to Cuba. I was dropping out, running away again just as I'd been doing since I was six, dressed as a spaceman, carrying my books about local birds.

Leaving Buffalo had looked to be easy. After quitting La Cité, getting drunk, blacking out, waking up, making my way home, blacking out again, waking up again, and burning through my hangover alone in an empty apartment, I realized that I could probably be gone in hours. Sam and I had been bouncing from apartment to apartment so often and for so long that we'd stopped even bothering to unpack most of our boxes at the conclusion of each move. Over time, they'd become tables, shelves. The boxes had taken on a whole new life as furniture. Looking around, I realized I didn't even know what was in them anymore, so figured them unnecessary. We could pack the car and be gone by evening.

My friend Kurt was down in Florida doing something technical with cell phone towers. He insisted that we join him immediately. But there was a money problem. I mean, a thousand or so dollars in IOUs look real nice on the dresser when you're working, but tend to evaporate quickly when you quit in a huff. Then there was the problem of Sam, who actually had a life upstate. She'd been laid off, but still had friends, family, appointments, places to be. There was the problem of our engagement.

Because Sam hadn't been there to see the way the schoolboy had looked down at me, the way he'd walked in like he owned the place (because, at least in part, he sorta did), I had to explain it all to her. And at the end of an epic, three-day-long battle—a screaming, crying flare-up, an apoplectic detonation after months of simmering border conflict and insurgency—I told her that I was going to Florida, with her or without her.

Then I told her she was coming with me whether she liked it or not—that she was going to be Bonnie to my Clyde, my wingman and passenger on whatever dumb-ass, unplanned, retard stunt I felt like pulling, because we were getting married, so with me was where she belonged. No matter what or who she'd be leaving behind.

I told her to just get in the car, please, and stop making such a motherfucking scene in the parking lot, please, because people were starting to stare.

KURT'S PLACE WAS IN BRANDON, a semidistant exurb of Tampa that was suffering through a spasm of new growth, a boom cycle that'd torn the main artery out of what was essentially a small, very Southern community, replaced it with a graft from some nouvelle Levittown— all big boxes, tract housing, twenty-four-screen movie theaters, enormous strip-mall Golgothas and T.G.I.McPtomaine's-style chain restaurants—but left everything else untouched. A block deep, it was just swamp, double-wides, bars, and cockroaches the size of mice.

Kurt had been in this pasteboard utopia maybe six months already—living in a two-bed, two-bath apartment, divided into an east and a west wing, united by a common living room and kitchen, in a complex filled with hundreds of identical numbered boxes that all backed up to a palm row that smelled like stump water and decay. The exterior walls of each building were stucco, cream-colored. Inside, everything was white.

He was already settled into the right-hand bedroom. Sam and I moved into the left, where the complete, loud and bitter dissolution of our five-year relationship began almost immediately.

TO SAY I MERELY DISLIKED FLORIDA would be an understatement of colossal proportions. I truly hated it, loathed every inch of the place with the kind of wild, sputtering passion that can generally only be mustered for the hating of another living thing.

But then, I still consider Florida to be alive, the land itself possessed of a certain collective animism and low, sentient cunning. Nothing so hot and smelly as Florida could be anything *but* alive. Nothing that buzzed and grew and sweated and stank like Brandon, Lakeland, Plant City and central Tampa could be only a place, only a location, and not some animate, vaguely menacing *thing*. Living there was like camping out in a Cuban longshoreman's underpants, and I felt from my very first day there as though someone or something was out to get me.

Yet as much as I hated it there, I was forced to acclimate swiftly as a matter of survival—putting my up-North self with its up-North ways and up-North metabolism on a down-South footing lest the environment just crawl down my throat and choke me. There was no getting-to-know-you period, no geographic honeymoon. On the day we arrived it was 170 degrees with 900 percent humidity, and as soon as I pulled into the parking lot, some kind of giant lizard fell out of a palm tree and onto my hood, dying there, sautéing itself. Sam and I would end up spending a few months. It felt like most of a lifetime.

I'd brought my knives with me, a couple pairs of generic whites and checks, my work boots. Because our bankroll had been seriously compromised by the journey and just a couple weeks without work, I took the first job offered to me, at the first restaurant I tried—a garish, oversize, rattletrap fish house close to a highway off-ramp. It was no different from the dozens of other garish, oversize, rattletrap joints surrounding it. I'd chosen the place more or less at random. The interview went approximately like this:

I walked in, saw what I correctly assumed was the restaurant's hostess sitting slumped at a nautically themed bar (graying wooden ship's wheel mounted on the backsplash, crab traps and shrimper's buoys depending precariously from the ceiling), running a sweating, half-empty bottle of Corona across the back of her neck. I asked if they were hiring. She asked what I could do. I told her I was a cook. She said to sit and help myself to a beer from the well if I cared to.

It was about nine in the morning.

The hostess turned away and shouted across the massive emptiness of the restaurant, "Jimmy! Cook for you!"

Jimmy, the owner, came out of the back wearing an Iron Maiden–tour T-shirt stretched over his ample circumference, a kitchen apron and bicycle shorts that fit him like two sausage casings and a codpiece. He smelled like he'd slept the night in a crab pot.

Exit the hostess. Jimmy and I took each other's measure like two unfamiliar dogs meeting for the first time but too domesticated by our circumstances to just come right out and sniff each other's asshole.

"Cook?"

"Yeah."

"Where?"

"New York, mostly." Which was true enough, and if he assumed I meant the city rather than the state, all the better.

"What brings you here?"

Those of you still reading at this point know exactly how long of a story that would've been to tell, so I abbreviated. "Just where I ended up."

"You work a fryer?"

I said that I could. And anything else that was needed.

"Ten an hour, cash. Mondays off."

"Ten an hour the going rate?"

"'S'what I'm offering."

"Deal."

Total time elapsed in my job search: twenty minutes, maybe. Not a record, but close. I didn't even bother fetching my knife kit out of the car. My tools—like any professional's—had a delicate constitution and stronger opinions on their employment than I sometimes had about mine. Had my good steel been exposed even for a moment to an environment such as this, they wouldn't have worked right ever again.

I WOULD LAST AT JIMMY'S CRAB SHACK* just long enough to get my legs under me enough to flee.

The place appealed to the Okie/cracker, white-trash highway trade and was successful for three reasons. One, Jimmy (or whoever

---

*Again, not the real name, but it may as well have been. If you're a cook, you've probably worked in a place just like it. If you're not, you've no doubt eaten in one. And in either case, God's mercy be with you.

had come before him) had invested long ago in a large sign on a tall pole. Two, he had an enormous parking lot. And three, he offered a daily seafood special for $17.95—fully two dollars cheaper than the seafood special of his nearest competitor. The special was the same every day: cold crab salad (made, actually, with pollack), a fried fillet of haddock, two crab legs, a fruit cup and half an onion in lieu of the classic baked potato—the onion sliced, battered, and fried in the style of the Bloomin' Onion appetizers so popular at the chain restaurants that encircled Jimmy's.

No one seemed to care that the daily special never changed. This was likely because Jimmy's Crab Shack had never in its long history seen a repeat customer. And no one ever complained, because anyone smart enough to know good food from bad would've taken one look at the limp fishing nets hung on the walls, the greening, foul-smelling aquarium that separated the bar from the cavernous dining room, and the pimply teenaged waitstaff and run for their fucking lives.

Lucky for Jimmy, the world was full of stupid people. And all of them vacationed in Florida.

Jimmy would later tell me that he'd actually invented the Bloomin' Onion (which he called an Onion Blossom) and had been serving it for years before the idea was stolen from him. The Onion Blossom was Jimmy's one claim to culinary immortality, and its alleged theft had wounded him deeply. Night after night, he took out the loss of it on every single customer unfortunate enough to find their way to his doorstep.

Fact or not, Jimmy's story of the Onion Blossom was true. Even if Jimmy's story was more or less dependent on the half case of Corona he habitually consumed before the start of dinner service (the balance of which he consumed during), it still affected his every action and spoke to the very human need of every man to feel that he will be remembered for something. Jimmy had no children who might someday fondly recall him. He'd done no great deeds—or at least none that he ever talked about. He'd certainly never satisfied a customer. What he had was a deep-fried onion in the shape of a flower, which was better than nothing, if only just barely.

I WENT STRAIGHT FROM THE BAR to Jimmy's kitchen, stopping off in the locker room only long enough to grab an apron and a dishwasher's jacket, but discovering in the process that stepping into the fetid stink of old sneakers, greasy linens, sweat, stale cigarette smoke and foot spray felt more like coming home than anything I'd ever known. Climates change. Borders get crossed. Cuisines may vary. But kitchen locker rooms will always smell the same. Some men might've found it disillusioning to realize that the length and breadth of their lives could be described by the smell of rotten feet and exhausted perspiration, but to me it just meant that everything came full circle and the world was really far smaller than advertised.

In the kitchen, the crew had been assembled into a bucket brigade and was stowing the day's fish and produce deliveries. They worked like a chain gang, all ropy arms, prison tattoos, steam burns and loose, easy conversation that riffed up and down along the line like some sort of freaky jazz improvisation, always returning to the central theme of who among them was the biggest fag and who among them sucked the most cock.

Ten bodies, all told, in various stages of breakdown, were variously employed to the task at hand—ten including Jimmy, who'd re-installed himself at the head of the line nearest the refrigerated trucks so he could check in every ounce of product he was paying for, abuse the Cuban drivers and scream into his cell phone over shortages, real or imaginary. I'd been plugged in just in front of Jimmy's head cook and kitchen manager, Floyd, so I could see where in the kitchen's one enormous cooler everything was supposed to go.

Floyd—who wore a white Danzig wifebeater, cutoff army fatigues, big hippie-stomper combat boots and a seemingly haphazard array of patchy black facial hair—cursed every case, carton, can, flat and bag that passed through his hands before tucking it away in the cooler, following some sort of bizarre stocking system that violated every single health code of which I was aware—putting raw meats (fish, in this case) over greens, mixing proteins on the shelves, and jamming freezer cases on the top shelf, right under the condenser.* The obscenities were amusing and lyrical and rarely repeated—*goddamn U10s, motherfucking dry packs, shitty celery, butt-fucking mushrooms* . . .

I watched Floyd work, knowing that my first night's survival on the line could well depend on being able to lay hands fast on a fish tub full of dyed pollack, some shitty celery or a can of motherfucking dry pack. For a line cook, no time goes so slow as time spent off the line during a hit; nothing breaks the rhythm like stepping away; no confounding, infuriating stress is like the stress of standing slack-jawed inside a walk-in or pantry, looking for something and not finding it.

I listened to the cooks talk, took the probing abuse when it came down my way—them calling me Cherry and FNG and saying how pretty I was. All of it was familiar, nothing more than depth-charging, a way for them to test the new guy's limits, the thickness of his skin and integrity of his emotional superstructure. It wasn't hazing exactly, but a highly stylized and precise assault. Hazing is juvenile and cruel without purpose. But calling the new guy queer, telling him you fucked his mother last night, that everyone around him is crazy, that he'll be killed if he can't keep up, and that the only way he's getting paid is to suck nickels out of your ass—that's a refined tradition, a jive as artistic as it is efficient, because if a crew could break the Fucking New Guy with language, it saved them the trouble of having to watch him shatter under pressure on the line. If they could rile him, offend him, disgust him, chase him off, make him cry, anything, it was better to know quickly exactly what it would take. Better to find out in the cool of the morning. Better to know than not.

---

*Later that night, I would realize that he was doing his stocking not according to any rule, law or safety regulation beyond the principle of easy access: placing that which would be needed most quickly or most often in positions where they could be gotten at by cooks in a rush. More, he was putting the heavy stuff—the fish cases and freezer boxes—at waist level to spare the knees and backs of his cooks from the constant strain of lifting. It was completely against the rules, but was done, like so many things in this kitchen, for the sake of expediency and speed, and for making it to the other side of the rush in one piece.

And I, as the Fucking New Guy, had to take it. I had to laugh and say, yes, I quite enjoyed intercourse with livestock, thank you. And, yes, my grandmother was available for a three-way. But at the same time, I had to have some spine, a little something *tra le gambe*. At least enough to look a total stranger in the eye, smile, and say I'd give five American dollars for that stranger's little sister to come over and lick a gallon of ranch dressing off my nuts.

Or, you know, something like that. These conversations were fluid things, covering a broad range of outrage and obscenity, so the Fucking New Guy had to pick his moment carefully. In prison, they say that the quickest way to earn the respect of your peers is to pick the biggest, meanest, ugliest bastard on the block and beat him to death with a chair on your first day. In a kitchen, the same was accomplished by picking anyone on the crew and telling him you'd gladly fuck his cat if his mother was otherwise occupied.

Or something like that.

I knew all these rules. I'd been the FNG often enough. So when, after a long battery of questions about my animal/vegetable/mineral sexual preferences, it was suggested that because of the way I was standing right up on Floyd, maybe the two of us were boyfriends already, I paused, looked down the line, and said, "No, but if I had to take any of you smelly fuckers to the dance, I think it would be Roberto there."

With the corner of the produce case I was holding, I gestured casually to the biggest of the cooks, a sweating Checker cab of a man with his four front teeth missing. "With that smile, I could just slip it right in and he'd never know."

Laughter banged up and down the line. The cook next to Roberto (a whippet in stained Chefwear pants named Stevie who looked like the spawn of a greyhound bitch and a yard of hemp rope) dropped the freezer case of lobster tails he was holding and Roberto cuffed him in the back of the head before standing up straight, blowing me a kiss, and snaking his gray tongue in and out through the hole in his grin.

I winked, passed on my box to Floyd, turned to grab the next one.

Things cooled out a little after that, and when the trucks were empty and the cooler packed, the work gang broke up. Jimmy retired to his office, smiling. All the cooks filed out onto the back loading dock to smoke cigarettes, pass a bowl around, and sniff—now a bit more delicately—at those things that were really important to them: where I'd been, what I'd cooked there, and how in the fuck I'd ended up here.

I'd been trying to figure out the answer to that question myself for quite some time. I'm still trying to puzzle it out today.

I MADE RICE AT JIMMY'S, ten hotel pans of steamer mix, each pan sealed in plastic, jammed into the upright steamer, then forgotten until my internal kitchen timer told me they were ready to come out again. Rice was the first test for any new galley hopeful, any comer who claimed to know a thing or two about a thing or two. Fifteen minutes in any pro kitchen, a guy learns how to make rice. After doing any amount of serious time, he would know how to make perfect rice in his sleep, standing on his head, underwater, with his ass on fire. Yet it consistently amazed me how often I would get guys who claimed direct descent from Escoffier, Paladin or Keller on their résumés but, when told to make rice, would stand and stare at the sack and the hotel pan like a cat trying to do long division.

While the rice steamed, I made mashed potatoes out of bagged dust and water. Once the mashers had sprung to life beneath my whisk, they were portioned out into steam-table six-pans, with the remainder scooped out into five-gallon plastic buckets that had once held olives or floor cleaner, then stacked at the end of the hot line as backup.

It was deep prep, and regardless of latitude, regardless of position or station, I loved prep. True, I'd gone from chef to fry cook in the space of a couple of weeks and a couple thousand miles, but that didn't matter to me. I didn't feel ashamed of the work or demeaned by it or too good for it. Work was work. I'd been making rice, coring tomatoes and stemming mushrooms at La Cité, so here at Jimmy's

I cored tomatoes. I stemmed hideous, leathery button mushrooms. I shaved racing stripes into the flanks of two cases of cucumbers with a dull peeler, then took an eight-inch chef's knife from the magnet rack on the wall and sliced everything in sight with veteran speed and machine precision. I was fast now. Finally Angelo-fast, after all these years.

Twice, Floyd came by to admire my chop, to fan a spread of cucumber slices with his fingers across the rough terrain of the plastic cutting board and nod in silent approval. I felt no particular pride in having done the job right because, at this point, right was the only way I knew how to do it. As with the mussels, after a certain number of years, a thousand repetitions of the same job, a thousand mornings spent doing it, right had just become second nature.

Looking around following Floyd's second departure, I saw elements of the same isolation and cool, surgical detachment on the faces and in the work of some of those surrounding me. On the board next to mine, a cook called Sturgis, with a giant, overhanging belly straining the snaps of his dishwasher's jacket and muttonchop sideburns that would've made Elvis blush, was stripping corn off the cob. He'd clip the ends off each ear with a double bang of his knife, stand it up, and denude it with six sharp strokes. On one side of his cutting board were kernels. On the other, bare cobs. He didn't leave behind a single kernel. Never missed. Never varied his motions. And he did it without looking, while staring dully at the label on a bottle of garlic powder on the shelf over the prep table with a loose smile hung between his sideburns.

Roberto, on the other hand, was splitting chickens like they'd said something nasty about his mother. And Lane—tall, shaggy blond, left arm bright with infected track marks and senior to me by all of two days—appeared flummoxed by the necessary interaction between lemons and a knife. That lovely Zen distraction came slow, sometimes not at all, and the appreciation of a thing done right had to be learned. But Roberto, at least, seemed to be enjoying himself.

On my side of the kitchen, bets were being taken on how long it would be before Lane (on the other side) took one of his fingers off; side bets on whether he'd even notice. They were measuring in minutes, not days or hours.

I just laughed and thought of tomatoes.

JIMMY'S DID NO LUNCH BUSINESS. There was neither the time, the space nor the need. Everything—every effort, every skilled hand (and not-so-skilled hand), everyone's concentration (however far it stretched)—was focused on the daily preparation for dinner, and as the day rolled on, things in the cramped, outdated, overcrowded kitchen got weirder and weirder. The endless chatter about dicks and waitresses and movies and which station the battered galley radio ought to be tuned to sloped off the closer the clock crept to two forty-five, which was when the hot line would be lit up, stocked, staffed and readied for the first early-bird hit at three.

The entire crew took lunch at one. It consisted of an ice-filled case of MGD longnecks and a pot of *ropa vieja* bubbling on one of the line's twenty burners. The *ropa* was Roberto's responsibility, and it was the best food served at Jimmy's by a long stretch—all dark and sweet and thick. For convenience's sake, it was spooned out onto slices of white bread or tortillas and eaten one-handed so work could be continued with the other. No one left his station.

At two, the sweet *tock tock tock* of knives on plastic cutting boards slowed slightly as half the crew rolled out for cigarettes on the dock, last beers, last-minute negotiations with their backs, knees and hands, begging their bodies to hold out just eight or nine more hours. When they returned, the other half went. I followed Floyd out the back door, my fingertips stained red from bell pepper juice, my calluses itching.

Floyd was wearing sunglasses now, had two utility knives in blond-wood sheaths tucked through the strings of his apron, a black skull-and-crossbones bandanna on his head that sparkled with fish scales like sequins inexpertly sewn. He looked like a Hollywood

B-movie pirate suffering from malnutrition and terminal scurvy. He heaved a sigh and sank down onto an upended milk crate set in the thin band of shade cast by the wall.

"Jason, right?" he asked.

I said yeah. Jay was fine. I hadn't been called anything but Cherry (or worse) since morning.

"Like smoking a jay," he said.

"Yup. Just like."

And that was it for the space of half a cigarette and a final bottle of MGD apiece. At the end of the dock, a dishwasher and a pantry cook (neither of whom had been in the kitchen when I'd arrived) argued in Spanish and looked ready to come to blows. The blacktop shimmered in the heat haze, a hot, tarry ocean. A car pulled up—a battered Ford Galaxie with its plates wired on and springs that squeaked like tiny birds having something terrible done to them. Two of the cooks, Roberto and a little kid called Dump, who didn't look a day over twelve, jogged out into the sun and leaned in through the passenger-side window.

Floyd picked at the label of his beer. "That's the dope guy if you're buying."

I said no. Not today, at any rate. But, as always, I found the idea of door-to-door drug delivery a brilliant innovation of the restaurant industry.

"I can stand you to a dime if you're broke," Floyd offered.

"No, it's not that," I said, although I was, nearly. "First night, you know? I think I'll stick with beer."

"Smart man." Floyd tapped the side of his skull with one finger and lit a second Kool off the stump of his first.

The car pulled away. Dump and Roberto were divvying up glassine nickel and dime bags between them, stocking their pockets, obviously (I hoped, for their sake) having bought for most of the kitchen. On the dock, the argument between the cook and the dishwasher escalated a notch, and without looking, Floyd side-armed his empty bottle at them. It shattered against the wall, showering the two of them with glass.

"Basta!" he shouted, cigarette bobbing in the corner of his mouth. *"Va a trabajar!"*

And they did, both slinking back in through the door, nodding in mortified fealty as they passed Floyd on their way.

After that, the only sounds were the full-throated thrumming of the highways in the distance, loud and constant, and the screaming of tropical monsters in the swampy greenbelts that separated one parking lot from another.

Floyd sighed, shifted his focus so that he was staring out across the shimmering, empty parking lot at the line of decorative palms dying at its far horizon. "Why don't you get back inside now," he said to me. "You're on fryers tonight. Light 'em up and don't disappoint me, okay?"

FOUR FULL STEAM TABLES. Twenty burners. Three double-wide fryers. Two deck steamers stacked one on top of the other at the far end of the line, three side-by-side, gas-fired charcoal grills with two salamander top-broilers mounted above. Two flattop griddles oiled to a high gloss, surfaces punctuated with hundreds of tiny nicks and scratches—the record of countless random impacts worked into the temper of the shimmering hot metal. Four enormous radiant ovens— two on the line, beneath the massive hot-tops, two more in the prep area—and two convection ovens stuck kitty-corner to the fryer station. Eight microwaves, six working, two with the doors wrenched off and used for storing spice bottles, smokes, speed-pourers, what-have-you. Six long heat lamps suspended on greasy cables over the gleaming aluminum pass rail.

With all the line's equipment fired, the kitchen went from a merely intolerable 100-some degrees to a murderous 140-degree hell above the equipment. Leave your dog locked in a car in the summer and Lassie will start to cook at 110, poaching in her own vital fluids. At 120, the human body starts to panic, pouring sweat until all you have left is a greasy, slick oil that oozes from your pores. Blood vessels burst in the eyes and on the skin. Your boots will literally fill with perspiration. Hydration and cooling the blood (usually done with frozen side towels wrapped around the back of the neck beneath the stiff collar of the chef coat) become life-and-death issues.

But 140 is like a weight, like swimming through soup. It hits you as a straight punch in the chest that never lets up. It sucks at your breath, crawls up inside you like a fever, chews at you and sits right on top of your head like a hot, wet goat. Unless you've been acclimated, unless you've made friends with the heat and accepted it, 140 degrees will just kill you.

We lit the line at two forty-five—at the last possible moment—and started sandbagging, carrying in stock in volumes that were difficult to believe. Someone gave me my fryer pars: two hundred pounds of precut french fries in waxy brown ten-pound bags; sixteen fish tubs full of breaded fillets (ten of haddock, six of cod dusted with cornmeal already going gooey in the humid air), then four more of portion-cut mystery fish to use for fish sandwiches that would have to be battered by hand. I had two five-gallon buckets of floury beer batter at my feet, six more stacked and waiting by the door of the cooler, and several hundred pounds of peeled onions, which, after being slammed through a sort of stamping press bolted to my station between the fryers and dunked in the same batter used for the fish, would be turned into Onion Blossoms. Lots and lots of Onion Blossoms.

My coolers were socked in with cases of Sysco breaded clam strips, already thawed, and more cases of calamari and more cases of rock shrimp and more cases of chicken cutlets and stuffed mushrooms and little appetizer things—all of it together probably coming out close to a quarter ton, most of it having been prepped in the last six hours. And as Roberto, Sturgis, Floyd, Dump, Lane, I and a tall, skinny, glaze-eyed Mexican that everyone called Chachi were all moving onto the line, a whole second crew of prep cooks and runners were coming in to take our places at the stainless. Their only job would be to keep the line supplied with whatever the line needed to keep working and, when necessary, carry off the casualties and stand stage until relieved.

"You need anything," Sturgis told me, "I mean *anything*, you just scream, Cherry, okay? Scream loud. Runner'll get'cha. You don't leave your station for nothing 'less Floyd says so. Not for Jimmy. Not to take a piss or nothing, cool?"

I nodded. I was walled in with stock, surrounded, in danger of being buried in a fish avalanche should any of it shift unexpectedly. Looking around at the rest of the stations—at the guys coolly laying in piles of side towels, fussing with their mountains of low-rent *mise*, stacking pans on wall racks in front of their posts; working silently now, hunched over, slotting knives into the spaces between cutting boards, angled for fast draws, and twisting the bottles in their speed racks snout-down; appearing doom-struck or expectant, bouncing in place, some of them, but all fated for some kind of disaster they all seemed to know was coming.

Jimmy walked through to inspect the troops and took up the expediter's spot at a long table right-angled to the pass. The hostess banged through the swinging doors. "Ready in front," she said. "They're already lining up outside."

"Go," Floyd said quietly, just loud enough to be heard over the roar of the hood ventilators. He still had his glasses on, had his hands braced on either side of the ticket machine, staring, waiting.

The hostess disappeared into the front. A moment later, she stuck her head back in. "Seating sixty," she barked. "Here we go."

A few seconds later, the machine began rattling out orders.

A chill ran down my spine. Like the one I'd get from a noseful of cocaine, a scare in a dark room. I cracked my knuckles and felt my eyes go wide, my pulse humming in my neck.

I couldn't wait.

A SOLDIER, *APRÈS LA GUERRE*, will tell you there is no way to describe combat after the fact in any human tongue. Anyone who tries, fails. And anyone who succeeds was probably never a soldier in the first place.

Likewise, a sailor cannot—likely will not—describe the sea or hard weather on it to anyone who's not another sailor because what comes of trying is a language of analogy and comparison. The wind was as strong as . . . The waves were as high as . . .

The truest thing ever said about a tornado? "There was wind. And then, after a while, there weren't any wind no more." I heard that once long ago on the TV news from some fat, florid hillbilly whose trailer had been flattened by a big twister while he huddled beneath it. There was wind and then there wasn't.

Cooks speak of their battles mostly in numbers: body counts, heads, tops, table turns and throughs. A hundred covers (meals actually served) is a good night for a straightforward, medium-size neighborhood restaurant. When Joe's Bar and Grill in Indianapolis does a hundred covers on a Thursday night, Joe is a happy man. He made some money. Joe's cooks are happy. They punched their weight.

A hundred covers means maybe 120 bodies through the door, 120 tops (chairs filled in the dining room), counting shared plates, nibblers, people who just want maybe a cup of soup, a dessert, and then those served jalapeño poppers and french fries through the bar or, better yet, not eating anything at all and just drinking watery whiskey or jug wine at double and triple markup—an owner's favorite kind of customer.

A hundred covers is good. Two is better. Two-fifty, better still. At 300 you're starting to talk some serious numbers, and unless the dining room is large and both kitchen and crew built for volume, 300 will begin to stress the systems of any normal restaurant. A topflight fine-dining galley with a veteran brigade can bang out 350, maybe 400 covers a night (taking into account long hours—maybe an after-theater rush, that kind of thing) without too much trouble, and a large, shitty, assembly-line corporate restaurant staffed by kids, moon-faced losers, jerk-offs and a couple seasoned shoemakers can do 300, 400, even 500, easy. Back at the diner in Rochester, Hero, James, Freddy, Juan and I could move those numbers—*did* move those numbers all the time. But at 500, you're talking a 100 meals an hour for five solid hours, on average—the length of a reasonable dinner shift. And that's *meals*—apps, entrées, desserts and ephemera. Setting aside *amuse-*

bouches, tasting menus, desserts, multiple courses and flights, dealing only with the core of a normal meal, one could conservatively figure two plates per customer and come up with a figure of roughly three and a half finished plates every minute being produced by the kitchen, a plate to the rail every twenty seconds.

On my first dinner shift at Jimmy's, the kitchen did 914 covers.

There was wind and then there wasn't.

PAST IS PROLOGUE

I f you read the prologue, you already know what came next—death, destruction, head wounds, the sudden realization of how badly I'd squandered what few gifts I had in taking this hideout job in the middle of this sucking swamp, in spending my waking hours deep-frying fisherman's platters for dimwits. But as with so many things in my life, this insight came just precisely too late. We were in Florida now, Sam and me, without the money or the resources to leave. I lasted only a couple weeks at Jimmy's, which was about the average for his cooks. The heat, the killing rushes and doomed, lost-outpost vibe got to me quick. An environment where the only pride was in survival turned me grim. I stayed only long enough to collect a couple paychecks, then left with a feeling that I was dodging some terrible inevitability. But afterward, I did worse.

I made pizzas, which might've been a nice kind of retreat—a full-circle return to my roots—except that these pizzas were all covered with shrimp and awful, sour olives and lamb, except that they were being bought and devoured by people whose shoes were worth more than my car.

For a while, I became a restaurant consultant (of sorts), poking around in the kitchens and coolers of suffering seafood shanties, hideous family restaurants and neighborhood bars, using every dirty trick I knew to help the owners squeeze an extra 4 or 5 percent out of their limping, jackleg operations even as two Olive Gardens, an Outback Steakhouse and an Applebee's were all preparing to open within sight of the front door.

Things were booming in Florida, the chain restaurants growing and spreading across all that fresh new cement being laid down over the swamps like kudzu. And while I could claim that I was trying to do the noble thing by throwing in my lot with the losers, fighting a holding action against the forces of evil and conformity and unlimited breadsticks, that wouldn't be entirely true. As a consultant, all I cared about was that the places stayed afloat long enough for their checks to clear.

But levels of betrayal exist between perfection and jalapeño poppers. You have to make your own choices about how low you are willing to sink. I'm not proud of anything I did while in Florida. Most of it, I'm downright ashamed of. But it was a weird time for me, a bad time, and I try not to think about it much, except on those days when I'm feeling good and feeling cocky and need to remind myself how I got where I am today. What I did in zip codes where I hope no one remembers my face or name.

I KNEW THINGS WERE OVER between Sam and me on the dance floor of the Castle in Ybor City, the old cigar district, Tampa's answer to Miami Beach, the French Quarter and Havana all at once.

She looked beautiful on the night I'm remembering, lit from above by the club's Intellibeams—white-hot, searching—and from below by the soft combined glow of hundreds of candles. And not to say there weren't other times she'd looked beautiful. She could be stunning in instants, frozen forever by memory: the line of her jaw when angry, her eyebrows raised in surprise, tilt of a hip, color of her hair against a car window rimed with frost, the curve of her neck when she stretched to talk to someone behind her. But on this night, she burned like a nova—dancing, half-smashed already, the crowds on the floor giving her room to move. The music was thundering, repetitive, numbing like chasing a faceful of blow with ice-cold vodka. It was "Pure Morning" by Placebo. I've always liked that song.

At the bar, I'd been buying another round: five Coronas and two shots, transporting them all in two hands through and around a mob dancing like a slow-motion riot, pierced by lasers, illuminated by strobes, wreathed in smoke. A life skill—to be able to do that without spilling, without freaking out. Maybe I was a cocktail waitress in a past life.

But when I saw her—saw Sam picked out on the floor—the circuit closed in my brain. We were done. Standing still with the dancers surging around me and the music crashing down on my head, I watched as she seemed to recede. Or as I did. Whatever. It was like she'd become a balloon-animal version of herself, slipping whatever tether had kept her near me through the years and just gliding away. I felt that trapdoor sensation, that feeling of stepping off the stairs in the dark having miscounted by one: a sudden falling away of solidity.

To my credit, I didn't drop the drinks.

SOME DEVELOPMENTS HAD LED UP to this moment at the Castle. It wasn't coming to me completely out of the blue.

We'd been having a rough few weeks, a difficult couple months, a pretty shitty year. Really, things had been not altogether good since we'd met, and had we met earlier, things would only have been bad for longer. When we were together, we were that couple who argued in public, who fought on the street, who made all their friends uncomfortable. Ever been stuck on a subway with a young couple who seemed right on the verge of strangling each other over some stupid little thing? The proper way to cut a lemon, perhaps. Or the capital of Iowa. Angry to the point where you can see their jaw muscles, the whites around their eyes? That was us. Or it might as well have been. If we'd been on that subway, if we'd been discussing lemons or geography, that's how it would've turned out.

Then, about a week prior to our night at the Castle, I'd absently been flipping through one of my notebooks and found a draft of a letter Sam (my fiancée) had written to David (my best friend) back in Buffalo. In it, she professed her love for him, her more or less total loathing for me, and apologized for ever having left home to follow me on this ridiculous, ill-fated, hopeless attempt at a fresh start.

How many "fresh starts" does one man think he's entitled to? she asked in the letter. *And when is he going to realize that he's never made a single one work?* Meaning me.

She'd closed by saying she was trying to make it home for Christmas (which was, at this point, in just over a month) with or without me (but preferably without) and, in any event, was never returning to the Sunshine State. It occurred to me then, as I sat there reading, that this kind of thing was probably going to put something of a crimp in our plans to wed.

And while a lot of our problems were my fault, they weren't *all* my fault. We simply did not match, her and me. And I think the only reason it took us five years to figure that out was that I spent so little time at home. Absence, heart, fonder—you know how it goes.

But lately, I'd been home a lot—stationed on the couch rather than in front of a grill, drinking coffee and smoking cigarettes, watching daytime TV and sketching fantasy menus in my notebooks, dream lineups like some freckle-faced Midwestern towhead fielding imaginary baseball teams in his backyard, like a convict listing everything he's going to do when he walks free.

Risotto twined with saffron threads, bresaola *with goat-cheese-stuffed whole Mission figs. White asparagus, peeled, rolled in oil and grilled, served in a bundle tied with a leek ribbon over a puree of white beans. White beans and onions tossed in vinegar and Chinese* shu mai *dumplings like the ones from the dim sum place where I'd eaten while negotiating for a job—so nervous, so unaccustomed to eating out (when would I have had time?), that I accidentally ate the flower garnish off a plate of tiny fried fish, not sure what on the plate was supposed to be food and what wasn't . . .*

They were the greatest hits of my spotty culinary career—worldly, border-hopping, almost surrealist expressions of my past, words with the power to recall old friends, old times, to stop the clock and roll it back to what seemed (sitting there on the couch) better days.

*Barbecue cooked over a kerosene fire to give it that chemical
stink just like at Hercules. Meat loaf.* Saag paneer. *Cream of broccoli soup. A bowl of littleneck clams and chopped sausage doused in
cheap wine and lemon. Fillet of sole looking so simple on the plate,
yet requiring the concentrated labor of three cooks cutting, adding
fish velouté, fish glace, maybe a shallow, almost invisible tarn of
lemon-scented, thickened cream . . .*

I'd been looking for one of these menus, one of these memories,
one of these unspooling, stream-of-consciousness inventories when
I'd found Sam's letter. She'd written it in one of my notebooks. And
even now, I half believe that it'd been deliberate, that she'd wanted
me to find it and knew when it would be seen.

*Anything in a Madeira or a bordelaise sauce mounted with
foie gras butter to give it a gloss like liquid velvet—one of the most
beautiful things in the world. Apple fritters dusted with cinnamon.
Red snapper in a sauce of butter, dill and anisette. Pho. Mexican
pork chops and ice-cold gin. Fried chicken with late-tomato jam
and Bresse chickens, split, rubbed with lemon, roasted slivers of
black truffle pushed beneath the skin and served beneath a veil of
sauce Périgueux. Bacon and eggs and bacon-wrapped sweet potatoes and soft-egg-filled Italian ravioli . . .*

The consulting thing had come to a crashing end just recently
when, in the classic film noir hit man's mistake, I'd let a job become
personal. There was an Irish pub and restaurant just down the road
from Kurt's apartment—dark wood, long bar, Guinness on tap, live
fiddle-and-bodhran music on the weekends and shepherd's pie on the
menu. Everything about the place was perfect except that it happened to be in central Florida, surrounded on three sides by the
crush of strip malls and Bennigan's franchises and backing up on a
lizard-infested slough. It was a real neighborhood institution. The
family who owned the place had had it for decades. They were honestly sweet, generous, hardworking people who wanted nothing
more than to keep the local Hibernian contingent liquored up and full
of lamb stew, but had instead found themselves staring straight down
the barrel of chain-restaurant fuck-u-nomics.

I'd gone in with every intention of spending a week helping them design a new kitchen and a new menu to go with it—convenience foods, depending heavily on the fryers and flat grills. But a month later, I was still there, working with a guy who'd race frogs and lizards down a greased prep table to entertain himself on slow afternoons and cooking alone most nights to save the owners a few bucks.

In a fit of idiotic inspiration, I figured that maybe playing *up* the whole Irish thing would help, so I started baking racks of Crucifixion soda bread, making pots of coddle, buckets of champ and colcannon, finding a supplier who could get me real Scotch sausages for bangers and mash, crusting expensive river trout in crushed walnuts and lacing them with whiskey-shot béchamel, doing fry-ups for the homesick Paddies.

Nothing worked. A word to the wise? When trying to save a floundering restaurant in the tropics, Irish cuisine should be the *last* thing you try. No one wants to be eating boiled bacon when it's ninety degrees outside and raining bathwater. Most people don't want to be eating boiled bacon under any circumstances, but even the Irish won't eat it once the mercury starts to climb.

Still, I was knocking myself out trying to help, working all day and all night, spending the family money, and accomplishing nothing except making a bad situation even worse. There were busy nights, but not *enough* busy nights. A lot of the heavy business we did beyond feeding the regulars was cooking for the overflow crowds that couldn't get a table at Red Lobster. And honestly, while there was nothing I could've done right that would've made the least bit of difference, doing everything wrong was certainly speeding the inevitable.

Then came the morning that I went into work feeling a little tired and achy and, ten hours later, was carried out, semiconscious, stoneblind and burning with fever. When one of the waitresses came looking for me and found me passed out with my head on a chair next to the dish machine, everyone had panicked. I couldn't walk. I couldn't see. They'd barely been able to get me up off the floor. Someone called the apartment. Kurt came to pick me up and bring me home. I went to bed. According to later reports from him and Sam, I ran a consistent temperature of 106 or better for three days. They doused me in ice baths, rubbed me down with alcohol, forced aspirin and water into me, took me down like mall cops submarine-tackling a teenage shoplifter every time I made a break for the door. Shivering, quietly humming Bing Crosby Christmas carols, totally gone in delusional fever-dreams and full Technicolor, Dolby-sound hallucinations, I didn't even know where I was. My theory: having finally given up on my body's ability to leave in the traditional sense, my brain—in a desperate attempt at getting out of Florida—had simply decided to stew itself into a coma fantasy of gentler climes and tall, straight pine trees dusted with snow.

The only thing Kurt and Sam didn't do was take me to the hospital. I'd never had health insurance in my life. We had no money for doctors. So as a result, I cooked internally for seventy-two hours— poaching my brain in its own vital juices, low and slow like a *sous-vide* lamb chop. And it wasn't until the fever broke that I agreed to go to one of the Tampa free clinics, where I was thankful for all the Spanish I'd picked up over the years.

No one in the place spoke any English except the young Indian resident who gave me my final diagnosis: double pneumonia, three ribs cracked from coughing, probable brain damage from the fever. He gave me ten days' worth of antibiotics in foil sample packs and a referral to a neurologist. I took the pills, tossed the referral, called the owners of the Irish pub and told them I was sorry—really, truly sorry—but I wouldn't be back. I'm positive I still owe them some money on an old bar tab. Maybe they'll find me when all is said and done.

I recovered slowly. For the first time since I was twelve or thirteen, I went two weeks without a single cigarette. It didn't make me feel any better. Rather, it made me wonder whether nicotine could be administered rectally, what would happen if I just ate the fucking coffin nails in a salad.

Once I was able to stand and take a deep breath without doubling over in pain, I took a job at the local Village Inn and flipped pancakes for eight dollars an hour, twenty hours a week. After years of sixteen-hour shifts and 115-hour weeks, it was the closest thing I'd had to a vacation. But it also gave me a lot of time at home, and really, that's what ended Sam and me: proximity.

Well, proximity and David.

THERE'D BEEN SOME PERSONAL STUFF in that letter, too. Things that led me to suspect (but did not damningly prove) that my fiancée and my alleged best friend had already had a relationshp before I'd packed us off for these terrible Southern latitudes.

And by *relationship*, I mean him fucking her, of course. I already knew there was a *relationship*—that they were friends, went out drinking together, bowling sometimes, that she spent an inordinate amount of time on his couch watching *Melrose Place* and putting away dime bags and once in a while slept there on nights when there was no chance of my coming home. But I'd thought that all so inno-cent, so platonic—was happy, in a way, that she wasn't just sitting around waiting on me every night because that would've made me feel guilty about all the hours I wasn't there for her. In the past, when I'd thought of the situation at all, it'd been confidently. I was glad I had a good friend like David who could watch out for my girl while I wasn't around. I pictured the two of them sitting together on the couch, laughing at the TV, pulling tubes, occasionally glancing up at the clock, noticing the late hour and commenting on what a respon-sible and hardworking fellow I was. I might just as well have imag-ined the two of them throwing quilting bees, floating around on magic ponies or lawn bowling with invisible teddy bears.

In any event, this had made the letter somewhat difficult for me to read, so, after poring over it only fifteen or sixteen more times, I stopped, closed the notebook, put it aside. I lit a cigarette.

I had finally become exactly what I'd set out to become all those years ago: a fucking mess. I was (and remain, to some extent) an ob-sessive, self-involved, needy, shamelessly egotistical, short-tempered prick; a workaholic who defines himself by his job to the near ab-

solute exclusion of all else, a borderline drunk, a control freak. If I'd
ever had a feeling that wasn't lust, hate, rage, envy or unconsciousness, I'd surely never shared it with anyone. Like any field commander,
I was accustomed to having my orders obeyed unquestioningly and
reacted badly when they weren't, when people (Sam, a traffic cop,
the teller at the bank) would bristle and ask me to, please, back off
and not tell them how to do their jobs. I was a chef. I'd learned from
chefs. I was awful. I get that. You know what was the final thing I now
had in common with all the rest of them?

A divorce. Or at least as near to one as mattered.

And if it seems from the way I've told Sam's part of the story that
every moment was bad from start to finish, that's just bullshit—a
function of soured memory and my own malicious nature. I'll say that
my time with her was like Disneyland in reverse: all I remember are
the lines. But buried in among all that is the way we fit perfectly together while sleeping, the smell of perfume behind her ear, the nights
I'd come home late and find her there, awake and waiting, and how
we'd sit staring out, through the snow and ice, at sunrises taking the
dark from the sky. We'd imagined great things together, and what I
was feeling that night at the Castle, I think, was simply the ruin of
potential—the sure knowledge that we'd made none of them work
and now never would.

As for David? We never really spoke again. We'd lived together,
drunk together, traveled together, done everything together. We'd
been best friends since grade school. Now that was over. A few days
before Christmas, Sam and I drove back from Tampa. I left her in Buffalo at David's front door with her things in boxes, in plastic trash
bags. Then I drove off, doing another exhausted sixty miles on an
empty interstate and ending up in the only place I had left to go.

The houses were all lit up for the holiday. Tiny candles in paper
bags lined the street and all the driveways in the neighborhood, glowing warmly in the darkness. Around 9:00 p.m., standing in the falling
snow just twenty-four hours out of Florida's heat, carrying nothing
but one backpack and one duffel bag, I rang the doorbell at my parents' house on Belcoda Drive and asked if I could come home.

In retrospect, seeing as it'd been almost five years since I'd spent more than a couple hours under their roof or said more than a dozen civil words to them in a row, it might've been better if I'd called first.

IN MY LAST WEEK IN TAMPA, I'd gotten a strange e-mail, totally out of the blue, from a girl I'd known forever ago. My mom (perhaps understanding somehow, even from a thousand miles away, that this was going to fuck with my head) had called me at Kurt's to warn me it was coming. This was also rather completely out of the blue. We hadn't talked in quite some time.

"Do you know someone named Laura?" she asked.

I was high and playing video games. It was four in the afternoon. I said no, that I certainly did not.

"Well, someone named Laura called. She was looking for you."

"I'm not difficult to find, Ma. Did you give her the number here?"

"No."

"Why not?"

She huffed, exasperated. "I don't know, Jay . . . Some girl calls here looking for you, what was I supposed to do?"

I chuckled, said, "Give her the number, maybe?"

Mom was quiet for a minute, seething. "She said you knew each other at college," she finally said.

I froze up a little inside, carefully set my PlayStation controller aside, and waved the pot smoke away from the phone as if, from several states away, mom might still be able to smell it. "This mystery girl have a last name?"

"It was something Russian. Wait, I wrote it down."

I said the name under my breath.

"That's it. So you do know her?"

Remember the girl who could put her feet behind her head? The one who didn't know how to make a woo-woo?

"No," I said. "But I remember her."

Mom had been right to call.

. . .

THIS MYSTERIOUS RUSSIAN GIRL had sounded funny* to my mom over the phone so, in her usual paranoid, protective style (and likely assuming this was just someone I owed money to, or worse), she hadn't given up my phone number, just an e-mail address. So we'd e-mailed back and forth a couple times, this funny-sounding Russian girl and me. At a totally inappropriately early moment, I'd spilled for her all the nasty details of my situation: Sam, Kurt, David, the letter, the pneumonia, the Village Inn and my comprehensive loathing for every oozing, stinking, humid, lizard-and-tourist-infested inch of the state of Florida. She responded by totally inappropriately spilling for me the details of the bad place she was in. Our stories were some-what similar—both involving illness, penury, betrayal and exile. She was in Colorado, suffering the dissolution of a five-year relationship, seeing to the equitable disbursement of cats, televisions and bed-room furnishings. She told me to call her, gave me three different phone numbers with three different area codes, said that she'd be at one of them. Maybe.

A BIT OF HISTORY: While at Ithaca, Laura and I had had something of a *thing*. It wasn't a romance because I was never really nice to her, and it wasn't really a friendship because we didn't much like each other. I once burned her quite badly on the hand with a cigarette just to see if she'd flinch. She didn't. And she mocked me mercilessly for pretty much everything—from my silly haircut to my taste in books and movies to my owning more coats than I did shirts and not changing my bedsheets often enough. Or at all.

But we also shared an attraction that I would, in later years, fi-nally be able to adequately describe only as atomic. Hers were the

---

*As I would later learn, she'd sounded funny because she was half in the bag when she'd called, drinking tequila from the bottle and drunk-dialing my mom, reaching out for me and getting Cindy on the blower instead.

ions that filled my outer valences, the heavy element made to comple-
ment and replenish whatever kind of straight freak radiation I was
throwing off. And me? I was just the bad thing she was looking to do
while away from home.

We both acknowledged this attraction. We talked endless, panting circles around it and, at least a little, got off on thinking that nothing was ever going to come of it. She wasn't ready. I had a girlfriend.
There was altogether too much static. The two of us together? When
people walked too close, their balloons would stick.

Flash forward a year or so. I'm working at China Town. She calls,
says I ought to come down for the weekend to Philadelphia because
Peter Gabriel is playing at the SuperUltraMegaDome or whatever and
she has an extra ticket.

So, okay. Why not? I tell Barney and Jake I gotta go see a girl for
the weekend. They make many dirty jokes, and I go—six hours' drive
all hopped up on goofballs, arriving cranked-out, fucked-up, twitchy,
sweaty and gross. But she's beautiful, sweet, happy to see me (which
made me suspicious right from the get-go), and we have a good time.
We see Peter Gabriel do his thing from decent seats on the upper
deck. She gets us a couple waxy buckets of beer, which is a nice
move seeing as she's as underage as I am at the time. Together, we sit
there, wrapped up in the peculiar sort of pulse-racing bubble of hor-
mones that often surrounds two young people in imminent danger of
doin' it.

Did I mention that she was a virgin? I should've mentioned that
she was a virgin. That's important to know here.*

The concert ends. Walking down the long sweep of steps in front
of the arena, she gets a little bit ahead of me, turns, looks back, and I
see her smile at me, her eyes flashing, face lit by the lights of passing
cars. It occurs to me that of all the people surrounding her—the surg-

---

*It's maybe more important to know that her virginity was not a moral one. She hadn't re-
tained it willfully or been saving it for anyone in particular. As she would be the first to
admit, it was simply a matter of having grown up in a nice neighborhood, attending a
nice school, and being the kind of nice neighborhood girl who chooses Fishbone, Metal-
lica, fast cars and college preparatory classes over dick. Though she was more than willing, no one had ever asked. Until I did.

ing crowd, the mob all making for their parking spots—she's the only one I'd give a second glance to. Now, true, this could be saying something bad about the people of Philadelphia in general, but I prefer to think of it as saying something really good about her. The way she looked when she smiled at me? I liked that. A lot. And even as it happens, I know it's one of those moments that's going to hang with me, burrowing into my head like one of those ear weevils in *Wrath of Khan*, impossible to dislodge. When I tell her this, she gets my weird *Star Trek* reference, laughs. Even more points in her favor.

We stay up all night talking. Some stuff happens. I'm not going to say what. But in happening, said stuff cements certain things about Laura in my memory forever. The powdery warmth of her skin. The expressive geometry of her face. The appearance of her disappointment.

At this point I go all weird. I freak the fuck out, say I gotta go, and—still not having slept a wink—literally *run* for my car. Confused, Laura asks me to stay, says we can just hang out, play Nintendo, have a nap. Anything. She wants to know what has so suddenly gone wrong.

But it doesn't matter. I'm in full flight mode now. Nothing short of a dart gun full of elephant tranquilizers would've brought me down. I mouth a couple stupid things about calling her, seeing her later, and that's it—I am out like bell-bottom pants. About halfway up the Pennsylvania Turnpike, doing ninety miles an hour trying to outrun my own bad decision-making and regret, fighting the urge to turn around and try it all again, I fall asleep at the wheel and drift off onto the shoulder, clipping a road sign.

I flee that accident, too; sleep a couple hours in the car on some frontage road, make it home, shower, change, go to work, and that's the night Stacy shows up, telling me all about this friend of hers named Sam.

LAURA AND I DIDN'T SPEAK AGAIN for almost six years. Over the phone in Florida was the first time I'd heard her voice since flannel shirts and Pearl Jam were hot.

If I was her, I would've spent those intervening years building some sort of small satellite equipped with a laser capable of burning a man's genitals off from orbit. If it was me, that phone call would've only been a ploy to get a positive fix on my location so a final aiming solution could be calculated. Then, bingo: instant eunuch, a radical wang-ectomy from space and no way to trace the crime back to me.

But for whatever reason, Laura wasn't like that. There was no space-borne anti-penis laser, and I appreciated that because she'd been on my mind, too. Not a lot, but sometimes. She'd become my what-if girl, my fantasy of an alternative life, like *I wonder what would've happened if I hadn't been such an enormous, spastic asshole back then?*

In my last e-mail to her before leaving Florida I kinda sorta half-apologized for my past behavior, explained that I was driving Sam back to Buffalo and that I had no earthly idea what was going to happen after that. Maybe I would keep heading north and find myself an island somewhere in the Maritimes where I could wear a sweater every day, cook mussels for lunch and live in a small shack by the sea. Failing that, I'd probably be staying with Mommy and Daddy, too humiliated for human contact. Figuring that this time I'd do the gentlemanly thing and warn her in advance, I told her I'd probably never talk to her again, again.

COOK'S HOLIDAY

hristmas in Rochester was strange, subdued, uncomfortable, but only slightly, with more left unsaid than said beneath the dulling morphine of family tradition. Waking on Christmas morning, I felt like a child waking on Christmas morning, only twenty years too late—missing the pad of footy pajamas on the stairs so going outside on the front porch for a first cup of coffee and three cigarettes instead. The tree was lit, the breakfast was laid out—coffee cake, eggs and bacon, slabs of ham left over from the night before, coffee in the same mugs my parents had been using since before I'd left: shallow things like teacups, twined with a flower pattern. From the stoop, with the heavy front door closed behind me, I marveled at the silence of the neighborhood, its blanket of snow unbroken by the gentle scars of footprints. It was nice in an Armageddon kind of way, a sense of my being the last man on earth complete but for the family gathered on the other side of the door, the countless other families behind other doors. Dad gave me a couple minutes of peace before following me out onto the steps, standing beside me, the two of us not speaking, the steam and smoke of our breath twining upward like Christmas wishes, roundly ignored.

Two days before New Year's Eve, I drove to Buffalo thinking maybe I'd see how Sam was settling in (read *try to get laid one last time*) and, when that didn't play out the way I'd imagined, decided to have dinner instead.

I went to La Cité, hoping to reconnect with some of my old friends, but trying the restaurant was a mistake. I barely recognized anyone. The menu had been changed. Even the smell of the place was wrong. Kitchens have an animating spirit the same way that people do—have living inside them better angels or worse, some spark of vitality or pulse of doom that is the attitude and temper of the chef, the cooks, the galley at large. La Cité used to be alive with it. This husk? Something had died here and I couldn't leave fast enough.

But at the bar down the street (old stomping ground for me, my crew, all the crews of all the restaurants in the neighborhood) I recognized absolutely everyone. Faherty's hadn't changed a bit. I opened a tab and just started buying. Matty was there, Al, Andy, Jose the prep mercenary and dishwasher, Max, Amy the waitress, Louis, Gay Jasie—everyone. It was just like a bad movie, like one of those things that never happens in real life. It was as if no one had ever left, which, I came to find out, was more or less true.

Squeezed in at the long oak, muscling my way through the press of other cooks and crews, crammed into a booth along the wall, I felt so happy, so buried in friends and good cheer. Washed by spilled lager and cigarette smoke, telling stories and roaring with laughter. It was like homecoming, only without the letterman jackets and date rape. The juke blared, beers were bought. I drank fast and recklessly, feeling the sizzle of carbonation against the back of my throat and tasting, vaguely, the caramel coldness of the beer, but having one of those nights where the alcohol just seemed to dissipate, floating up and out of my body like a ghost.

Still, we drank until we were full, then stepped out into the alley to pass a joint and just kept moving. It was like trick-or-treating. We'd stop at one house, pick up a sous-chef and a bag of weed, move on, trade the sous for two sauciers and an eight ball, move on. Eventually, we ended up in someone's attic chopping lines of cocaine mixed with ephedrine* on the frame of a foosball table and snorting it through rolled pages torn from a *TV Guide*. Tabs of ecstasy were

---

*Which hurts like fuck, by the way, and is an unwise thing to do for many reasons.

being passed around, hand to ruined hand, prescription painkillers, bottles of terrible Greek white wine (Chateau Diana, with a screw top), Ritalin and pale orange and dusty Dexedrine the same color as an old Flintstones chewable vitamin. We were celebrating something, but I couldn't tell you what. The New Year maybe. Maybe just a Wednesday. Since restaurant people work while the rest of the world relaxes, cooks tend to invent their own holidays, generally focused around any time or place where two or more have gathered with a bottle between them. Sometimes these revels spin quickly out of control.

Actually, most of the time they do. Pretty much always.

I WAS TWENTY-FIVE YEARS OLD, back sleeping again in the childhood bedroom I'd left at fifteen, the shelves crammed with my books, the dresser's lowest drawers still holding some of my cast-off clothes, the desk crowded with pictures in stand-up frames, in albums, in pewter hearts from Things Remembered, bordered by cheap black photo matting board. The house was small—a hobbit house made up of three-quarter-size rooms and narrow, low-ceilinged hallways perfect for turning out bonsai Irish with small goals, small dreams, low expectations. Unlike most prodigal sons returning to the womb after a long and confusing absence, I never found this a surprise. The house had *always* felt small to me, cramped, turned inward so that even the smallest of the rooms felt smaller for being clenched against the outside world.

In the hallway by the stairs, there was the Wheel O' Jay. In the closets, forgotten Christmas sweaters, broken model tanks, a Cub Scout uniform, an old Misfits T-shirt with one sleeve split at the seam that had immediately been drafted into service, bringing my current wardrobe of shirts to two.

Mornings, I'd wake early to the smell of coffee and my father's music on the stereo—the Chieftains, the Pogues, Black 47 and old R.E.M. in heavy rotation on WDAD; the kind of folk music that only serious audiophiles ever even hear, let alone own, with songs about tree-huggers, Irish Republican martyrs and dead smoke jumpers in the Pacific Northwest.

Dad was on permanent disability—multiple sclerosis—but was handling it well. He'd quit smoking after a lifetime of Marlboro cigarettes and his pipe, but along with the habit had lost the smell of burley and bright I'd so long associated with him. He filled his days now with painting, woodwork, carving, carpentry—anything to busy his hands, covering every flat surface in the house with ducks and dragons, bobcats and faeries. When the flat surfaces were all used up, he covered the walls. When the walls were full, he started on the garage. On nice days he'd get this wild look in his eye and I'd be worried he was thinking about paneling the lawn.

Mom was working full-time and then some at a marina on the bay, doing the books for the owners and learning TIG welding from the guys in the yard. Bren was off somewhere living his own life. So mostly, it'd been just me and my dad for the few days after Christmas, before I left. Other than laments for Bobby Sands and dead firemen, the house was very, very quiet. If we talked about anything at all during the day, it was books,* the weather, his newest projects ("I'm thinking of carving tree stumps into bears with my chain saw. What do you think?"), or me when I was a boy. It was nice. The funny thing was, even when Mom was around, no one asked me what'd happened in Florida. No one mentioned how I'd left with a car full of stuff, two cats, and a fiancée but come home empty-handed and without.

---

*Dad has phenomenally bizarre taste in literature, leaning heavily in the direction of swords and spaceships and stories of wilderness survival. He will read anything, but makes his choices almost exclusively based on the subject matter portrayed on the front cover. Forget abstraction, pretty colors, a famous name—none of that matters to him. After careful study of his nightstand over the years, I've determined that if a book doesn't have a flaming spaceship, a busty woman, a brooding knight or someone locked in mortal combat with something on the cover, he's not even going to pick it up. As a result, he has read some of the best and almost all of the worst fantasy and science fiction novels published in the last fifty years, always telling me about the good ones and almost always finding something worthwhile in even the most awful. The downside of all this is that he's probably never going to read this book unless my agent can convince its publisher to take my advice on a cover: me, dressed in a chef's coat and holding a butcher's saber, riding on the wing of a flaming spaceship, clutching a busty woman in one arm while fighting off a half-alligator/half-lion with the other.

And despite my overly dramatic musings in Florida about becoming a hermit in Canada and saying I would probably never speak to her again, I'd called Laura the minute I was through the door. She'd gone to Philadelphia, retreating to her own parents' house without telling me, to her own childhood bedroom, which I had her describe for me in great detail once I'd figured out which of the three numbers was her parents'. Her room sounded much cleaner than mine, but her TV didn't get cable.

I called her again. She called me. I called her, mostly late at night. It was rude, but she kept a cordless on the white table beside her narrow bed below the painting of the irises so she could pick up before the ringing woke her folks. Also, she had the sexiest voice I'd ever had in my ear. Especially when she was whispering.

"Say my name."

And she would. Then I'd say hers. Then we'd talk about anything—her ex, food, *Star Blazers*, what we'd each thought of such and such a song or such and such a movie that'd come out during the years we hadn't known each other. Mostly, we talked about failing.

"The problem was, my mom and dad always told me I could do anything I wanted. They never stood in my way, told me I should be, I don't know . . . that I should just do something with computers."

"Mine, too! I mean, my mom would tell me I should get a good job on an assembly line or something—for the benefits, you know? But, no, they never told me I *couldn't* be something."

"If they'd ever just said 'Do this' or 'Do that' I might've been inspired to actually do something else."

"Or if you had, like, one leg or flipper hands."

"Right! If I had flipper hands and the doctors told me they were very sorry but now I could never be a painter, I'd *be* a motherfucking painter right now."

"Yeah. Flipper hands would be cool . . ."

I'd told her I was going to Buffalo, but not why. I think she had some ideas of her own. She'd been cold to me on the phone the night before I left, an edge of pained bitterness in her voice.

"Just don't do anything stupid, okay?"

. . .

BY TWO IN THE MORNING, the attic was crowded with bodies and the air heavy with smoke. Tom Waits was singing "Innocent When You Dream" in one corner, and somewhere else a radio was playing the New York Dolls, a duet of line cooks singing along, becoming a sextet, an octet on the chorus, the scream: *And if I've got to dream / baby baby baby yeah / I'm a human being.*

I was on a gut-sprung couch, anxiously flipping through old copies of *Saveur* as torn up as roughly used pornography, the pages just as sticky. Because I felt that I had nothing to lose, I had no fear, so I kept drinking, kept taking whatever was handed my way, reaching for something beyond the bottle, the straw or the roach, but getting the paraphernalia every time.

For most of the people there, this was a final hurrah before a grinding, long weekend. New Year's Eve prep would've already begun at most of their houses. Some of these guys would be working straight through for the next thirty- or forty-some hours, counting down to the prix fixes and parties meant to bank enough green for their owners to keep them solvent through the lean weeks ahead— five months of low counts and slow nights broken only by the saving graces of Valentine's Day and Mother's Day.

For me, it was . . . something else. I had nowhere to be, nothing to do, no plans. Eventually I got just epically fucked-up. And why not? Tomorrow, all my friends, my guys, this adoptive dysfunctional family of cooks and chefs, prep specialists, mercenary bakers, floormen, *sur de la Frontera asesinos* and black-eyed, rough-handed frog-humpers who'd taken me in time and time and time again, who'd forgiven me every quirk, perversion, trespass and personality defect, who'd worked with me and for me and beside me until all those kitchens I'd been in bled together into one enormous, smeary flashback-kitchen full of sound and fury, blood and fire, the stinging scent of hot wine, boiling vinegar like tear gas, old sweat, garlic in the pan, howling punk rock in one ear, the rattle of the ticket printer in the other and the sweet cant of the wheelman, "Firing six, twenty-two, eighteen and twenty-two and service, please! Oh, you motherfucking darlings, *service!*" Tomorrow they'd all be headed back to their own kitchens and I'd be nowhere again—headed back to Rochester, to Mommy and Daddy's house, to loose ends and a life apart that I didn't quite know how to continue.

Maybe. Maybe all those things. But in the meantime, another line. Another moment of feeling like I was a part of something that I no longer was or, at least, of feeling nothing at all.

In the sour gray light of dawn, those of us still conscious (plus the bakers and pâtissiers who were already due in at work) were downstairs watching *Apocalypse Now* on an ancient floor-model TV—the kind with the stick-on wood-grain exterior and faux-scrollwork mesh over the single speaker. I was on the floor, head resting against a couch cushion, barely able to see, mush-mouthing lines of dialogue along with everyone else.

"Saigon . . . Shit, I'm still only in Saigon . . ."

Whoever's house it was, I'd already thrown up on their cat. I'd already blacked out in a hallway trying to find some door or another, some way out, walking with my cheek pressed against the wall so I wouldn't get lost. I'd already thought I was going to die a little.

"Disneyland. Fuck, man, this is better than Disneyland."

I didn't. I ended up here instead, following the sound of Captain Willard's voice downstairs to where there was Café du Monde hot in a huge French press on the table and bodies scattered everywhere like the victims of a gas attack, sprawled where they'd fallen, in sometimes unashamedly intimate closeness. I'd gone down close by the couch, someone's hand tenderly patting the top of my head as my consciousness fuzzed in and out like a radio station in the mountains. I watched as a dozen mouths, a half dozen, mine, too, all moved in weird sync. Everyone knew the words. They were dust on our tongues, spoken so often. Everyone played along.

"PBR Streetgang, this is Almighty. Over."

And out. Way out. When I decided it was time to go, I left, saying goodbye like I was never going to see any of these people again. As things turned out, that was pretty fucking prescient of me because I never again did. Life went on. I found my car, got in it, got it started and headed back for Rochester—not realizing until I crossed the Pennsylvania state line near Erie that I'd gone the wrong way on I-90 and was headed for the Midwest.

I didn't bother turning around.

PEOPLE WERE GATHERING IN SANTA FE. Old friends, mostly. Civilians from back in a time when I used to know some, plus Kurt, who was flying out from Florida. As I flashed past the wet greenness, melting snow and gray office parks on a good stretch of Pennsylvania highway almost completely devoid of traffic, I thought to myself, "How far can it be?"

Thirty-two hours if you drive pretty much nonstop, riding a wave of borrowed chemical focus, adrenaline and the high, clear buzz of flight. One of the unexpected thrills of intermittent drug bingeing is finding out what's in your pockets on the morning after. In a rest-stop bathroom with the door locked, I did a quick inventory and discovered that I'd walked off with a bunch of pills, three cigarette lighters, a badly rolled joint that sifted down dry marijuana dandruff when I twisted it between my fingers. Two bottles of Chateau Diana were in my backseat. Not bad. I still had some cigarettes and about a hundred bucks cash, no insurance and only a vague notion of exactly where in New Mexico Santa Fe was and where in the United States New Mexico was. I was golden.

I CALLED MY DAD from Ohio to tell him I'd gotten sidetracked and was headed for New Mexico.

"In that car? You're never going to make it."

"It's the only car I got, Dad."

He thought about this for a minute, but my logic was unassailable. "Okay, well, it's your choice then. But you understand that you're on your own. No one's going to be able to bail you out this time."

"I know, Dad. Happy New Year."

. . .

I CALLED LAURA from a Village Inn about twenty hours later, in bad shape.

"How was Buffalo?"

"I got lost."

"Lost? You lived there for years, Jay. Where are you?"

"Rolla, Missouri."

I CALLED MIKEY AND RONNIE, at whose house the party was happening. I got Mikey—a nice guy, proud hillbilly, accustomed to strange phone calls late at night. Even though I hadn't seen or spoken to him in years (not since he and Ronnie had been living in Ann Arbor and I'd dropped in unannounced on another long, weird weekend with friends in tow), he acted like I'd just gone around the corner for a pack of smokes and some Doritos.

"Where you been?"

I laughed. "Everywhere, it feels like."

I gave him the short version of the story, including my current location. He asked if I wanted him to come and pick me up. For those of you as geographically challenged as I am, Rolla, Missouri, is about nine hundred miles from Santa Fe, but to him, that was nothing. He said he could be there in ten hours or so if I didn't mind waiting—and meant it. I said thanks, but I'd try to get through on my own.

"Be careful," he said. "We'll all be waiting on you."

I ATE BACON AND EGGS and drank a pot of coffee at the Village Inn, staring down at the imitation-wood-grain tabletop like it was TV. By this point, I was having heart palpitations and couldn't get the stink of ammonia out of my sinuses, the taste of chewing old nickels off my tongue. I was suffering intermittent road hallucinations—weird foliage squirming inside the liquid shadows of the breakdown lane, creeper vine and terrible labial suck-flowers crawling along the edges of my vision like long tendrils of Gulf Coast bog flora reaching all the way up from Tampa to try and drag me back down into that swamp of Cuban sandwiches, palmetto bugs and betrayal.

But with a destination in mind (and some direction, courtesy of Mikey, who seemed to know where everything in the world was in relation to everything else), I was feeling okay. Like I could maintain. I gassed up the car at a truck stop where they sold elk jerky off a rack by the door and gravity knives and ninja throwing stars under glass near the register. For hundreds of miles, nothing was on the radio dial but sports talk and damnation.

THEY HAVE A RULE IN SANTA FE that every construction—even things like gas stations and Denny's franchises—must be done in keeping with a rigidly defined Southwestern "look." Everything was adobe, red tile, rounded in a way that looked both sleek and ancient at the same time. It was like taking a wrong turn and ending up on a movie set. Or in a cult compound.

Because of this, I found it difficult to navigate. How does one find his way when all the roads are named after dead Mexican revolutionaries or vicious desert foliage?

Eventually, I found the right white adobe apartment complex, the right Spanish-style door, and knocked. I was still up—burning like an amphetamine supernova, all psychotic giggles and clenched teeth, twitching like Peter Sellers in *Dr. Strangelove*. Kurt hugged me like a long-lost brother even though it'd only been days since we'd last said goodbye and inside, the party was already in full swing. In an attempt to counterbalance my overintake of accelerants over the past fifty or sixty hours, I began self-medicating with red wine, verdant New Mexican reservation weed and Hamburger Helper cheeseburger casserole. When the crash came, I figured I was going to end up in the hospital and ruin everyone's fun. An overdose on New Year's Eve? How déclassé.

Out in the living room, Mikey broke a glass, Ronnie was in tears. Things were unraveling. Sometime before midnight, I saw the

fireworks, the ghost lights swimming behind my eyes, and felt my
stuttering heart threaten to stop. The carpet boiled and twisted
around my feet in fractal representation of infinite Fibonacci se-
quences. When I fell down, Kurt caught me, lit my cigarettes for me,
talked me down to some cold and aired-out piece of real estate somewhere in the center of my brain: a solid toehold on sobriety, swept
clean of junk or consequence, that would only grow as the New Year
began. With my head on his shoulder and his hand on the back of my
neck, he told me everything was going to be all right. I believed him
because I had no other choice but surrender.

I called Laura. We talked for a long time, listening to Mikey and
Ronnie's birds-of-the-world clock tweet and screech away the hours.
Long after midnight but with the New Year still young, she told me to
do whatever I needed to do to hang on in New Mexico. Lie, steal, murder. Be creative, she said. She was going to fly back to Colorado as
soon as she could—a few days, week at the most—and would then be
just a few hours' drive away.

"Come up and find me," she said. "I'll buy you a taco."

I said that I would, faked a coughing jag to cover the lump in my
throat that wouldn't go down. This relationship was still new. Without coming off creepy, I couldn't tell her how happy she'd made
me, how blissful and filled with joy. I had plans again. I had somewhere to be.

Around dawn, I hung up the phone, curled up on the floor and
slept until the following night. When I woke up, Mikey was crouched
over me, having just taken my pulse to see if I was still alive. I was. He
handed me an iced cappuccino fresh out of the blender in a big plastic cup with a clown on it, and a cigarette, then sat down on the floor
next to me with his back against the cabinets.

"Man, you snore," he said. "Loud."

I'VE FOUND THAT ONE of the other benefits of the indiscriminate drug
spree—beyond pocket joints and the acquisition of too many Bic
lighters—is a certain contrapuntal rearranging of one's mental lawn

furniture into patterns more in line with effective feng shui. It is puri-
fying, so long as you survive. And if you don't? Well, anyway, you're
cured of all life's mortal sorrows.

This time, I felt as though I'd come a little bit too close to the Big
Black and, on a whim, quit the drugs. It wasn't a resolution or anything. Just one of those things that happens. Suddenly, I had no taste
for them anymore, and, believe it or not, since that night in Santa Fe
I've managed to stay more or less completely away. Other than
whiskey, rum and vodka, cigarettes and beer, tequila and mescal, Am-
bien and Prilosec, a variety of pills prescribed by actual licensed doctors, antibiotics, four or five pots of coffee a day and a little weed
now and then, I haven't touched drugs since December 31, 1998.

And I don't miss them at all, except for almost every day.

TRUE TO HER WORD, Laura bought me that taco. After I'd been in Santa
Fe about ten days, she called to say she was back in Colorado, staying with her ex-boyfriend, and did I think I could make the drive? I
told her I'd walk if I had to.

I headed out for Boulder the next morning, wearing my only pair
of jeans and a clean sweater that I'd found in my trunk and saved for
just this event. It was a six-hour drive. I gave myself ten just in case.
Also unnecessary. Other than work, meeting Laura was probably the
first thing in my life I'd ever been early for. Also, probably the last.

I drove around Boulder for a while, doing my best not to get lost,
just driving in circles. It was gorgeous, idyllic, snugged up against the
snowcapped foothills and sparkling like some hidden stronghold out
of a fairy tale, only infested by hippies and their mangy dogs.

We'd agreed to meet at the Dark Horse.* I pulled into a parking
spot with a good view of the door and settled in to wait, determined

---

*A well-worn and rambling bar just off the highway, visible from any direction and im-
possible to miss. Laura had chosen it because it would be easy for me to find and because decades' worth of college students had met and made bad choices there. True, we
weren't in college anymore and we weren't meeting for the first time, but trust me: it's
never too late to make a bad choice you should've made long ago.

to get the first look at her, not even knowing if I'd recognize her after all this time.

I needn't have worried. I caught sight of her walking across the lot with her back to me, wearing a cocoa-brown leather pimp jacket from the seventies, the greatest pair of blue jeans in the world and a pair of stack-heel boots. She was shorter than I remembered, but her hair was short and flaming red, her skin like milk. I was actually up and out of the car before I even thought of getting up and out of the car, already striding across the ice toward her. I called her name and she turned to look at me. She smiled—a gorgeously mean and sardonic thing—while she looked me up and down.

"You're shorter than I remember," she said.

There was wind and then there wasn't.

MAL CARNE

Sheehan! Gnocchi, baby. Dragging ten. What's up?"

I'd been so good at this once. Ten gnocchi? Two-step prep. Step one: boil fucking gnocchi. Step two: plate fucking gnocchi, nap of red sauce, sprinkle of parsley. Put it to the rail. Nothing easier. It was a retard's station, the pasta trench. Made for cripples, casualties. Just heat and serve, heat and serve, like slorking out cans of Chef Boyardee, only easier. How had I gotten so far down?

"Thank you, ten gnocchi," I parrot back. "Ten gnocchi, ten gnocchi, ten gnocchi, ten gnocchi . . ."

"SHEEHAN! Anyone seen Sheehan?"

I can hear them yelling for me. Can't make myself care. Standing out back, sitting out back, folded up on an overturned milk crate, a broken chair, I'm staring at the grass. I'm attempting to close my nostrils against the scent of the breeze off the Dumpsters, the dusty gravel of the parking lot soaked down by grease and leaky trash bags. I'm watching a sparrow up a tree, its branches hanging spidery over the fence beside me, waiting to see if the bird will fly away.

"Sheehan!"

Bird flies, I fly. He goes, I go. But the bird is fucking stubborn. I smoke cigarettes I don't want or need. Two, three packs a day, taking any excuse to step out front, out back. My throat is raw. My chest hurts. I stare at the bird, willing him to go, concentrating on the scrape of his bird feet, the tilt of his bird head.

"What are you waiting for?" I ask him under my breath. "You're a fucking bird. You can fly away."

"Sheehan! What the fuck?"

One of the cooks pokes his head out the door, sees me, shouts at me to get back on station. The sparrow explodes upward off the branch with a fluttering thump of wings like a racing heartbeat and a rattle of disturbed leaves. I stand, grind out my cigarette with the toe of my boot and slouch back into the kitchen. What can I say? I'm a pussy.

MY DAD HAD BEEN RIGHT about the car. It hadn't quite made it home with me from Colorado.

Laura and I had spent a night at the Dark Horse. We'd gone up into the Boulder foothills and, at some point, fallen into each other's arms in the snow. Later, standing, leaning against a boulder in the darkness, she'd folded herself into my chest and the warmth of her body against mine was like an early spring. I wore the imprint of her shoulder, the point of one hip, the palm of her hand on my chest, like a tattoo for days. Later still, descending a switchback road in the dark in her car, I had a feeling like if she was to miss a turn and send the car slipping off into air, tires spinning, it would simply fall forever through a bottomless night, never touching ground.

But it couldn't last. After spending a few days with her, sleeping (sometimes with her) in the basement of her ex-boyfriend's place, I decided it was time to go home. The living arrangements were getting weird. Not weird-dangerous, just weird, period. The three of us— Laura, me, the ex—had all gone out for Chinese food one night and had nothing that we were willing to say to each other or in front of each other. Just trying to figure out who was going to sit where was so complicated it was like dancing.

On the day I left, I decided to take a northern route back East and try to rush out ahead of a wicked storm that was blowing in,* but that hadn't worked at all. I made Cheyenne okay, turned right, and drove smack into the worst blizzard I'd ever seen. For the past several months, all I'd had to contend with were the daily four-o'clock rainstorms in Tampa. They happened every afternoon like clockwork, lasted ten minutes, and were vicious—the rain pouring down like the clouds had been unzipped, like rain was a new trick they'd learned and couldn't wait to try. But when it was done, everything would be a little better. The smell would get beaten down, the dust knocked off all the limes and palm trees. If nothing else, all the lizards would be washed off my car.

But this was apocalyptic—serious Old Testament shit, merciless, devoid of all the Hollywood fire-and-brimstone pyrotechnics. One minute, Wyoming highway in the dark. The next minute, white blindness, ice and frigid silence. It was spooky beyond words.

I ended up spending the night in a truck-stop parking lot barely fifty miles away, at first trying to sleep in the car under my borrowed blanket, then giving that up, kicking my way out through doors that'd been glazed shut with ice, and sleeping inside the truck-stop restaurant. It was twenty below zero. No one got moving again until late the next afternoon, and only then with the help of generator trucks, engine blankets and a wrecker.

I'd survived, but the car had developed a tick in the engine that slowly became a knock, then rather quickly became a cataclysmic banging—blown gasket, thrown piston rod, maybe worse. I'd made Indiana by this point, which wasn't bad. Muscling the dying car into a gas-station parking lot just off the interstate, bringing it to a chugging, final stop, I was already thanking the machine for getting me as far as it had.

---

*Though not before borrowing a blanket, a hammer and sixty dollars from Laura, none of which she ever got back—a point she brings up whenever she feels the need to remind me of what an untrustworthy little prick and shameless hustler I've been for most of my life.

Still, a dead car is a dead car. I sold it on the spot to a tow-truck driver who'd stopped at the same gas station for coffee, asking $200 and a lift to the state line, taking his counteroffer of $150, then sorting quickly through my belongings, taking only what was absolutely necessary. The rest I left behind, my possessions being winnowed by circumstance, and climbed into the truck's cab.

The driver took me as far as the Ohio line and left me by the side of a four-lane frontage road. I hitched the rest of the way to Rochester, arriving once again on my parents' doorstep unannounced, this time without even the car I'd left with.

Every time I went out, it seemed I came back with less—less people, less cats, less stuff, less large American automobiles. I was okay with this. It felt appropriate somehow. Like butchery, like taking down a nice steak, I was only losing my fat cap, my chain, my inedible silver skin and rind, and I trusted (hoped, anyway) that there was still good meat in me somewhere, beneath all that trim.

My folks thought differently, though, and my dad was angry that I hadn't at least had the common sense to pull the plates off the car before handing over the keys.

"SHEEHAN, CHICKEN?"

The head cook is talking to me, nominal chef, maybe even a short sweat-equity partner with some piddling 2 or 3 percent, which was still more of anything than I'd ever owned.

"Chicken, man? You hear me?"

I do, but I am not responding, staring at the side of his face as he stares down at the sheet tray in front of me, neatly laid out with chicken breasts, immaculately cleaned, butterflied open, half of them already split along the thin hinge of flesh where the breastbone would've been had they still been possessed of their skeletons. I have the knife in my hand—my knife, a solid and beautiful Henckel classic with the little finger hook at the butt end of the grip—and am watching the play of muscle under the head cook's clean-shaven cheek, the lines of veins and tendons running down the side of his neck.

"Chicken man, get it? Chicken man Sheehan." He chuckles to himself. This is the eighth sheet tray of chicken breasts I have done this morning. Not because we needed eight sheet trays of chicken breasts for parms and paillards, but because I'd just sort of gotten into a thing. A rhythm. When he looks over at me, I don't look away. Our gazes collide like two cars on a blind corner, with their full weight and violence.

"Jesus, man," says the head cook. "I was just trying to make conversation, you know?"

"Chicken man," I bark, then laugh too loud, too hard, too joylessly—really forcing it. "I get it, yeah."

"Hey, these are nice, but how many trays you done?"

"Eight," I say. "Eight."

"Eight?"

"Eight."

"Yeah, you might wanna lay off now, huh? Do something else? I think that'll cover us. By the way, Friday night? What happened to you?"

"Left," I said. "I was done."

"Well, that isn't really your decision to make, is it? What the fuck, you think you can just leave whenever you want?"

"I was *done*. No one needed me to stick around."

Which was mostly true. What was more accurate was that none of the other cooks had wanted me to.

Home again, I'd taken a job at a thoroughly mediocre but well-loved neighborhood Italian restaurant walking distance from my folks' house. I pounded out veal paillards, breaded chicken for parms, made thousands of really excellent gnocchi by hand—bringing the dough together, rolling it out, pulling each little thumb-sized blob across the tines of a fork to shape it. During service, I worked the pasta trench or the fryer station—low man again, the FNG—but couldn't get into it. It all seemed so ridiculous, so pointless. And I was so angry all the time. I could do the job when I chose to—could go through the motions, watch the pastas, set my *mise*, keep the fryers rolling—but I took no joy in it. Those things that would once have thrilled me (the fine work of making the gnocchi, the precision and care of it, and breaking down the veal for paillards and the hectic pace of a busy line), I found only dull. Something was broken in me now; something had soured and cooked off in my head, some nugget of rot and frustration and rage that couldn't be dug out no matter what I'd lost, how close to the bone I'd been trimmed over the last month.

When doing prep butchery, sometimes you'll find a piece of meat that can't be saved. Cutting fish, you'll occasionally find an entire loin or side ruined by some marine worm that has bored through the flesh to die, curled in a knot, deep inside the powerful muscle. It's the kind of thing that can put you off fish for a long time. Breaking down beef, it's usually a vein or artery that can't be pulled without wrecking the steak or a hump of tough fat in the wrong place. And it doesn't matter how good you are with the knife, how clever with your anatomy— it's just bad, ruptured, decayed, tumorous, *wrong*, and you have to just let it go.

That was me. All of a sudden I was showing up late, fucking with the radio too much, not pulling my weight during cleanup, and would occasionally just walk off for no reason. I was breaking all my own rules about conduct on the line, a disgrace to my borrowed white jacket. The owner was always pissed at me. The other cooks, likely smelling bad meat—that bit I was never, ever going to be able to dig out—wanted nothing to do with me. I never even learned their names and could go whole nights without talking (except to my ingredients). Those were the good nights.

From the corner of the front parking lot, I could see Ferrara's, where all this had begun. And usually when I disappeared, that's where the owner or one of the waiters would find me: standing there, smoking a cigarette, just staring.

MOST NIGHTS WHEN I GOT OFF WORK, I'd hitch into the city, to the Rose & Crown, where my buddy Sparky would already be waiting for me— hunched up like some kind of troll over his pint, a pub golem made of creamy black Guinness, stale pretzels, broken glass and wisps of cigarette smoke. He'd been haunting this particular stretch of long oak for years now, since the three of us—Sam, him, and me—had come back from California, living almost directly across the street, on the second floor of a rambling old Victorian made up of too many small, unusually shaped rooms all crowded with his stuff. He could walk to the Rose & Crown in the afternoon, stumble home after last call, and often did—having become the kind of guy who closes bars on a Tuesday night.

I had no idea what he did for a living that wasn't this. It wasn't something we talked about. He was and sometimes wasn't dating a girl who was and sometimes wasn't a stripper. We didn't really talk about that either.

What we did talk about was the past. Constantly. Both our real pasts and an invented collection of pasts that we could shake up like a box of dominoes, pulling out one, then another, then another. Lay them out on the table and they made a story, a different one every time. We'd tell them for beers, for dinner, for kicks. We told them to each other when no one else was around like a two-man manic-depressive vaudeville act practicing, polishing up our licks and timing.

We were just doing it as a way to pass the time, the lies more fun than the truth, sometimes the other way around. And we did it at the Rose & Crown because the Rose & Crown was Sparky's home away from home and because the Rose & Crown was where an entire generation of Flower City kids had grown up drinking, where they all eventually came back to when their lives elsewhere imploded and, like me, they came running back home, defeated. We'd sit about halfway down the bar, near the center run of taps, because from there we had a good view of the door without looking like we were looking to have a good view of the door. Sparky with his badly shaved head, sweatshirt hood up and Carhartt jacket on. Me with my long hair, bandanna, white button-down oxford and greasy blue jeans. Both of us wreathed in cigarette smoke, rolling single well whiskeys between our palms.

But everyone, when coming to the Rose, was looking for some-one. Even when people didn't know they were looking, they were looking. Sparky and I just tried to be what they found, especially when they were people of the female persuasion, or people willing to buy drinks for two guys who maybe they knew ten years ago and now were here, telling stories about kitchens, about working one of those cannery jobs in Alaska or for NASA or whatever.

When there was no one to talk to, we threw darts. Sometimes, when closing time rolled around, I'd crash at Sparky's. Sometimes not. Sometimes I'd bum a ride from someone headed back out to the burbs. After Colorado, I didn't have a car anymore, was shortly to lose my license as well.

True, this made that whole NASA story a tough sell. You tell a bunch of people you're a rocket scientist, they sorta expect you to have your own wheels. But whenever it came up, I'd just say my license had been revoked over multiple DUIs, which, by the end of almost any night out, was both perfectly believable and less embarrassing than the actual truth.

BEFORE LONG, I got pulled off weekends at the Italian restaurant—a worse punishment than simply being fired because it was a highly public shaming in front of one's peers, an acknowledgment that you just didn't have what it took to hang with the swingin' dicks on Friday and Saturday nights.

"You come in here telling me you're this Mr. Big-Time Chef," the owner said, "and this is what I get? I'm not saying you lied to me, Sheehan, but just get out of here. Come back for Tuesday dinner."

I was fine with it. I just didn't care. Weekends off gave me more time for hanging out at the Crown, for staying out late and feeling bad for myself. Misha (the long-lost high school ex-girlfriend) would sometimes join us and play along with our stories. Otherwise we'd meet her at the Bug (an old punk bar with Day-Glo decor and a good juke), have a few, listen to some music, then retire to Gitsi's or Mark's for eggs, fish fry, chili dogs and coffee, to Nick Tahou's for Garbage Plates at two in the morning. We'd go to Joe's—a coffeehouse down by the Eastman Theatre—and make fun of the slam poets there. We'd just drive, playing the same game we did at the bar, only now just for our own amusement, passing playgrounds and schools, buildings where we'd lived, train tracks and alleys, all of them blurring in the windows of Sparky's car, seen through handprints, the smudge of our breath, these half-forgotten benchmarks of our childhoods.

Mornings and nights, I had Laura for company: e-mails and phone calls, thousand-minute interstate phone cards burned through in a matter of days. Ours was becoming a kind of old-fashioned/high-tech courtship. Love letters. Whispered conversations. My memories of the few days I'd spent with her out West still fresh and vital, my memory of leaving still an ache that wouldn't go away.

"You know what else would be cool? Gills. So I could stay in the water all the time."

"Really? Gills? No way."

"Why not?"

"I'm afraid of fish."

Later, I would go to see her, back in Philadelphia—borrowed car, borrowed cash, borrowed time. We had a weekend, no more. She cooked for me (that took balls), and it was nothing complicated— *rotini* pasta with chicken, fresh herbs stripped from the stem—but I loved it. How long had it been since someone had cooked for *me*? In her bed that night, the two of us curled together, exhausted, forehead to forehead, like parentheses with nothing between, I smelled the sting of fresh thyme on her fingertips and never forgot it. Messed up as I was, that memory burned itself in deep. Ditto the memory of the next day when her ex showed up at the door, having flown in unexpectedly from Colorado with a ring and a proposal, trying to make the big romantic move. I stayed upstairs. She dealt with him in the basement. When the dust settled, I was the one who went to bed with her that night, the two of us laughing about it. No regrets.

Some weekends, I'd take the Greyhound bus to Buffalo to see my buddy Gracie—a civilian with a *grillardin*'s heart and tastes in everything from music to booze, who I'd met while he was still in college and liked immediately because he was just as profane, black-hearted, miserable and funny as most of the cooks I knew, but was just smart

enough to have found something better to do with his life than cooking dinner for strangers.

Sometimes I'd see Sam. Sometimes not. Mostly not. I'd walk
around the city, ride the subway, sit in the diners. I never had to worry
about where I was going to sleep because by this point I wasn't sleeping much, sometimes at all.

I wasn't well. I was getting fevers that would come on out of
nowhere, have me boiling in my skin like a steam radiator sweating
through its paint, then break and vanish a few minutes or an hour
later. I was talking to myself (which I originally chalked up to my being alone all the time, until it occurred to me that I wasn't actually
alone all that much and that sometimes I'd be chattering away to myself while surrounded by other people) and seeing things that weren't
there. Sometimes I'd just space out for an hour or so. Sitting in a
restaurant, my coffee would go cold in my hand. Often, I'd just
stand there. It wasn't a problem unless I was on a bus or walking—
suddenly coming back to myself in neighborhoods where I'd never
before been. In any event, I was keeping it all to myself pretty well.
I was handling it. More or less.

ON MAY 1, I had plans to spend the day with Gracie in Buffalo. May 1
was the day before Sam and I had originally planned to wed, and I
think most of my few remaining friends had been waiting on the call,
the request for company. Gracie was just Mr. Lucky.

I didn't understand what the big deal was. I had no intention of
getting all weepy or maudlin. Things had ended. That was that.
Really, I just wanted someone to hang out with. I even had other
plans to meet with David and Sam later that night. We had tickets to
see the Jim Rose Circus Sideshow,* all of us together. Though I don't
recall exactly why any of us thought that would be a good idea or a
nice time, I believe it had something to do with Sam and me feeling

---

*You know, the freaks. Contortionists and geeks, guys who hammered nails into their
faces and hung car batteries from their genital piercings. Good, honest showbiz folk.

that it would be a suitably ironic way to celebrate the dissolution of Us. We could all say goodbye and good luck and, along the way, watch a man eat lightbulbs. Fun for everyone.

I left for Buffalo in the morning by Greyhound, arrived in the city around noon, stopped at a liquor store between the bus station and Gracie's second-floor apartment on Main Street—situated above the hippie coffee shop and Chinese herbalist's store—and carried two six-packs of Killian's the rest of the way. Gracie and I had a couple of beers at his place, sitting in his window frame and taunting the Deadheads and poets arrayed below, the hairy-legged girls all trying to play Ani DiFranco tunes on their rattling pawnshop guitars. When that got dull, we went down the street for a late breakfast at Amy's Place—a great, dirt cheap Lebanese diner always full of radical feminists, student Buddhists, hungover professors of cultural anthropology from the university down the street and tables crammed with anarchists all drinking watery tea and sharing a single plate of hummus.

Some friends of Gracie's met us there. We spent the afternoon relaxing, hanging out in the sun, just knocking around the city. It was one of the better days I'd had in a while and I was feeling fine.

Night came. I thanked Gracie for his company and for drinking more than his share of the beer I'd brought, then left to join Sam for dinner. We talked lightly about the good old days, joked about our various failures, were both self-deprecating and sweet. Later, David* met us at the club where the show was happening. We found our reserved table, ordered drinks and some snacks, made (I assume) some slightly uncomfortable small talk. And then, at around eight-thirty, just before the show was supposed to start, some vital system inside me finally failed and all my lights went out.

I REMEMBER FEELING A LITTLE ILL, like maybe I was going to throw up. I was right in the middle of telling a story about New Year's Eve in New

---

*I know I said earlier that I never spoke to him again. You'll see why that's still basically accurate in a moment.

Mexico, and I can recall, with sometimes uncomfortable clarity, the sudden rush of cold sweat. I remember thinking, "Man, I better find the bathroom."

Like *now.*

I do remember standing up, but at this point, the clock is running down on lucidity. I remember excusing myself politely from the table, turning and feeling the whole room twist like a Möbius strip. I remember the sudden tunnel vision, the fireflies in my eyes, a sickening, loud bang like a lightning detonation somewhere deep inside my head, and lurching crazily toward a four-top of horrified yuppies all frozen with shock.

Miffy, Buffy, Biff and Chet certainly hadn't anticipated this. They'd come here looking for some tame, cultivated freak-show experience— to see the fire-eaters and Mr. Bendo at a comfortable distance, giggling behind their hands while they drank their white-wine spritzers and ate their ahi tuna appetizers. But now, here they were, about to receive a highly personal lesson in inevitability; watching me come toward them with mounting horror, maybe even thinking, right up until the last instant, that I was a part of the show and would stop at a respectful distance and pull a bouquet of flowers out of my ass.

No such luck. I hit their table going down—groaning, clutching at them—then slid off and, seeking shelter, dragged myself underneath. I knew something had gone bad wrong inside me, but knowing it, I had no idea what to do about it. Pushing legs and feet and ankles out of my way, I wrapped my arms around the table's center post, hanging on like a tempest-tossed sailor to the mast, blubbering and speaking in tongues. I was scared. I had no idea what was happening to me.

And after that, all I remember is the hospital.

ACTUALLY, I don't *really* remember the hospital, but I remember being there because I remember leaving, because I've been told I was there, because, somewhere, there's paperwork that proves it.

The human brain has this remarkable ability to edit out pain and trauma—a mercy of limited recall that keeps us from obsessing over every hurt, little or large, which is the only reason any woman has ever had more than one baby and why Evel Knievel kept jumping his motorcycle over buses and vats of flaming badgers well into his middle age.

The problem is, the brain is an indelicate editor. It spills a lot of Wite-Out and, in excising the bad stuff, inadvertently takes a lot of the laughs with it, a lot of the sweet detail. For me, the forty-five minutes or so immediately following my one-man gravity demonstration are almost completely gone. Things are spotty for a couple hours before (like, I can remember eating dinner with Sam, but not where; I can remember meeting David, but not precisely when). The six or eight hours after are something of a wash, too. The part of my brain skilled at stringing moments together into scenes, and scenes together into a story, had checked out. All I was left with were the loose moments, free of context. As a result, it's quite possible that some or none of the following things truly happened, and it's absolutely true that plenty of other things happened that I'll never recall.

Regardless, here's what I know.

THE ER DOCTOR WHO FIRST SAW ME was absolutely convinced I was fished out on drugs when I was brought in. Five months earlier, this would have been a fair diagnosis. But since January I'd remained remarkably clean. Hunched over me, his face way too close to mine, knuckles digging into my chest, he demanded loudly that I tell him what, *exactly*, I'd taken and in what amounts. I thought he was going to slap me when I insisted I was sober.

THE OWNER (OR POSSIBLY THE MANAGER) of the nightclub where the show was taking place had been walking from the bathrooms back to his office when he saw me go down. Thinking I was drunk, he'd first moved to call in the bouncers, but then he saw me twisting and flopping around on the floor and knew I was having a seizure. He ran over, scattered the yuppies and the gawkers who'd gathered, grabbed me under the armpits and dragged me into the office, my heels furrowing the carpet. He was also the one who'd called the ambulance.

I was laughing hysterically, speaking what he thought was French and pouring sweat like I'd just run a marathon. Every time he tried to put me in a chair, I'd fall out.

He told all this to the paramedics when they arrived, asking, "Is he gonna die?"

THE PARAMEDICS WERE UNABLE to get any information out of me because all I would do was mumble, laugh and seize. Twice, while they were attending to me in a back hallway outside the club, I snapped into what appeared to be total consciousness, leaped up, thanked them for their concern and efforts, then tried to run. I'd black out before I got far, but it was always a surprise, so when they got me on the gurney, they put me in restraints. Outside, it was snowing. Seems like a rare thing in May, even for Buffalo, but that's what I remember. Everything had a beautiful halo around it and it was bright as noon. I tried to catch snowflakes on my tongue.

IN THE ER, when my tox screen came back negative for everything but a couple beers and some tabbouleh, the doctor decided he wanted nothing more to do with me. He sent me upstairs for a CAT scan. An orderly with a gigantic Afro came to wheel me off and, when I asked, took me outside so I could have a cigarette.

"Ain't no rush," he said. "Doctor thinks you faking it."

AN AMBULANCE RIDE OF FIVE BLOCKS in Buffalo cost $750 in 1999, making it the most expensive cab in the city. But then this also included all the crack medical care I received en route: the two full-bore IVs they stuck in me, stabbing me so many times trying to find a vein that the bruises didn't heal for a month; the twelve-lead that required them to take a pair of surgical scissors to my favorite party jeans and the British SAS commando sweater I'd received as a gift; the fingertip pulse monitor that fell off during the ride, filling the ambulance with that screeching electronic *eeeeeeee* sound that, thanks to the glut of hospital shows on TV, has finally surpassed the death rattle as the sound of impending mortality in this modern age.

Sam, who was riding up front, heard that and freaked out—twisting in her seat and trying to claw through the partition behind her like a cat. A trainee on the rig, not thinking to first check the monitor, started chest compressions that nearly broke my ribs.

THIS PART I REMEMBER CLEARLY:

"We didn't know what was wrong with you, but you sure seemed to be enjoying yourself," one of the ambulance crew later told me, standing outside the hospital. They'd come back to check on me, which I thought was nice. He said I'd been laughing, telling jokes between blackouts, but not speaking any language he'd ever heard. Also, I'd pissed myself. And tried to bite one of the medics, for which I sheepishly apologized.

"Don't worry about it," he said. "Happens all the time."

IN THE CAT SCAN MACHINE, I fell asleep and couldn't be woken. That's when the hospital called my parents in Rochester, waking them with the 4:00 a.m. phone call that they'd probably been expecting for years. As always, my mom picked up.

Mrs. Sheehan? This is Buffalo General Hospital. We have your son Jason here . . .

"GOOD THING WE'RE NOT GETTING MARRIED TOMORROW," I said to Sam at some point.

• • •

I WAS STILL UNCONSCIOUS WHEN MY FOLKS ARRIVED—coming out of it around six or seven in the morning with them already in the room and the doctor attempting to explain brain disorders to my mom.

"A seizure can be triggered by many things," he was saying. "At this point, we really don't know what happened, but he appears to have had one large . . ."

He paused here as if searching for a word that would neither confirm nor deny the veracity of what several different people had told him had happened to me, the validity of the eyewitness explanations, reports from the ambulance crew, the blood work, the tests that had shown my body to be completely spent and exhausted, if not in any specific way broken.

"One large *episode,*" he continued, as if suddenly I were a supersize prime-time drama. "And about a dozen smaller ones. These are like aftershocks, but they seem to have stopped now."

Brainquakes. I liked that.

"Jason hasn't been very helpful," the doctor added.

My mom sighed scoldingly. I knew that sound all too well, having heard it roughly ten thousand times before this night. Lying there, I'm thinking, "Here it comes . . ." It was the perfect moment for her to swing into her routine, her whole *You know, up until he left home, he was a perfect angel* act. Never before had she been set up so cleanly, had an audience so willing—eager, even—to hear and have entered into the official record the full litany of mistakes, screwups, poor choices and bad behavior I'd engaged in since leaving her protective custody.

But then, Mom has always been full of surprises.

"Helpful?" she asked, fixing her eyes on the doctor. "Does it look like he's in any condition to be helpful? Aren't *you* supposed to be helping *him*?"

The doctor made another attempt. "We're trying to help him, Mrs. Sheehan. Do you know of any drugs he might be using?"

"Drugs?" Mom laughed. "Oh, no. He might've smoked a little marijuana in college, but if he said anything different, he's lying. I always say, it's like he has this whole other life sometimes." She paused. Through slit eyes, I could see her turn to look straight at me, half smiling. "This whole other, made-up life."

She looked back up at the doctor. "So tell me, if you don't know what's the matter, can we take him home?"

Making one last feeble effort, the doctor asked again, "So, no drugs then?" He had his pen poised over his clipboard, his eyes on my mother, waiting.

And Mom paused a moment, tilted her head, looked at the doctor with a quizzical eye as if to say, *Who is this little man that makes me repeat myself when I am in a rush?* When she did finally speak, her voice had grown perhaps half a decibel louder and the ambient temperature in the room had dropped five hundred degrees.

"Can we take him *home* now?"

WE WERE GONE FROM THE HOSPITAL in about twenty minutes. Dad helped me out to the car, stopped on the way out of Buffalo so I could pick up a couple of gas-station sandwiches and a pack of cigarettes, but I was asleep again before he even made it out of the parking lot.

Having never had health insurance before, I went on Medicaid. Once I had my wits about me somewhat, I was not much other than tired. Well, tired and pissed. Because of the nature of my hospitalization, the DMV pulled my driver's license for six months, pending a doctor's note promising I wouldn't seize behind the wheel and run into a bus full of nuns. I felt as though my second-favorite organ was betraying me with its weakness, further screwing up my already amply screwed-up life.

Three days later, I went back to work at the Italian restaurant, and it happened again. Again, it came on out of nowhere. Dizziness, cold sweat, a wave of nausea and the smell of cooked wiring, then out. This "episode" was different only in that the cast of guest stars had changed—cooks now, not yuppies—and there wasn't that sickening crack in my head, no flopping around. I went down on the flattop this time, on my left forearm (where I still have the raspberry-colored scar), and slammed my head on the edge of the cutting board behind me. I was carried off the line and dumped outside the back door. Bad meat. Nothing for it but to toss it aside and move on. Again my folks were called. They picked me up. And I never went back to that restaurant again, either—something that was, at this point, becoming a pattern.

Two days after that, I was having a cup of coffee and reading the paper at the diner when I felt the panicky sweats wash over me. This time I had the presence of mind to drop a couple bucks and make a dash for the door. Almost made it, too.

After it happened again (at a hamburger restaurant this time, with me fading to black in the back parking lot), I stopped leaving the house alone, wouldn't go anywhere without chaperones who understood that I might, at any moment, just hit the ground and start swimming away. For a week or so, I was afraid. Subsequently, only annoyed.

That's why, when I was out at the bar with Sparky, I'd tell people the reason I needed to thumb a lift was multiple DUIs. It might not have been the truth, but it sure was an easier story to tell.

Besides, I wasn't really a motherfucking rocket scientist either, was I? Or an ex-con, or fresh back from the bayou or whatever other story Sparky and I had decided on telling that night. I wasn't even a cook anymore. I was just a goddamn cripple. And no one wanted to hear that story.

CHICKEN HITLER

I never really cooked again seriously after that.

I mean, I cooked. And I would collect a paycheck, at least for a couple more years. But the fire and the magic had gone out of it for me—had gone out of *me*, really. The food was still food, was still as good or as bad as it'd always been. Only now I looked at it with dull eyes rather than love, and at kitchens mostly with dread.

I remember wishing (for the first time, not the last) that I had pictures of me and my time spent on the line, in my whites, a pan or a knife in my hand; that I or Sam or Matty or anyone else had thought to just pick up a camera and snap a couple. Something to look at—to seed the memory, make it all come back in a cold rush like those weird intersections of meth and memory where you'd end up taking a bump that would trigger some amphetamine-fueled cascade effect of devastating perfect recall. I didn't realize it then, but I was already chasing a past so recent the scars had hardly healed; trying to scramble over the wall and back into the garden of better days. It was an addict's mind-set: constantly reaching for the voodoo of that first, best hit. But no matter where I was, where I went, on what line or in what galley I found myself, I would be disappointed and was always looking for a way out. Always found one, too, right up until the moment I found the last one: final back door, last goodbye.

· · ·

I WAS IN THE HOSPITAL AGAIN when Laura called from Colorado, my skull covered with mad-scientist electrodes, long hair chunkily gummed down with sticky, milky conduction jelly that made me look like the victim of a particularly well-attended gang bang up in neurology. By the time I got home (Dad and me stopping on the way for McDonald's cheeseburgers and coffee, eating together in the car in the parking lot, happily not speaking at all about what'd just happened and how bad I looked), Laura was already booking a flight back East. She was using the computer only because it was easier for her to lay hands on than a pistol, buying a ticket because one was available and because it was quicker and less complicated than hijacking, which she later told me had been her first instinct.

She flew to her folks' house outside Philadelphia and made the six-hour drive to Rochester in a rented car, twice in a week, arriving determined and with an air of cool, green-eyed competency, meaning to do what, for centuries, women have done to cure and comfort men who've been broken. It didn't take, but I sure did appreciate the effort. Since she'd also brought magazines and snacks, beer and hotel reservations, we spent a lot of time lazing around in a big hotel bed eating beef jerky, flipping through Hollywood gossip magazines and watching *Red Dawn* on cable. Her considered and well-researched opinion was that no malaise, spiritual or physical, can't be fixed by a change of zip code and room service.

Failing that, there was always brain medication, which she took in the form of prescription mood stabilizers and tequila. Chasing her own elusive happiness, she'd been to Munich, Salzburg, Zurich, Gstaad and Saint Moritz, the Virgin Islands (both British and American), Key West, Aspen and to the offices of a variety of medical professionals who specialized in difficulties of the noggin. The doctors had been a waste, she informed me. But a passport cures everything.

She spoke fluent German. She knew the names of beaches in the Leeward Islands, hotels in Morocco and the capitals of all fifty states. Her makeup was better traveled than I was, and I was jealous of even just the airline tags on her luggage. She claimed to have never once been lost in her entire life and that she could go coast to coast, Philly to L.A., in thirty-eight hours flat with no map. She'd spent the intervening years—the ones between Ithaca and the Dark Horse, the ones I'd spent learning only how to cook—teaching herself all those things she thought might be necessary for living an interesting life, things that included, but were not limited to, playing blackjack, how to drink a man under the table, knowing the names of weather systems and the proper way to start a fire by rubbing two sticks together. Being as equally dislocated as I was—a true child of the interstate— her things were currently scattered across three different addresses in two states, and she was terminally short on underwear because she'd packed most of it away, then immediately forgot where the box had gone.

I had a few good stories, I thought. A couple, anyway. But mine, at that time and in that place, couldn't even compete with her underwear. Having always seen myself as a man who could not stand to see an opportunity pass, a bad idea go untried, this left me floored. How had I missed out on the kind of life that she'd already had? What was wrong with me that I didn't know the name of a good hotel on the rue Michelet in Algiers?

Cooking, which I'd always seen as a sort of concentrated form of life—a distillation of its best bits, the sex, drugs, blood, fire and rock and roll, a reduction of the stuff of it down into a *glace de viande* of experience—suddenly paled a little. Had it really been all that? Or had my time in the back of the house been an evasion of life, of responsibility and growing up? There's a Peter-and-the-Lost-Boys vibe in the best kitchens, a kind of J. M. Barrie sense of great and piratical adventure. But it is also isolating, insulating, an outright and considered rejection of straight and normal life in favor of a few loud, uncertain hours of action: playing with knives and fire, shouting, hitting people, staying up late, reaching for excess and doing everything a proper grown-up isn't supposed to do. Hook once asked Peter who and what he was. Peter haughtily replied, "I'm youth, I'm joy." He might just as well have added, "I'm rage, I'm violence, I'm the blood-mad, knife-crazy, firebug junkie boy in all of us who, for some, refuses to ever go away." I loved my time on the pirate ship so much that I never noticed it hadn't ever gone anywhere.

To this day (because even though I know better now, I still essentially remain the lurching, provincial, mush-mouthed dumb-ass I was then) Laura is the worldly half of our crooked dyad. In airports, over dinners with friends, she can speak about Pacific beaches and streets in Austria, about properly made crêpes suzette and troubles with passports. All I can talk about is the pirate ship and what I saw there, who I knew and what I made for dinner.

WE SPENT MOST OF OUR TIME TOGETHER AT THE HOTEL, but did manage to get out long enough to go and have a few drinks at the Rose & Crown one night. I smoked cigarettes and we tipped pints, fed the jukebox until we'd run through everything good and closed the place. I wanted to drive around with her until the sun came up, to show her my hometown, the places where I'd grown up, in fits and starts, a little bit at a time. I wanted to keep her talking, to keep me talking. I wanted to stop time and stay in this moment, living perpetually in the embodiment of some midnineties power ballad—dopey, loud, timeless and just a little bit sad.

I wanted all of this, but I felt awful. Shaky, sweating, exhausted, sick, my internal architecture and the good face I'd been putting on things for most of the night rapidly crumbling. We ended up parked under the shattered streetlamps in an alley near Sparky's place, her rental car nosed up against a Dumpster, the two of us kissing with a starving hunger like we'd just discovered it; like we were the first two people on earth who'd ever thought of doing such a thing.

And while it might be cute or poetic to say that, after that, I was cured, it would be a lie. When does real life ever really go that way? I ended up half-conscious on her shoulder, gasping for a breath I couldn't seem to catch, mumbling stupidly to myself. She took me back to the hotel, helped me inside and put me to bed—joining me, curled like a question mark against my back, only when she was sure that I wasn't going to die on her.

When she packed up to go the next morning, I thought I was never going to see her again. I hadn't exactly been the most charming company. As things turned out, she was gone for only about twenty-four hours before turning right back around and coming back. I asked her why. She said she'd missed me and had nothing better to do.

This time around, we didn't bother leaving the hotel at all.

I USED TO HAVE THIS RECURRING DREAM, and I think it started around this time. I would be sitting in a room. Bland, boring, like the waiting room of a small-town dentist's office or the kind of place you're forced to sit while being turned down for a car loan. Paintings of seashores, hung perfectly; dull plastic flowers; the walls done in the kind of pastel shades used in hospitals or medium-security psychiatric facilities—meant to induce calm, achieving only a blunted sense of crawling paranoia.

The room was small, yet, in dreamland physics, every animal I'd ever killed was in there with me, waiting. Every lamb whose loin or chop or gigot I'd ever prepared was there; every cow that I'd ever called in a hit on—talking to my meat guy on the phone, asking for a hundred pounds of ground, two cases of T-bones, tenderloin, shoulder, steamship round. All the pigs who'd given up their bellies, backs and trotters. The veal calves. The ducks. The rabbits whose necks I'd broken with my own hands (the sound like cracking stalks of celery, the feeling like breaking a green twig wrapped in a blanket). And the chickens? God, the chickens. All those breasts. All those wings. All those tens—maybe *hundreds*—of thousands of eggs. I was the chicken Hitler in my time. My name the one that mama chickens invoked to scare baby chickens who wouldn't behave.

They were all there. And they weren't angry at me. They weren't threatening. Like me, they were just waiting. Resigned. And we would sit there, all of us together, listening to the Muzak, until finally a door would open, and on the other side there would be a kitchen. Sometimes it would be a crazy kitchen—bloody aprons and gouts of fire and everyone screaming, cooks with their heads thrown back in gory exaltation, impossibly wide and insane smiles on their faces; a huge, massive industrial kitchen that seemed to stretch away into infinity, all stainless steel and nonskid mats and roaring, grinding machinery. But most of time it was just a plain kitchen with a few guys quietly working at their boards, and I would stand up and all of the animals I'd killed for dinner would stand up and I would walk into the kitchen and all the animals would follow along behind me, all of us knowing that we'd never really had a choice in any of this. That this was simply what we'd been made to do.

COOKING FOR DANNY

n the help-wanteds one day, I found a listing for an institutional cook's job at Wegmans. It sounded good: forty hours a week and no more, no line work, just production, cafeteria-style, two meals a day. A trained monkey with a sharp knife could do it.* And considering the condition I was in, I figured I could at least give that monkey a good run for his money.

After spending months unemployed and unemployable, still visiting the occasional doctor, still having to stand in line in a succession of terrible water-stained and shabby offices to defend my Medicaid eligibility, and still skittish about venturing too far from home alone lest that little black snake in my brain decide to uncoil and knock me down again, I'd started looking through the employment ads in the newspaper, purely as a tonic against boredom. I'd also started doing crossword puzzles, sipping green tea and watching a lot of daytime television. Basically, I was just a crocheted shawl, a pair of bifocals and nineteen cats away from becoming someone's creepy, shut-in grandma.

It wasn't pretty, and as each doctor I saw utterly failed to come up with a reasonable diagnosis,† the side table in my bedroom started

---

*It didn't say this in the ad, of course, but it was implied.

†Their quackery and befuddlement ran the gamut from a small panic over my low blood pressure, which resulted in the novel (and delicious) treatment of prescribing me a pound of bacon a day, to some kind of stomach medication given to me by a doc more concerned with my nausea than my *fucking unconsciousness*, which had the unpleas-

to become crowded with transparent orange pill bottles, every one of them filled with some kind of ridiculous snake oil bought on the tab of the State of New York.

It upset me, seeing all that money and all the well-meaning (though ultimately useless) efforts of strangers going to waste. Finally, I just flatly refused to see any more doctors. I was no longer bothered by what had gone wrong with me that night in Buffalo, only by its aftermath, and I no longer required any Grand Unified Theory of my fucked-up-edness. Mostly, though, I was just bored. Time to move on.

So I called Wegmans, sent a résumé, had an interview. Figuring I'd be cooking in one of the warehouse lunchrooms—steaming cheeseburgers and baking french fries for a thousand every day—I didn't take it very seriously, joked around a lot with the HR people. It wasn't until they told me I had the job that the job was actually explained to me: cooking for the suits in the executive offices on Brooks Avenue, doing parties for birthdays and retirements, catering business meetings and Danny Wegman's company jet.

I did crab Benedicts for breakfast, Italian *muffaletta* sandwiches and wild-mushroom salad for lunch, finger sandwiches, bruschetta and strawberries glazed in black balsamic vinegar for the plane. I stocked two buffets a day, plus specials, and never once had to worry about food cost or labor because that was all handled elsewhere.

There were issues, of course. I didn't exactly fit the mold of the corporate chef. Unshaven, with long hair and the slightly wan and wasted look of showing up to work, more often than not, still blearily hungover, I would walk the halls between the front door and the kitchen door and get looks like I was there to rob the place. For a normal kitchen, I could've been considered fairly well put together. I was conscious. Ambulatory. But for this place, I was like the bootblack or

---

ant side effects of massive weight gain (eleven pounds in a week before I stopped taking it) and truly extraordinary flatulence. I was given some kind of pharmaceutical superspeed that jacked my heart rate up into the two hundreds while I was strapped upside down to a steel table, and something else that made me sleep about twenty-three and a half hours a day—getting up only to piss and wonder why it was always dark outside. Other than the bacon prescription, none of these did me any good at all.

chimney sweep in something out of Dickens—purely backstairs help and best kept there.

In the kitchen it was worse. My boss was a woman. The crew who set up, stocked and broke down the dining room were all women, mostly older, high school cafeteria ladies made good. The dishwasher was a middle-aged black guy who they treated with care and condescension, like they were dealing with a child. And I was like a strange pet that'd been brought in on a whim one day—amusing for a short time but, after that, just a nuisance. I worked the way a cook works when doing deep prep, when stocking up a line. I had the radio on, my head down, my brain full of lists and strategies, pulse ticking down like a clock in my neck set to go off for every breakfast rush, every lunch. I talked the way a cook talks—with a certain obscene flair and curses like commas. People would complain when I got my apron dirty, when I would wipe my knife on a side towel rather than having it washed, when I walked the floor with my chef's jacket open, Wegmans baseball hat turned backward and the neck of my T-shirt garlanded with Sharpie markers and probe thermometers. When I would stand in front of an oven counting down its last minute and talk to it, saying, "Come on, you cunt. You motherfucker. Cook, you fucker, cook" (which any chef will tell you *does* make food cook faster because food loves being talked dirty to), it put people real uptight. And when, getting upset over the hideous cooking characteristics of those little portable butane burners, those camp stoves that kitchens with no hoods, no legal ventilation system, are forced to work with, I would occasionally, accidentally, drop one and kick it to death against the door of the lowboy, my fellow employees would avoid my company for hours afterward.

Still, I showed up on time every morning and worked late every night I was allowed to. I did my work, then did extra work whenever I could because working, still and all, was better than not working, and because I liked being the guy that could be depended on to knock out apps for thirty at the eleventh hour for a retirement party that'd been forgotten about until Friday at quitting time, or doing something special (prosciutto and melon balls, crab *tartiflette*, cold sausage with port-wine jelly) for the plane. Something in it—its simplicity and lack of stress—felt comforting, like therapy. And something else felt like I was clawing my way back from somewhere bad in a kitchen padded with foam, with all the rough, sharp, dangerous edges taken off. The orders that I took in would be massive, brought straight to the loading docks from the warehouses, and I liked walking through them with a clipboard, feeling officious, making sure that everything I was getting was the best, the absolute best, that Rochester could provide.

And it was fun, in a low-impact kind of way, until my boss decided that I needed another boss and so brought in another girl to run the galley, who was, near as I could calculate, a billion times more wrong in the head than I was. She had a terrible, thick Jersey-girl accent and a long scar that ran across her throat from one hinge of her jaw to the other—the only smile I ever saw within fifty yards of her face. One afternoon, after screwing up an *aglio e olio* that she swore was her mother's recipe (the *aglio e olio* sauce already being done as an apology for screwing up an unbelievably simple pasta salad the day before), she planted her ass on a cutting board, took all the knives in the kitchen, and systematically ruined every one with a diamond steel.

She was fired shortly after that.

Then I believe she killed herself.

But the upshot was, she didn't take any of us with her. So, you know . . . good timing.

BALLROOM BLITZ

few months later, Laura called to tell me Colorado was too small a state to share with her ex. She said she was leaving for San Diego, where she intended to eat meat loaf at the Antique Row Café, hang out in Balboa Park, temp and wait for me to come to my senses and join her.

I told her I'd think about it, then didn't—until a few days later when a postcard from San Diego and a California State lottery scratch-off ticket arrived in the mail. The world traveler, she'd actually left the afternoon she'd called me, figuring on arriving by morning so as not to waste any time.

I scratched the ticket and won a hundred bucks. I'd never won anything on a scratch ticket before. The only complication was, it had to be cashed in California.

I called Gracie and asked if he felt like taking a drive.

"Sure. Where to?"

"California."

He waited a couple beats. "Okay. Let me pack some stuff."

I quit my job at Wegmans. Gracie quit whatever he was doing. Though not quite so impulsive as Laura, we were on the road in less than a week. Unlike my first trip cross-country with Sam, where everything was looked on with scorn, or my subsequent trips, which were seen through somewhat different eyes, this time around I was enthralled with everything, wanted to see and smell and eat it all. We chewed chicken dumplings and drank watery coffee at sundown in a small mining town in West Virginia where the entire population seemed to cower in the shadow of the smelting machinery on the river. In Memphis and Graceland was everything that was wrong and beautiful in the American character—an entire city of sex and barbecue and sex and booze and sex and poverty and velour jumpsuits. In Austin was a bastion of sensibility amid the overwhelming Texasness of Texas and a real good place for pancakes. We found a Greyhound station somewhere in the Middle West that serviced no buses but still had an operating lunch counter and looked like a church for those involved deeply in the worship of soft angles, neon and chrome. In Arizona, we hit the state fair with the express purpose of stealing a life-size cow made of butter and, in Kansas, accidentally stumbled across America's only surviving atomic cannon, rusting away on a hillside. In Vegas, I won forty dollars in nickels at Circus Circus and, not knowing you could cash them in for actual folding money, walked my four buckets of silver down the street to a gas station and used the coins to buy microwave burritos and cigarettes.

By the time we reached California, Laura had gone missing. Depressed, she'd walked off one day, crossed into Tijuana, and tried to renounce her citizenship in trade for a couple six-packs and a used Ford Galaxie. There were no takers, and in a snit she'd gone off the radar.

Concerned for her safety and well-being, Gracie and I did what we thought was best: retreat. We stopped in Blythe, just over the California border, cashed in the lottery ticket, bought two bowls of chili and a tank of gas, drove up to Barstow (for the scenery), and fell back to Tucson, where we stayed for a week with a friend who bowled a lot and had a band that played very loud music in some very suspect bars. With no word from Laura forthcoming, we withdrew again for Santa Fe and set up a bivouac in Mikey and Ronnie's living room.

Two weeks after entering Mexico, Laura was escorted back across the border by two *federales* and asked not to return. She reentered *Los Estados* with nothing but the clothes on her back and a white plastic Corona hat that she'd won dancing on a table at some subterranean expat bar in the American quarter popular with bikers and renegade dope smugglers. She called from fifteen feet inside the country, at the first pay phone she found.

"If those fuckers don't want me in their country, I guess this one is stuck with me," she said. Then she told Gracie and me to stay put because she'd meet us in Santa Fe by morning.

LAURA'S STILL NEVER TOLD ME what she did to get kicked out of Mexico, always insisting that it was just "a misunderstanding," but saying it in such a way that it is absolutely clear that whatever she'd done, it'd been quite deliberate.

We've been back to Mexico a few times since, but never to Tijuana. And the Mexico story has become one of the central mysteries of our suspicious, distrustful, secret-filled and enigmatic relationship.

I think we still have the hat somewhere, too.

LAURA WAS IN SANTA FE in time for breakfast, tan and happy and sexy as hell. I felt faint when I saw her—through the front windows of a diner on Camino Consuelo, parking her car, stepping out of the driver's side into the sun—and for the first time in a long time, it didn't have anything to do with the faulty chemistry in my head, just blood following instinct and gravity to more southerly environs and the thoroughly wholesome biology of lust.

We hung out awhile with Mikey and Ronnie. I cooked steaks slathered in whiskey cream sauce, penne in a Gorgonzola béchamel with potatoes, and we all ate crusty French bread with chèvre and drank terrible, cheap red wine fit only for hoboes and teenagers, but perfect for that place and moment. I told Laura that this was all I wanted out of my life anymore—a few good friends, cheap wine, crusty bread, some good cheese. I told her that we could stay together forever if she was cool with our never wanting for anything more than that, and she agreed.

Afterward, the three of us—Laura, Gracie and me—continued on into Colorado again, where Laura rented us a one-bedroom, off-season ski chalet for a long weekend spent mostly soaking in the hot tub while floating an expensive bottle of tequila back and forth, watching *Sid and Nancy*, *Buckaroo Banzai* and *The House of Yes* on TV and wandering around the Front Range. I told her to forget about the cheap-wine-and-cheese thing, that I could live quite happily like this, too, if she was willing, and she just smiled and passed me the bottle.

For the entire trip to this point, I'd offered Gracie the better bed wherever we were. I was always the one sleeping on the pool table, the folding chairs, the floor. I was fine with this. It was the least I could do since, with my license still suspended, he was doing all the driving.

But for a couple nights in Colorado, he had to sleep on the couch. I felt bad about this, but not so much that I considered even for an instant offering him the bedroom with the soft mattresses and the locking door that I was sharing with Laura.

I'm pretty sure he understood.

WHEN IT CAME TIME TO LEAVE AGAIN, we stalled. Made excuses. Had a long lunch and went to see a movie—anything and everything Laura and I could think of to buy ourselves a few more minutes together. When we finally couldn't stall anymore, driving away felt like getting my heart pulled out through my throat. I hated leaving her now. No matter what direction I ran in, it was wrong.

But this was rubber-band time for us—a love affair for the permanently geographically dissatisfied. We kept bouncing, stretching and rebounding; connected, but perpetually in flight. She'd go to California, I'd be in New Mexico. I'd chase her to Colorado, she'd surface in Philadelphia. All we were living for were the collisions—in hotels, on friends' couches, in off-ramp Mexican restaurants whenever our roads crossed. There was another New Year's Eve, another party, this one in Ashtabula, Ohio, with a cast of characters similar to the last, a house out in the middle-of-midnight nowhere. Everyone was supposed to bring something, so I showed up with about forty pounds of steaks that I'd taken out the back door of a friend's restaurant in Rochester, and Laura brought a bottle of ridiculously expensive tequila that she'd paid honest money for. She'd also bought me a beautiful Celtic knotwork pin that I stuck to the lapel of my black jacket, going around the party loudly announcing to anyone who came close that I was "the sheriff of party town," literally yelling in their faces because I was blind drunk already and because, having had so little experience with holidays as a civilian (I was always at work), I had no idea how to behave myself other than how I'd behave when surrounded by cooks.

Before the night was done, I'd picked a good-natured fight with someone's brother or cousin who turned out to be an all-state college wrestler. I held my own for about twelve seconds, until he got his hands on me, at which point he completely wiped the floor with my dumb ass until I cried uncle. Laura found me on the stairs dabbing blood from my lip and laughing. I asked her if she'd seen it and she said yes. I asked her if she'd been impressed, and she said no. But she took me to bed anyway, and waking the next morning, I felt bad about what an asshole I'd been so apologized the only way I knew how. I made everyone breakfast.

If we'd been richer, the map of my and Laura's tumbling for each other might've been more cosmopolitan, more intriguing: finding each other under gas lamps in the Marrakech night market, a white-washed *pho* shop in Saigon, amid the clattering pachinko machines of the Ginza or the worshipful quiet of the main floor at Taillevent.

But I liked the course we charted, the Americanness of it and its unique, dirty glamour. Through snowstorms and over mountains, in the steamy heat of Chinatown bars, in lobbies and interstate rest stops, motels, taquerias so bright they bled neon like a wound, and over plates of chicken croquettes in scuffed chrome diners where even the air was antique, we earned every minute we had together, and no matter where she was, going to her was always like going home.

She was my best girl and I loved her.

• • •

OF COURSE, I neglected to actually tell her this. I thought, considering the circumstances, it was one of those things that went without saying.

That was, to put it mildly, an extremely unwise assumption on my part. If I've learned anything since I was fifteen (and probably I haven't), it would be that *nothing* ever goes without saying.* But when I finally asked her to move in with me in Rochester, my reason was not "because I adore you," not "because I don't want to be away from you anymore." It was "Think about how much money we'll save on gas and phone cards and hotel bills."

"Well, sure," she replied. "When you put it that way, it would be stupid of me *not* to move in with you, wouldn't it?" And the whooshing sound on the other end of the line was me totally missing the sarcasm in her voice—hearing assent and giddily ignoring everything else.

But because Laura is a sweet, forgiving, understanding and angelically patient woman, she came anyway. I found us an apartment that afternoon (taking Misha's old one-bedroom as a sublet, sight unseen, because she'd found a bigger place across town and was looking for a way out of her lease), and Laura showed up the next day with everything she still owned packed into the backseat of her used Chevy Celebrity. We met at Gitsi's on Monroe Avenue, had lunch, giggling all the while like a couple of kids eloping, then, together, we went home and locked our own door behind us for the first time.

BECAUSE LAURA IS A CRUEL, vindictive, capricious and psychotic screwhead, she dumped my punk ass that night—after about six hours of our living together.

I talked her down. She came back inside and stopped screaming at me in the middle of the street. We smoothed things over.

Then she did it again the next day.

On our third day living together, she managed to dump me

*Those of you still reading can no doubt see where this notion has gotten me.

twice—which was no small trick because I had to work and was gone from seven in the morning until well after midnight.

Thanks to my being able to put something like "Wegmans Corporate Chef" on my résumé, I'd gotten myself a slot as an executive sous at one of the downtown hotels. We had a fine-dining restaurant, bar, lounge, 250 rooms with a full room-service menu, meeting rooms and conference rooms and ballrooms and banquet space for a couple thousand. The kitchen was enormous. The dish room alone was bigger than some restaurants I'd worked in. And on a busy night, I was like Patton at the Kasserine Pass, with an army of about seventy-five people working beneath me (including cooks, prep and pantry, captains, bartenders, floor, dish and support staff) and only two above: the executive chef and the hotel manager.

Because I was the chef's right hand, his backup and the instrument of his considerable will, it meant I was essentially living in the kitchen—in early, out late, with only the occasional two-hour span, midshift, when I would duck out for a nearby driving range (still in my whites and checks) to knock back a few beers and hammer a bucket of balls. I was terrible at it, but the job was pretty high stress and hitting something that I knew wasn't going to hit me back felt pretty good. I'd explained this to Laura before asking her to move in—the hours, the stress, The Life. That part she understood.

So to get around the complications of my schedule, she broke up with me first thing in the morning just as I was getting ready to leave for work—informing me that she was moving out and heading back to Philly immediately—then dumped me again when I got home, stinking and exhausted, after a seventeen-hour shift.

This went on for about a week. Then, on my first day off with her, I woke to the blinding pain of an abscessed tooth and spent most of the next forty-eight hours either rolling around on the floor moaning or half-whacked on OxyContin, drooling my way through an afternoon showing of *Girl, Interrupted*.

Not even an opiate coma could make that movie tolerable. We left halfway through.

Anyway, she didn't try to dump me then, but instead took care of me as best she could. But once I was feeling better?

Dumped my ass again.

THE HOTEL GIG WAS A GOOD ONE. A fun one. Also the worst one—coldest and most distant of all. Hotel work is peculiar in the food service industry in that it attracts some of the best and a lot of the worst characters in the business. It's a middle step between the dignity and nobility (and, often, penury and insanity) of the legitimate independent restaurant world and selling out to go work for the chains or one of the innumerable "Restaurant Groups" that operate multiple properties and multiple concepts spanning cities, states and continents. Hotel work pays well, sometimes ridiculously well, and employment generally comes with things like health insurance, 401(k)s, and pension plans—perks that are virtually unknown elsewhere in the industry unless you consider ready access to the neighborhood drug dealers a kind of health insurance or the ability to walk out of the kitchen with a case of frozen 30–40 shrimp under your coat on a Sunday night a savings plan.

But the trade-off is often a complete loss of control, a surrendering of one's creativity to the nightmare groupthink of Corporate Chefs and focus groups and one's balls (or at least one of them) to the organizational necessity of large-scale operations. Not a single thing on the hotel kitchen's menu was mine; everything had been passed down, hand to hand, complete with cost breakdowns and illustrated prep and plating instructions, through the corporate hierarchy (which existed as a whole separate stratum of bosses, above and beyond my exec and the hotel manager). Not a single thing would I have proudly cooked had the choice been mine. Cedar plank salmon was already a dead trend by the time it made its way onto our dinner menu. Cheeseburgers topped with a clot of the cheapest American Gorgonzola. Red snapper in a *beurre noisette* and flamed with well anisette that made it taste like a licorice fish stick.

And even when we were given our own head somewhat, the exigencies of costs and tyrannical P&Ls, food and labor targets, dictated what could and couldn't be done. We stocked a happy-hour buffet in the bar with the worst dregs of the collective house memory (Swedish meatballs, mini–beef Wellingtons, chicken wings and tacos by the thousands) and pulled down something like four hundred dollars to provide ten people at a breakfast meeting with a platter of stale pastries, coffee and bottled water. It was embarrassing sometimes, but was really just a question of scale, of having been promoted like a soldier—moved from the field where I'd been down in the trenches and concerned exclusively with small-unit tactics, to a comfy post in command, where, suddenly, complete armies were at my disposal and the disposition of entire battlefields my responsibility. In Florida, at Jimmy's, I'd nearly been defeated by a siege of a thousand customers. Now, a mere thousand was a slow day, was one wedding in the ballroom on a Friday night being handled by my banquet division while I was also seeing to my restaurant hot line, holding down the northern front, organizing resupply for the beleaguered bar staff dying on their own hill, and fighting a holding action against two hundred blind-drunk regional sales coordinators in Meet-C, in town for the annual Widget Manufacturer's Convention and breaking their lines to sexually harass wandering bridesmaids and snort blow off the polished brass rails in the courtyard.

Jeff, my exec, was totally around-the-bend, double-bat-shit crazy, but also a tactical genius who could make the operation run like clockwork even under the worst conditions, in a place where all conditions were bad. The staff were hard-core veterans, some of them having come here of their own volition, others starting as prep cooks on a prison work-release program, then getting hired full-time once their sentences were up, with still others on staff for so long nobody remembered anymore where they'd originally come from.

Some I loved, some I hated. I had dumb ones and useless ones, lazy ones, ones that stole, ones that lied. That's the way things are with a big staff. Most of the ones I disliked, I detested simply for their necessity. I couldn't fire them because I had no one else to fill their posts. This wasn't Lutèce or Daniel. Guys weren't exactly lining up for the chance to do *coulibiac*, beef Welly and cheeseburgers under Jeff's command. Or mine. I couldn't fire them because for some of them it was this or G-pop; because I didn't have three days or even three hours to spare to teach someone new where we kept the chicken breasts or how to mount the snapper. I couldn't fire them because, technically, firing was Jeff's job, and Jeff kept his own byzantine counsel when it came to giving someone the ax. He had his own rulebook, the principles of which were never explained, and sometimes you could show up late for a shift (which meant less than ten minutes or an hour early, depending) and be just fine, but break an egg in his freshly scrubbed walk-in and he'd chase you down the long hallway between banquet prep and the dock waving a hot saucier over his head and screaming threats of murder. I knew this because I'd seen it happen. And Jeff didn't even fire Carlos. Carlos just hit the back door running and never came back.

"Less paperwork that way," Jeff said, laughing about it later that night on the dock. He was a big man, neckless, heavy around the middle but deceptively quick. "Man, did you see him run?" When he smiled, the corners of his mouth disappeared up into the rough of his mustache.

WE DID MULTIMILLION-DOLLAR WEDDINGS where everyone wore walkie-talkies and earpieces like Secret Service agents and the floor staff all worked in tuxedos. We did nights when the restaurant served three people and, still, the insane FOH manager (who looked like a Rat Pack throwback and talked like Telly Savalas in *Kojak*, relentlessly upbeat and calling everybody "baby") would come into the back smiling and saying, "Just you wait, boys. Next week, the week after, things'll pick up. And then, when we get one of those critics in here, baby? Wow!"

I did good work there, took care of my crew as best I could, pulled my weight. I was feeling better, too. During staged events (held out in the courtyard, with me and the best of my guys wearing long-sleeve chef coats to cover their track marks or tattoos, standing ramrod-straight and carving steamship rounds to order), I could put on my white Bragard jacket with the black button covers and my name embroidered over the breast pocket, the white paper toque (only time I'd ever worn one), and solid black exec pants (mark, in the color-coded galley hierarchy, of an above-the-line, command position) and act like a human being—passing jokes, filling orders, not falling down at all. I could walk the room during a fancy event and, with my hair tied back and my battered work boots traded in for a pair of shiny black clogs (only time I ever wore those either), almost look the part of a chef: hard and competent and polished like stainless steel.

It was an act, sure. But what job isn't? Just on the other side of the swinging doors there would be bedlam, fire, blood and harsh language; twenty guys who, in another life, were maybe the guys who'd stolen your car or your credit-card numbers, who worked two jobs or three jobs under two or three different names to keep their own families fed, who you wouldn't let into your house without locking away your daughters and liquor; twenty guys arranged in a double line, facing each other across three prep tables lined up end to end, working assembly-line fashion to arrange those lovely plates of plank-roasted salmon, whipped mash, mixed veg and garni, of tenderloin in red-wine demi with grilled asparagus and sautéed mushrooms; passing them hand to hand, sliding them, spinning them down the table so that one guy could pipe the potatoes, another sauce the beef, another spoon out the veg so delicately, another carefully arrange the three stalks of asparagus just *so* (tied with a leek ribbon when Jeff was feeling frisky), another wipe down, another plant the chervil top or sprig of parsley, another wipe again. Twenty guys, all talking, all busting each other's balls across and up and down the table, all singing along with the galley radio, tuned to a classic rock station, blasting out Billy Idol doing "Rebel Yell" (the Mexican guys singing in Spanish,

Con una rebel yell, ella lloró, ¡Más! ¡Más! ¡Más!), all feeding those plates down to Jeff, standing at the foot of the table, yelling, too—encouragement, threats, curses, calling everybody cocksucker, calling everybody motherfucker, saying he was gonna call INS, that he was gonna call everyone's parole officer (he knew them all by name), that he was gonna break his big fucking foot off in someone's motherfucking ass if they didn't move faster—even as he's slapping cloches on plates four at a time with his big, mauled hands, shuttling plates to sheet trays, shuttling sheet trays onto the Queen Marys standing beside and behind him, screaming for runners, for service, for captains to take the loaded Queen Marys and wheel them out into the hall between the banquet kitchen and the service side of the ballroom, where fifty waiters are all loafing, smoking cigarettes, passing beers back and forth, waiting for all the Queen Marys to be filled with all the trays of all the plates so they can be arranged, reset onto service trays and brought onto the floor of the ballroom to be French-served to three hundred at a time.

I walk back into the kitchen from my tour of the floor, out of one world, across a hallway (stealing a drag off someone's smoke and swallowing a half a glass of wine in one gulp), and into another in ten steps. I pull off the fancy white jacket and hang it on the end of an ANSUL nozzle over a cold rack of flattops. I'm wearing three walkies (one for service, one for bar, one for the kitchen) and am still talking into one of them as I pull on a dishwasher's jacket over my T-shirt, tie on an apron, look in on the hot line (firmly in the hands of Indy, my best lieutenant, my friend, with Louis, the Puerto Rican gangbanger, pulling his first shift on the dinner side under Indy's care), then step to the banquet line, beside Jeff, and start stacking plates.

"What are you smiling about?" he asks me, though I hadn't realized I was. Jeff is deeply suspicious of smiles in the kitchen, of happiness in general. It always means something is about to go wrong. "What, you going queer on me? What's wrong? Why are you smiling like that?"

Just because I'm alive, baby. Just because I'm alive.

. . .

LAURA AND I, we'd cut a groove in those first hard days of living together that was tough to jump. So it continued, on and off, for a couple months, the fights and breakups interposed only by long days and nights at work (fourteen hours a day, sometimes sixteen, sometimes more, for six days a week, then a short day on Sunday—twelve hours—with every other one off), the exhausted collapse into bed, forays out to the grocery store—considered neutral ground, both of us totally in love with the idea of food shopping together because it was just so normal and domestic—and restaurant meals taken at odd hours, in strange neighborhoods. Essentially, we were at peace only when food was involved: *bánh mi* sandwiches, Vietnamese egg rolls over noodles and duck sausage from Dac Hoa, mai tais at the Chinese restaurant down the street, *saag paneer* and chili dogs and Chester Cab pizzas, salt bagels with cream cheese on Sunday mornings when I didn't have to be in until eleven, wax-paper bags of cannoli from the Italian restaurant around the corner.

We slept on the floor because I'd never owned a bed, under a pile of blankets and a sleeping bag made out of an American flag. At six o'clock in the morning, sunlight as thick as white butter streamed in through the big windows, which is only a nice thing in a real estate listing, not so much in the real world where neither of us ever got enough sleep. Since we had no curtains, we taped newspapers up over the windows. And once we were informed by the building manager that the apartments on the ground floor were all infested with cockroaches that were probably headed up our way, we looked around and realized we were living in a crack house.

Okay, maybe that's an exaggeration. There was an *actual* crack house across the street, and our building was more like the place that the crack house's former customers moved into after completing a treatment program, finding Jesus and a job selling aluminum cookware door-to-door.

But we decided to move again anyway, only couldn't figure where. Laura had taken a job delivering pizzas—the perfect gig for her, combining her love of fast driving, precision route mapping and the fact that she couldn't stand most people for more than thirty seconds at a stretch—so her money, together with my salary, left us plenty of budgetary leeway. Especially since we weren't out there spending all of our disposable income on window treatments. Or furniture. We had some cash put away. Not much, but some. Enough, we calculated, to get us somewhere and settled provided we did it on the cheap and didn't go crazy, blowing all our folding money on Chiclets and hats.

I CAUGHT JEFF IN THE OFFICE doing paperwork. He was a magician at it, able to make numbers turn themselves inside out at his command, to jump and flop and twist into whatever he needed them to say to keep his masters pleased, the money flowing, his pension intact. To the day, he knew how long he had to go until he was fully vested. To the hour, the minute. He talked about it incessantly.

Like a crooked accounting firm, we kept two sets of books: one for us, which told us the unvarnished truth about what was in our coolers, our stock levels, labor costs, then another set for the bosses, which told a somewhat more rosy picture.

"We still have top rounds left over from the carving stations last night?" he asked me without looking up, tapping a pencil on the clipboard in front of him. I stepped inside the tiny, cramped office and closed the door, opened his desk drawer where we kept the ashtray, lit up.

"Two," I said. "Maybe three." I'd been on last night, seeing to the breakdown and demobilization for a party of eight hundred at one in the morning—tail end of a day that'd begun at 8:00 a.m., seventeen hours on the front lines—so knew right off the top of my head what'd been salvaged. "Lots of fruit left, too. Backup trays of veg."

He looked up at me. "Did we overcount?"

"No. They underate. Most of them were shitfaced before the buffet was set. Bar got slaughtered."

"Nice . . ." Jeff smiled. "Looks like we're going to be doing a lot of roast beef sandwiches and fruit trays."

He started scratching numbers onto the paper, altering our stock levels to represent the new reality—three top rounds of beef and about fifty pounds of assorted produce popping into existence like he'd conjured them, free because it'd all been paid for by last night's party. We didn't re-use food in the kitchen, but neither did we let anything go to waste. If the Smith wedding paid for dinner for eight hundred on Friday and only ate for six hundred, then the Jones graduation paid for buffet service for a hundred and only fifty showed up, that put us up two hundred and fifty meals' worth of supplies— enough, if we were careful and creative, to cover both the Women in Business symposium on Sunday afternoon *and* the snack trays for the "Lose Weight Now, Ask Me How" seminar on Monday afternoon. It's not like the chubbos ate much, anyway. Too guilty. Double up on the bottled water, put out a half-count of sandwiches and consider it money in the bank.

"Chef, you got a minute?"

"Does it look like it?" He took a drag off my cigarette.

"It's important."

Jeff stopped, looked up at me sideways. He must've known what was coming even if I didn't exactly. "Jesus, you're not gonna cry for me are you?"

"No, Chef. I'm not going to cry."

"You coming out of the closet?"

"No, Chef. I still like pussy. Sorry to disappoint you."

"Funny. So what, then? You quitting?"

"Yeah."

Jeff took another drag off my cigarette. I lit a fresh one. I'd had this whole speech worked out, argument and counterargument; had held to it with a debater's confidence all the way in to work, through my first cup of coffee taken standing quiet and peaceful on the expo side of the line listening to the plastic-wrapped radio in the dish room playing Spanish love songs and the long walk down the hall to Jeff's office. I'd wanted to tell him how awful it'd been—the hours, the yelling, the violence and pressure—and how great; how, a few nights ago, in the middle of a big party in the ballroom, these two guys had come into the kitchen, sharp suits and polished shoes, and pulled me aside, asking me, could I do a couple special plates for their table, lasagna, maybe, or a rigatoni? They hadn't said, "Just like mama used to make," but it'd been implied. Wiseguys, or guys pretending to be wise, anyhow. And one of them had pulled me close, patted me on the cheek with his paw and tucked a bill into my pocket. "We hear you're very good."

I'd made rigatoni. A really good rigatoni—ricotta and mozz, red sauce worked up from pork scrap and espresso-ground coffee beans (always one of my secret weapons). And I'd had it delivered special to their table by Johnny, my best banquet captain. The bill Joey Mafia had put in my pocket? A five-spot. Laughable, but this was still Rochester, after all. Tough times for everyone. Where else but this industry was that actually going to happen?

I'd wanted to tell Jeff that I'd done my tour, that I'd seen enough; about fighting with Danny in the hallway—knock-down, drag-out, because he'd lied to me, called in with a bullshit excuse about hurting his ankle and left me a dishwasher short on a Friday night. I'd caught him out in his lie—someone else I knew having seen him out drinking on Friday, sans crutches, then snitching to me—and told him so. Called him all sorts of names. I couldn't fire him. I needed him. He was a great dishwasher. So we'd fought instead, punching and wrestling and rolling on the floor until it became ridiculous and we started laughing. Where else but here are HR issues resolved so quickly? And I'd wanted to tell him about my late-night dinners with Indy—me making him burritos out of house stock and tortillas I'd brought in from the grocery store, or him offering me some of the food his wife had cooked for him: samosa and *saag* and *biryani*. We'd sit on the stainless and eat, cross-legged, talking about anything but work. Indy was married, had about seven hundred kids. He wanted to be a writer and was good. He would bring me things to read now and then because I'd told him that I, too, occasionally put pen to paper. He was Indian (hence the nickname), and his writing reminded me of Rudyard Kipling or that guy who wrote *The Sheltering Sky*. He'd collected rejections from *The New Yorker*, which he kept, proudly, because even if they were noes, they were noes from *The New Yorker*. We'd make coffee at midnight, one in the morning, and talk about writing. I'd encourage him, tell him that he had to keep trying because anything had to be better than this, right? Indy was the only one who knew I was planning on quitting.

But standing there, my argument collapsed inside me. I don't know why. I told him that I just had to go. West, I thought. Fast. And out of nowhere, a lie on my lips: "I've got a chance to become a food writer and I just can't let that go without trying."

I had no such chance, no such opportunity. It wasn't even something I'd been thinking about (much . . .) until right at that moment. To this day, I can't figure where that thought had come from or why I'd given it voice. But there it was.

"Food writing?" Jeff asked.

"Yup."

He shook his head and looked away. "You gotta do what you gotta do, I guess."

He asked if I could give him two weeks and I said sure. I think I gave him three. And when I left, I just left. Indy slid into my exec-sous slot, wished me luck, and I just stepped out the back door for one last time and was gone.

A FEW NIGHTS BEFORE MY LAST NIGHT, I'd met Laura at the Rose & Crown after work with every intention of hashing out our travel plans over a few pints and accidentally asked her to marry me instead. I didn't have a ring or anything, but I did have a few drinks in me and had seen her and some smooth-talking British fellow making eyes at each other across the bar. So really, it was a defensive proposal—much more civilized than just jumping up and punching the other guy in the face, I thought—and I did get down on one knee. She threw me by asking me to state my reasons for wanting to marry her. I told her it was because she was mine and I didn't want some caddish twit with an accent and the gin sweats thinking he had a chance at walking out with her.

Actually, what I said was "Because I love you. Because you're the one I want. So marry me."

She smiled, shrugged, and said, "Okay."

And that was that.*

---

*Which isn't to say she stopped trying to dump me or anything. In fact, she threatened to divorce me the first time she read those last couple paragraphs, claiming that it didn't happen that way at all. I asked her what the problem was—did she remember there being tea cakes and unicorns and circling cherubs? Something I forgot? And she said that, yeah, I fucking forgot something. I forgot that there actually *were* rings. A matched set of silver six-dollar Celtic knotwork rings that she'd bought for us and brought with her to the bar that night. I asked her if that meant she'd been planning on asking me to marry her, and she got all defensive, saying, no, she'd just bought the ring for me to replace one that my ex had given me, then bought one for herself because she thought it looked nice. Of course, I knew she was lying because whenever she lies, one of her ears turns bright red. But I let it go because that's just the kind of sweet, sensitive motherfucker that I am. Which I told her, of course, saying, "I'll let that go because that's just the kind of sweet, sensitive motherfucker I am."

At which point she threatened to divorce me just as soon as she could find a decent lawyer, pounded upstairs and locked herself in the bedroom. So really, not that much has changed in our relationship since the beginning.

But I have been wearing that six-dollar wedding ring every day since that night. I always wondered where it came from . . .

BAKED

We met my parents at a greasy chrome-and-Formica diner in Rochester a couple days before Thanksgiving and broke the news of our engagement over turkey loaf and watery coffee. We looked at it like a practice run, and in keeping with my character I botched it suitably—stammering, hedging and chain-smoking, saying something along the lines of, "So, Laura and I have been kinda thinking about maybe . . . ," then hanging my head like I'd just copped to a bank robbery, or worse.

I don't know what I was worried about. The folks weren't exactly keen on keeping me around. It wasn't like I had a lot of other prospects. They certainly weren't going to be having this conversation with my brother anytime soon—what with his penchant for waitresses, one-night stands and generalized debauchery. Plus, they were crazy about Laura, figuring her for a stabilizing influence and the kind of girl who'd handle the important stuff like paying bills and remembering birthdays while I was out there doing my little nonsense things with duck breasts and chervil.

So my mom got a little weepy from relief and smiled a lot, her voice rising several octaves whenever she tried to speak. And my dad, who never used three words when none would do just fine, said simply, "It's about time," then got down to business with his turkey loaf and pie.

It was a short meal. No one lingered. And when we were done, on my way out the door, I caught myself wondering if there'd been anything important in my life that'd ever happened outside a bar or restaurant; if there'd been anything, ever, that didn't have food at the core of it.

It was a short accounting. I hadn't really done much important. But the consensus of my jumbled, fucked and sour memory was no. Everything following the loss of my virginity (which had happened at fifteen, right about the same time I was discovering kitchens for the first time—food and pussy and fire and sex and knives and girls being the consuming and defining passions of that magnificent year) had occurred in a dining room, a kitchen, a bar, on a loading dock or in some filthy alley outside a restaurant's back door. Somewhere in there, at the wet and meaty heart of everything that'd meant anything to me, was a meal. Perversely, this pleased me. It made me feel as though there'd been some sort of structure buried deep beneath the mess I'd made of myself, some purpose, however ridiculous or pathetic. Some people have church. Some people have large families, which form comforting parentheses around everything they experience. I had the galley, the floor and the long oak, and because I'd never been a man who'd expected much or wanted much until meeting Laura, it was enough.

On my way outside, I stopped and patted the center post between the in and out doors like the restaurant was a dog that'd just brought me my slippers.

In Pennsylvania, I went all old-fashioned and decided that I was going to formally ask Laura's parents for their permission to marry their daughter. Then I blew the surprise by asking her brother first. I'd been Dutching up my courage for most of the afternoon, which might've contributed somewhat to my poor aim—red wine and bourbon making me think that maybe an ally at the table might come in handy. But when we sat down to Thanksgiving dinner, I finally did it right: "I'd like to marry your daughter. Can you please pass the mashed potatoes?"

Being prudent and rational people, her parents had a long talk with us about marriage in general and our plans in particular while the plates of turkey and stuffing and cranberry sauce went round and round. And while Laura and I were deliberately vague about our plans, I had no problem talking about the various pitfalls of our impending connubial fusion. At this point, my courage was somewhere north of Amsterdam, so what did I have to lose? They asked how I knew that I loved their daughter and I told them it was because I'd never hated anyone quite so much as I could hate her when I was angry, and that no one can hate like that without loving a little on the other side. Her mom asked if I regretted not doing anything before deciding to get married, and I said yeah. I was a little disappointed that I'd never banged a cheerleader.

After that, everything else was pretty much a blur.

Still, they'd said yes and I was planning on holding them to it. Once again, to make things right, I cooked for everyone the next night. Laura's mom had always told her that she was going to marry an Indian cook, someone who'd make her samosas and curried chicken salad. Instead, Laura had a hungover mick with a galley tan, fucked hands and bags under his eyes knocking around her mother's kitchen making crème brûlée and something involving puff pastry, leftover turkey and cranberry rémoulade. Too late to back out now. The night after that, we all went out to celebrate at a restaurant in Conshohocken called the Spring Mill Café, where we ate *bastilla* and black bass in a saffron broth and I decided it would be wise if I didn't drink quite so much. The night after that, Laura and I went out to celebrate again in Chinatown, at Penang, over *roti canai* and curried-beef *rendang* and icy bottles of Tsingtao beer. Afterward, we stumbled around in the steam and chilly rain, ducking in and out of different shops, buying packs of Chinese cigarettes and chopsticks and Hello Kitty condoms, walking arm in arm until we were sober enough to drive.

LAURA AND I DID HAVE A PLAN. We'd decided to move to California with the idea of renting a bungalow in some toxic suburb of L.A., running a gypsy cab service and becoming screenwriters. Not the rich and powerful kind, but shameless hacks, pounding out genre buddy pictures for C-list stars and shoot-'em-up action comedies while sitting beside a scummy swimming pool and drinking heavily in the sun. I'd buy a cowboy hat. She'd wear a Stars and Stripes bikini. We'd get a lot of plaster garden gnomes and a shotgun, which, for kicks, we'd use to shoot the gnomes when we got bored, blasting away somewhere out in the desert where we could do it naked.

It was, in short, the perfect scheme. Love would get us by. And when love inevitably failed, there would always be the drinks, the gnomes and the typewriter to pay the bills. From our stools at the bar in Rochester, lying together in bed on Sunday mornings, sitting against the steamy windows at our favorite Chinese restaurant drinking rum-heavy umbrella drinks under the buzzing neon while it pissed down mercury rain outside, it'd seemed infallible. Absolutely flawless from any perspective.

Where we ended up was Albuquerque, New Mexico, because Albuquerque, New Mexico, is where a lot of high desert trash blows up, where a lot of dreams go to die, and where the most recent in our long string of four-hundred-dollar used cars crapped out on us. We took a room at a pay-by-the-week motel full of alcoholics, recent divorcées and itinerant construction workers, figuring we'd only be there long enough to figure out how to get the hell gone. But one week turned into two, and two weeks turned into a month, and before we knew it, we were *living* in Albuquerque—neither of us exactly clear about how it'd happened but knowing it had something to do with New Mexico being dirt cheap, always sunny, full of really great places to eat tacos, and the closest a person could get to living in Old Mexico without filling out any paperwork.

From our little third-floor efficiency, we could step out onto the walkway and watch the prairie dogs zap themselves on the electrified fence, the roadrunners get squashed beneath the massive tires of the construction workers' shiny new six-wheel pickups. In the morning, we could see the sun rise over the trash midden in the vacant lot next door. At night, we drifted off to sleep to the sound of accordions, gunfire and Indians beating the crap out of the drunken cowboys in the parking lot, rolling them for their wallets and fancy silver-tipped ostrich-skin boots. It was delightful.

We moved into an actual apartment just before Christmas when I got a job working at a place called the Blue Crow. An Italian guy, an East Coast transplant like me, ran it, now doing Nuevo Latino cuisine for tourists who didn't know chili from chile. He hired me even though he had no place for me on the line—seeing the back-East area codes on my résumé and thinking he'd found a kindred spirit, I guess. Another shit-talking, name-taking, no-nonsense mercenary who'd somehow gotten blown West and decided to stick it out. He brought me on as a baker/pâtissier because that was the only slot he had open, but promised he'd find a real kitchen position for me eventually.

"But I don't know how to bake," I told him, thanking him for the offer but being very clear about what I saw as a fairly serious flaw in his reasoning.

"You'll do fine," he told me. "Make some table bread, some rolls, do a couple desserts. It's easy. Then you can help out the guys during dinner."

"I've never done any pastry work."

"What?"

"None. At all."

He seemed to consider this for a moment, then said, "Well, you'll figure it out. You can do all your own ordering, right?"

"No," I said. "I can't. I've been in town a couple weeks. I don't know any of the suppliers." It was like talking to a robot, programmed to give only positive responses and vague encouragement.

"Don't worry about it," he said. "Draw some cash, get some supplies and get going."

IT OCCURS TO ME, looking back on this now, that the chef (Robert, I think his name was) was probably as confused as I was by this exchange. He was a fairly young guy with maybe five or six years on me, tops. He'd probably come up the way I did, been trained in a similar fashion, had the same kind of rough education. But I remember that his kitchen at the Blue Crow was staffed with a surprising number of white kids for its being in the Southwest. I remember that they threw around a lot of French culinary terms and wore their uniforms spotlessly—pressed and ironed and turned out in a certain way that said that they were serious about their business and the way they looked while doing it. Serious the way a marine will look on the parade ground. Serious like they'd been taught. These were probably not the kind of guys who were collecting their paychecks on Friday night and blowing the rent money on cases of Labatt's Blue and scag. They were the kind of guys who thought it would be a kick to stay late after a full-book Thursday and just play around in the kitchen—practicing their *tournée* cuts and frenching lamb chops and using the pastry station to make bombes for show.

Robert had hired these guys. Robert had no doubt shown them the ropes. And I'm thinking that Robert had come to a point in his career where he just assumed that everyone coming up below him and now asking him for a job was coming to him out of culinary school where no one—not even the most serious, dedicated and brilliant grill artist or saucier—would've made his bones without doing the required courses in baking and pastry, without having had at least some glancing contact with a piping bag and loaf pan.

What I think he must've assumed I was saying was that I didn't *like* doing pastry or perhaps considered myself not good at it. What I was actually saying was that I didn't know the first thing about baking or pastry—was as deaf, dumb and blind as Tommy when it came to the gentler side of the menu and couldn't have made him table bread or a couple simple desserts if he'd put a gun to my dick and said, "Bake." No lie, had someone told me back then that they needed me to pull some sugar, I would've gone into dry stock, taken a bag of sugar off the shelf and set it on the floor in front of the shelving unit because, to a cook, that's what "pull some sugar" would've meant— take it down from its place in storage and put it where the person who will come along behind you needing it will be able to find it easily.

Realizing this now only makes what followed next even funnier to me.

AFTER GETTING MY ORDERS, I did the only thing I could think of: I drove to the grocery store, bought them out of baking supplies, loaded my car down with fruit, then stopped by one of the big chain bookstores to buy a copy of Payard's pastry cookbook.* Flipping through it in the parking lot, I started taking notes, trying to cram an entire pastry and baking master's class worth of knowledge into my head in a half hour while also desperately attempting to translate the language of bakers into cook-ese.

It was like trying to teach long division to a hamster. Cooks and bakers are two totally different breeds with two totally different brains. Cooks work from the gut, from sense memory, by rote, blind but focused repetition. Cooks taste and adjust flavors on the fly, can improvise, riff, repair mistakes; are constantly tinkering, working a thousand variations on "crispy outside, soft in the middle," which may as well be our guild motto because it's the most succinct explanation of our primary duty and an apt description of what we've all dedicated our lives to accomplishing.

But bakers are just magicians. Scientists. The Jedi knights of the kitchen. Their work is mysterious and arcane and precise. They measure things, use scales, work from recipes, do math more complicated than trying to figure a three-way split on an eight ball or how to stretch the last six ounces of sauce in the lowboy across four plates for the last table of the night.

Theirs is also a more pure galley faith than that of cooks because it encompasses daily miracles of transubstantiation. When I make a beurre blanc, a béchamel or espagnole, I am intimately involved in every step of its creation. I watch it coming together in the pan or pot, tasting it all along the way, adding salt or fat or stock or cream—

---

*I didn't see this as a standard text or anything, just recognized the name, knew it was French and saw it had a lot of pretty pictures. And even though it all turned out badly in the end, I still have the book—a fantastic resource for would-be pâtissiers.

babying it and shaping it into something that eventually matches the image of sensual perfection I have in my head. Cooking professionally, after a certain amount of time, becomes mechanical. Foie gras is only exciting the first couple times you work with it. Truffles, too. And doing the job well on the line requires, more than a passionate love for food, the masturbatory intensity of the stage magician practicing endlessly in front of a mirror, his passes and fakes worked out a million times until they are flawless. The cook is in the same position, shaving seconds and motions away from his nightly act until a kind of elegant conservatism results. It's grunt work, miraculous only at table, only by dint of all the work you, the dining public, *don't* see.

But a baker or pâtissier puts a vat of liquid in my oven, walks away, and when he comes back to pull it out, it's a soufflé. He lays out an ugly, pale, scraggly twist of gloop on a glossed baguette pan and an hour later it's a steamy, light, gorgeous loaf that tastes of butter and yeast and life and sunshine. A baker must have trust and confidence, must know when to step aside and let his ingredients be. They are Buddhists among the kitchen's rough pagans, Kinsey to us hopeless sluts, carefully observing, taking notes, beginning reactions that take hours or days to reach fruition, then just walking away while those of us left on the line are still taking it in the ass from the early pretheater dinner crowd for fifty bucks a day plus lunch.

I did the best I could—about what I could've managed had someone thrown me, in my boots and blue jeans, onto the stage at Radio City Music Hall and told me to dance the fucking *Nutcracker*. I made maple–sweet potato dinner rolls that smelled like heaven but turned hard as rocks three minutes after they came out of the oven; a tiramisu that tasted wonderful and looked lovely but collapsed into liquid the minute it was unmolded. I learned that when translating on the fly between metric and American measures, one cannot just estimate. Or rather that one *can*, but that the resulting *pâte à choux* will be like eating cement, only less palatable. I worked Payard's book to death, took it with me to bed at night, and did manage one decent dessert—poached pears crusted with icing sugar like ice crystals and set on a slant in a tarn of cabernet reduction sweetened with simple syrup—but could only pull that one off because I actually understood such words as *poached, reduction* and *pear.*

After four days, Robert called me into his office and said, "I'm sorry, Sheehan. But it's like you don't know anything about baking at all . . ."

ATOMIC CHEESEBURGER

lbuquerque is a great place to visit but a terrible place to live, and the trick is to just visit it every day without ever getting attached or drawn in. Because once you start living there—in it and in the moment—it tends to reveal itself, like an old man showing his ding-dong to Girl Scouts, as the obvious third-world city of exile and grim ending place it has always been. The Land of Entrapment is what the locals call New Mexico, and anyone who stays more than six months is given special license by the city to make vicious fun of all the Texans, Californians, New Yorkers and Sun Belt refugees, newly arrived, and still prattling on about all the charming architecture and inexpensive turquoise jewelry.

Soon enough, they'll be mugged. Soon enough, the cops will show up to raid the meth lab in that charming little casita across the street. Soon enough, they'll leave, suitcases loaded down with faux-authentic Indian trade blankets and Kokopelli statuettes, taking their gringo dollars with them and leaving their credit-card numbers for the identity thieves.

Albuquerque has a gang problem, the severity of which is complicated by the fact that most of the gangs there seem to be splinter sets composed of three guys with a broke-ass lowrider rolling on a doughnut spare and one pawnshop pistol shared among them. It's also the only city in America where I've been beaten up for reading. Granted, it was probably my fault. It was a Friday night. I should probably have been out getting drunk on mouthwash, knocking up one of my cousins or robbing a bank like everyone else. And true, the book I was reading didn't have any pictures in it, which could've been seen as provocative—as acting intellectually uppity by the standards of the 3:00 a.m. crowd at the Waffle House on Central Avenue, where I was sitting.

But even I was shocked when the four-foot-tall cholo with the crazyweed eyes and yellow bandanna leaned over my table and yelled, "Hey! Wha'choo doing, mang? Reading?"

I allowed that, yes, I was, in fact, reading. I even went so far as to hold out the book to show him. You know, in case he'd never seen one before.

And he batted it out of my hand (on the second try), looked at me as hard as he could, and said, "What're you, some kinda faggot?"

Now, I've been called a lot of names over the years. Sometimes I've deserved them, sometimes I haven't. But I was boggled by what leap of logic my diminutive friend must've made in that tiny, fogged-up little brain of his to equate reading with flagrant homosexuality. Sitting there, I tried to think how he'd arrived at one from the other, but gave up and instead shouted back, "Why? You looking?"

He slammed his fists down on the table. I laughed at him. And he punched me square in the face. He was then immediately set upon by two waiters, a very large cook, three customers, and one homeless guy who dragged him, kicking and spitting, out the door and into the parking lot, where they proceeded to beat the mortal shit out of him and stomp half the teeth out of his head.

Meanwhile, I went back to my book. I'd been going to that particular Waffle House almost every night for several months at that point and had made a lot of friends. I was a regular. My little buddy, tragically, was not.

NOT UNTIL LATER THAT NIGHT, while walking home without even a black eye to show for my trouble, did I finally figure out the poor little fella's logic. I'd been reading *The Sailor on the Seas of Fate*. The author? Michael Moorcock.

Get it? Moor-cock?

Shit, I thought. Maybe that little prick had been smarter than he'd looked.

DUMB, BRUTAL, POVERTY-STRICKEN AND CORRUPT, a city where you could be shot just for venturing into the wrong neighborhood in broad daylight and punched in the face for reading in public—but Albuquerque is a beautiful city, too, held in the embrace of the Sandia Mountains, surrounded by flat-topped mesas and the black snouts of cold volcanoes. You can't walk a hundred yards without bumping into art—a gallery, a sculpture, the work of taggers and guerrilla muralists. When it's not on fire (as it is two or three times every year), the cottonwood bosque along the Rio Grande is damn close to heaven.

It's a cheap city, so it tends to attract artists and writers, amateur thespians, young freaks and dangerous fringe elements; in turn attracting the kinds of businesses and services required by such a population. In Albuquerque it's never difficult to find a futon, a payday loan, a gallery opening featuring photographic vaginal self-portraiture, a good jukebox, a fish taco or a pawnshop television. Usually, this can all be found on the same block if you know where to look, the mattress stores and fly-by-night shopfronts sharing space with Mexican *panaderías*, Eritrean markets, Vietnamese after-market auto parts shops and Korean bodegas selling lottery tickets, Enramex phone cards, Chinese cigarettes and baklava.

It's an international city. English is not its primary language. Or its second or third. And it can be an incredibly friendly and forgiving city when you least expect it. Shortly after arriving in Albuquerque, at the same Waffle House where I would later be assaulted for flaunting my literacy, I was relaxing at the counter with a bunch of locals, all of us talking about Christmas. When I mentioned that I'd just moved to town and that Laura and I were planning on spending a quiet holiday alone, three complete strangers each individually invited Laura and me to join them for the holiday at their homes, to share their deep-fried turkeys, *chicharrones*, posole and mashed sweet potatoes with them. A few months later, Laura and I would also accidentally find ourselves caught up in some other family's Fourth of July celebration just because we were close by when the party kicked off—everyone lighting things on fire, singing mariachi music and firing their guns in the air.

My favorite Vietnamese restaurant was also a regular stop for the teenage prostitutes who worked the stroll on Central Avenue, old Route 66. I also liked the *pho* shop that shared space with the crooked emissions-testing station that would sell clean inspections for forty bucks cash: Château Tailpipe.

Laura and I couldn't chuck a brick downtown without hitting someone selling tamales or shrimp cocktail out of a cooler, piñon off the bed of their pickup. We spent many long afternoons cocooned inside a knockoff Chinese tiki-bar restaurant on Central Avenue with soggy dim sum and glacially slow service just because it always felt as though no one who worked there had been allowed out since sometime in the middle sixties. To them, Kennedy was still president, the Beatles still a bunch of wild longhairs, the streets still full of sexy 'Vettes and pre-fastback Mustangs. When whole days and nights would go by without a single diner coming in, I could picture the entire staff—cooks and waitresses, the house band, managers in dusty tuxedos with frilled shirts, bartenders wearing arm garters—all sitting down and discussing in hushed tones whether this whole trend in Polynesian cocktails and Don Ho covers might finally be coming to an end.

Just an hour south of the city, the greatest green-chile cheeseburger in the world was being made the same way it'd been since the 1940s—beef ground every morning and hand-formed, chiles roasted and chopped, shredded lettuce, mayo, onions and mustard, all slapped together wetly, overhanging the bun, and served with a side of green-chile beans. It was in San Antonio, New Mexico, at a dusty joint called the Owl Bar—a dim and rambling adobe roadhouse famous for many things, but mostly for having been the place where the Manhattan Project scientists working at the nearby Trinity Site came to live, eat, drink, carouse and use the phone. The detonation of the first atomic bomb was actually watched from the front porch of the Owl, the flash of white and towering mushroom cloud convincing all the residents of San Antonio (except the owner of the bar and a handful of dorky gringos packing slide rules in their pockets) that the Rapture had finally come.

The Owl remains one of my favorite restaurants in the world. I've never found a cheeseburger I loved more.

COOKING LIVE

wo or three weeks after being fired as a baker, I took a job as chef de cuisine at the Ranch—a restaurant loved and respected by the locals, offering comfort food and New Mexican cuisine, downscale charm and fine-dining quality. In style, it reminded me a lot of La Cité: rustic but polished, the dining room done all in bold primary colors with plates to match and cowboy-kitsch knickknackery hanging from the walls. The food hit that sweet spot of American appetite: a fixed point stuck halfway between haute and coddling, a classless middle-mark of caviar pretension cut with meat-loaf dreams. Chefs and owners in Albuquerque and Santa Fe—in the West in general—are masters at hitting that bull's-eye because of the West's essential cultural disconnect: the prevailing wisdom that the best dinner you're ever going to have is one eaten off fine china while wearing your favorite blue jeans.

So the Ranch did meat loaf and mashed potatoes by the ton. It did flat blue-corn enchiladas with chile-marinated chicken flashed under the salamander and chimis with fried potatoes on the side in a one-off riff on Michoacán cuisine. It also did a perfect pork loin, wild-mushroom polenta, rough-cut filet mignon under a glaze of maître d' butter, and trout with poblano-corn relish. After being hired and doing a week's immersion training at a second Ranch location out in Bernalillo (which consisted mostly of a crew of serious, name-taking *asesinos* teaching my punk white Frenched-up East Coast ass exactly what a burrito was supposed to look like, what an avocado was, how to make a proper posole and what it meant when a check came off the printer saying XMAS*—all invaluable lessons), I took the sauté post on the dinner line at the Albuquerque location and went to work. I cooked every night, handled specials, did ordering and costing. Figuring to load most of the weight of change onto myself at first, I started doing scratch sauces, fruit chutneys for the pork, and bringing tough, durable fish onto the menu: halibut cheeks with dill and lemon, sea scallops dressed simply in a grapefruit mignonette, sometimes just a squeeze of lime, served over jicama slaw, and blacktip shark marinated as a kind of demi-seviche, then seared in a pan with salsa *cruda* for upscaled shark tacos.

I probably pushed it too far with the poached lobster tails plated curled around a dollop of Japanese squid salad over a fan of perfect soft green avocado slices. That may have been a bit esoteric, a bit Alfred-Portale-at-Gotham, for what was essentially a jumped-up three-a-day New Mexican diner. But I didn't care. The specials always moved, even when the traitorous waitstaff went around making fun of me to the customers. The parking lot was always full. The dining room was always crowded, always loud, and when the rush came, it would hit like a wave—building and building until it broke over the kitchen in a wash of cursing, spinning and droning house music pulsing from the greasy galley radio. In the kitchen, we worked with a giant skull-and-crossbones pirate flag hung on the fryer end of the line and comported ourselves accordingly.

IT'S FUNNY HOW CHEFS AND COOKS of a certain age love and know by heart *Apocalypse Now*—the movie that most speaks to our condition, to the total freak-out madness, stupid macho bullshit and occasional lost-outpost resignation of even the most successful among us. In Buffalo, at La Cité, we would start off some nights with Jim Morrison

---

Christmas is Southwestern cook's slang for any plate getting both red and green chile together. The first time I saw it, I thought it was a leftover holiday special off some menu I'd never seen and was laughed at for twenty minutes after asking where the Christmas was, how it was cooked and why everyone was laughing at me like that.

singing "The End" on the galley radio and lighting the trench on the flat grill with 150-proof rum or cooking vodka in homage to the opening scene: the napalm strike lighting up the treeline. When we were feeling particularly expressive, Matty and I would pack the trench first with mesclun greens or broccoli florets, then pour on the liquor and FOOM! *This is the end, my only friend, the end . . .*

It's funny how many cooks I know who love the book *Dispatches* by Michael Herr and feel that, more than any other writer (myself included), Herr got it just right. He nailed the language, the shattering dislocation, the weird, kinky, hateful love of doing a terrible thing with terrible consequences night after night after night. And, yeah, he was writing about men at war, but that's only a detail. Take away the guns, the choppers, the bombs. Put all the grunts in white jackets. Dress the VC like a hungry pretheater rush, and he could've been talking about us.

And it's funny how kitchens—or at least the ones I've known— are so much like the fighting ships of the British navy as described, say, by Patrick O'Brian in his Lucky Jack Aubrey books: so full of strange vernacular, stranger tradition, both equally loved and fiercely kept. There is an element of the piratical, the tyrannical, a sense of always being called upon to do the very nearly impossible on short supplies, while desperately undermanned, with no hope of relief in sight. As on the lower decks, we had harsh discipline, our own superstitions, our own jet-black humor, our Sunday plum duff in the form of staff meals (fine or foul, depending) that would cause harsh feelings when denied, and our daily ration of grog, which translated into the shift drink—one freebie, on the bar, at the end of a long night. A shift drink could easily become five or six if the bartender had been properly inducted into the galley family, would be added to all the regular drinking done in the course of any night's service (of the cooking vodka, the beers squirreled away in lowboys, the speed pourers of gin and tonic or cheapjack *tinto de verano* of red wine and orange soda mixed up by the bus crew).

It's rum, sodomy and the lash on Saturday nights. Anything—any threat, any promise—to keep a line going through the last hard push,

final tables, last calls. I've seen chefs hit. I've seen them scream
(never knew one who didn't). I've seen them pay cash to guys just to
keep them on the line for twenty more minutes and seen them carry
off the casualties (of heat, drink or misadventure) on their own
shoulders. I've done all the same myself in my time. And as in the
navy, the hope always is that you have a good captain at the wheel, a
lucky one, one who has all the knowledge, the training, the dirty
tricks and just plain illegal skills required to make a kitchen run
smoothly in rough waters. You hope he's a guy who came up through
the ranks himself, who understands the heat, the noise, the furious
pressure; who knows what it's like to go home—bloody, exhausted,
stinking of truffles, liquor and rancid grease—at the end of the night
to a woman (or a man) who doesn't get it at all, who wonders why
you don't just take a luff gig folding T-shirts at the mall, who com-
plains incessantly about the stink, the suppurating wounds, that time
you came home with a mauled chicken foot stuck in the tread of your
boot. You hope you find yourself laboring under a chef who loves it as
much as you do.

At the Ranch, I had a sense of almost coming back to myself, of
almost finding the groove again. But the vibe in Albuquerque was too
diffuse, the work—even on the busiest nights—too simple to be engaging on the gut level I'd once known. I tried, but I couldn't get into
it deep enough that the job took on a life of its own—became the
thing that I was, not just the thing that I did, showing up every day for
a paycheck.

I remember a night, a few months in, when I burned myself on a
pan handle. It was the veg pan—a big, heavy saucier full of butter and
mixed vegetables, squashes and corn and chiles and what-have-you—
and it was a slow night, lots of enchiladas, lots of salads. I don't know
how long the pan had been sitting there undisturbed, racked up on a
back burner, waiting while the smaller sautés got juggled across the
front six, but it'd been a while. The handle, which should've been
turned out to hang above the cool of my sauté *mise*, had gotten
bumped or moved and was, instead, toasting like a marshmallow
above the blazing flame of an open burner. Ten minutes it'd been

there. Maybe fifteen. Loaded with veg, it probably weighed six or eight pounds. Then there's me, not thinking, needing to flip the veg in the pan so it doesn't scorch, in a rush and reaching back, grabbing the handle bare-handed (stupid, I know—should've used a side towel) and lifting it right off the burner. I didn't feel the heat for about half a second—long enough for me to bring it across the stovetop and near my body, to start the motion of flipping. But when the pain came, it was *awesome*.

I dropped the pan, spilled the veg all over the nonskids, bellowed like a wounded bull and went down to my knees—ruined hand clamped between my thighs, short of breath and wide-eyed from knowing, almost instantly, that this was going to be a bad one.

The story here is not of the burn. The burn itself was meaningless—I'd gotten them before, had survived, had certainly hurt myself worse. All part of the action. The story is in how I reacted.

I went home.

Not immediately. I iced the hand (palm burned slick and shiny and white, not even blistered but *hardened*—like some kind of antique hand under a thick coat of varnish). I got a wet towel and swabbed it down, calmly assessing the damage, impressed by how the actual shape of the pan handle had been burned neatly into my flesh, complete with the oval hole at the end of it and the faint tracing of the embossed maker's name tattooed now on my hand. I swallowed six ibuprofen, and with a side towel full of ice gripped in my claw, fingers forced to curl as the skin tightened, I stood another hour or so at my station, sweating through the pain, thinking of my father, who I'd once seen tape one of his own fingers back together after cutting it halfway off, then go back to work without a word, and cursing my own stupidity and weakness under my breath.

But after that, I left—abandoned my post, thinking, "You know what, fuck it," and just walking out the back door. This was something I would never have done two years before, three years before. I would've stuck it out like that night in Buffalo—cooking one-handed so as not to fuck my guys on a busy Friday by leaving them short-handed. Like all the other cooks and chefs I'd known who played hurt, who soldiered on no matter the damage, who treated every night like it was their last one on earth—not wanting to miss one minute of the fun. Down in the trenches, in the muck and the heat and the fury of it, the impulse to just keep cooking is, I imagine, a lot like that thing they say about soldiers at war. They don't fight for a cause, for a flag or a country or a commander. They fight—and *keep* fighting even when everything around them is going to hell—for the guys squatting next to them in the foxhole, crawling next to them in the sand. They do it because it is assumed that the guys next to them will do the same, because the thought of possible death and certain horror is not so bad as the sure knowledge of personal cowardice and absolute weakness. Soldiers fight because it is worse not to. Cooks cook because to give up means knowing forever that you backed down when things got bad and having to live with the cold wisdom of failure.

Even though I know why I did it—why I left, why I walked away on that night—and even though I can rationalize it (it was a slow night, the rush was pretty much over, I just didn't give a fuck), I am still ashamed of myself even today. I'd done a lot of bad things in my life. I'd become something of a flake over the past year. But that irrevocable step out the back door of the Ranch was worse than anything else. It was like a negation of all the good I'd ever done. This was the life I'd chosen, that I'd worked for. I loved the kitchen the way any man loves his work when he is happy and productive and useful. I loved the kitchen for what it'd made me, how it'd saved me more times than I could count. I loved it for breaking me and burning me and screaming at me, for shaping me and giving me a language and a family and a home. I loved it for being my life, for seeming, in its best moments, a *good* life, and in its worst, always offering a second chance at something better tomorrow for those who could just pick themselves up, brush off their whites, pull the crab leg out of their hair and stand once again at their station, waiting for greatness.

Walking out the door was a betrayal of all that. And even though I did go back the next night and did stand my station like a man, the damage had already been done. I knew there was a point in me now where I would break and give up and surrender, and felt exponentially weaker for having to carry that knowledge in me.

AT THE RESTAURANT, I got a call from one of the local TV stations asking if I could do a three-minute live cooking spot to cover some dead zone in the middle of the morning news broadcast. I said sure. No problem. Since I didn't faint when the red light came on, one segment led to another a week later to fill in for another local chef who'd bailed out at the last minute, and that led to a regular, twice-a-week slot with me bantering with the anchors and lighting shit on fire.

I had no illusions. I knew these callbacks had less to do with my winning personality, sweet voice and telegenic good looks than they did with my always bringing extra supplies and making lunch for the news team. But the hustle worked. I always wore the pristine white jacket with my name stitched over the breast pocket and my Ranch baseball hat. The lead-ins and walk-offs always sold me as "Jason Sheehan, chef at the Ranch Restaurant." So no matter how much it cost the owners in product or how much the exec was bothered by my name being associated with the restaurant instead of his, there wasn't dick anyone could say about it. The free publicity was too good and the floor counts went up by a significant percentage on the nights following every broadcast.

Moving dangerously close to small-time, whorish celebrity chefdom, I then started teaching cooking classes at a show kitchen downtown, extolling the virtues of gas cooking for the local utilities company in trade for three hundred bucks an hour handed over at the end of the night like a mob payoff in an unmarked envelope. Again, in my starched white jacket and a ridiculous soufflé hat, I'd titillate and horrify packed rooms populated mostly by bored yuppie housewives, grandmothers and couples desperate for a night out by making jokes, simple desserts and sauces that required eight *pounds* of butter, then telling half-raunchy stories about life in professional kitchens before sliding into my smooth pitch for open-flame gas cooking over electric or induction elements.

"Look, you want to cook like a pro? You want your sauce to taste like the sauce you had at the restaurant last week? Then you gotta have *fire*"—pause to upend the bottle of cooking wine, flaming the preheated pan I had set up and making an enormous fireball that tickled the hoods—"there simply is no substitute."

While all this was going on, Laura and I were making wedding plans. We were going to do it small, in Las Vegas, at the Treasure Island Casino because there were pirates there and I (obviously) liked pirates and everyone else loves pirates, too. After that, we had a big reception planned back on the East Coast, just outside Philadelphia. We hoped to honeymoon in Bali, in a little hotel on Monkey Forest Road. We had the chapel booked for mid-September 2001. Then, a couple months before the wedding, everything that'd been going so well started falling apart.

It began when, in a fit of unwise (but entirely justified) pique I quit my job at the Ranch. Over the past few months everything had been coming together. Business was good. The TV spots, the cooking classes, and in particular the daily ops at the restaurant were all ticking along smoothly. I'd been talking with the owners about special-event menus and possibly collaborating on a cookbook. But the one thing I'd forgotten to do was ask for a raise. And when I finally did ask, I (again unwisely) went to the executive chef, not the owners. It's the white jacket and the title, man. I'm a sucker for them every time.

I caught him in his office during a lull between services, hanging out in T-shirt, shorts and sunglasses, using the computer to download music. I made my pitch, and unsurprisingly, the exec (who was hardly ever at the restaurant anyway—always either away on vacation, recuperating from some mysterious injury or "in meetings" all day—and who'd laughingly passed on both the TV gig and the cooking classes, thinking them below his station until, all of a sudden, it was my name, not his, on TV and on the big sign out front of the restaurant) refused my opening shot: a request for salary-plus-benefits commensurate with his. Sort of surprisingly, he also refused my compromise position. Then, just to be a dick, he said he thought he might be able to see his way clear to offering me another fifty cents an hour. A dollar, though? That was out of the question.

I was currently making nine bucks an hour. I told him to go fuck himself. He just leaned back in his chair and smiled as I pulled off my apron and stormed out.

ONCE MY JOB AT THE RANCH WAS GONE, so was the TV gig because now, rather than being "Jason Sheehan, chef at the Ranch Restaurant," I was just "Jason Sheehan, long-haired weirdo who's touching your food."

With the regular TV spots gone, so went the cooking classes. It was a trifecta. In the course of about two weeks, I'd lost everything. Again. Though really, at this point losing was less of a shock than a habit to me. I took it all with what I considered remarkable equanimity.

Laura, on the other hand, regarded my apparent lack of concern, this grinning, mercenary élan I'd worked so hard to cultivate, as just maddening carelessness and irresponsibility. But one of the things that normal people don't understand when dealing with enduring fuckups is that the last pride the fuckup has is in not showing just how wrecked he is by each successive failure. The fuckup has seen this coming, of course. The fuckup is prepared. The fuckup can say, with mordant aplomb, that these things just *happen*—truly believing that they simply do—then move on along to the next job, relationship, term in the White House, whatever. It's a calculated pose, dignified only in that it is a denial of panic (which is worse), even though those who affect it (like me) are often just too fucking dumb to know when they're licked.

It was like this with Laura and me—one of the many imbalances in our bond that kept us forever orbiting at a wicked tilt. Despite all her own endemic oddness—and perhaps only because I'm measuring her against myself—she was, at the time, the normal one in our relationship. The rock, in the same way that, if presented with a pile of mud and a plate of Jell-O and asked, "Which one is a rock?" a person would have to say the pile of mud, if only because of the chance that, someday, the mud might *become* a rock while the Jell-O is never going to be anything but dessert.

Laura got things done. With her around, bills got paid (most of the time), dishes got done (most of the time), birthdays got remembered, plans got made and (most of the time) were stuck to. She finished things—jobs, chores, college degrees. When she left a job, she gave reasonable notice, filled out all the necessary paperwork and was missed after she was gone. My life she didn't understand at all and saw each of my concurrent losses as a hammer blow to our plans. Biting her lip, making her eyes anime-big, she asked me what we were going to do now.

We cracked two beers, sat down on our thirdhand couch in front of our pawnshop TV, put our feet up on the cardboard box we were using as a coffee table and I told her we should go to Juárez for tacos. It was just a few hours' drive south of us, and, come on . . . no problem seems too serious when looked at from Mexico. I said we'd figure everything out when we got home.

I HONESTLY WAS NOT WORRIED, because I had no cause to worry. I'd been through this before. It'd always worked out okay. I used to look at it like this: Being a cook is a great way to live but a terrible way to make a living. Cooks don't get benefits. We have no retirement package. Most of us have no union looking out for us. We're on our own. The pay is crap, the work is hard, the hours are long, our masters are often dumb or crooked or out-and-out criminals, and our fellows— those with whom we surround ourselves daily—are often worse. But we do all have one thing going for us, which is that whenever things get too harsh or too intolerable in one kitchen, any cook out there worth his whites can simply quit, walk out the door on a Thursday afternoon and be reasonably sure, if he's not too picky, he can have a new job by first seating Friday night.

That's job security right there. That's comfort like you wouldn't believe. And I was confident in my view of the industry because I'd done exactly that a half dozen times or more. Granted, this mercenary mind-set had landed me in some fairly shitty posts (that St. Paddy's Day Irish joint in Buffalo, Jimmy's, working at a place that specialized in pizza and burritos made by guys who, culturally speaking, had probably needed to look both words up in a dictionary before their first shift just to know what they were going to be cooking), but work was work—was a paycheck, new friends, new connections, a continuation of the lifestyle, which, in many cases, was what I and a lot of guys like me were signing up for in the first place. One of the toughest things about being out of work? Having to pay for my own drinks like some kind of friendless schmuck. Another drag? Not knowing where to find a drug dealer when I needed one, a cheap used car, a lawyer, bail bondsman, quick loan, new bird's-beak parer or a computer that'd fallen off the back of a truck somewhere and was now being sold for a hundred bucks out of the trunk of some dishwasher's Honda Civic. When I was working, I could find all of that in one place, plus a hundred other things. A kitchen could get me drunk, get me high, get me laid, see me fed, find me a fight if I wanted one or a shoulder to lean on. Without one, I suddenly had to read the classifieds if I needed a car, go on dates if I wanted my junk touched and score on the corner or down in the park. And you know what? That shit is *scary*. The kitchen is a game preserve for the weird. But like any game preserve, it comes with walls, protections, dikes against the inrush of reality. As weird and wild and dangerous and frenzied as the back of the house could get, it was also insulating and comforting and coddling to those on the inside. Once you become acclimated, it's easier to be in a kitchen than not. Kind of like jail or a mental institution: all one's needs are seen to by professionals.

In Albuquerque, though, something went wrong. Once Laura and I got back from Mexico (where we'd found not only tacos but a million piñatas, dusty backstreets full of pharmacies, girls in white church dresses and dudes on Japanese street bikes making deliveries for Pollo Loco with the grace of motorized dancers, dollar Coronas at any bar outside the American quarter and seventy-five-cent packs of Marlboros being sold out of briefcases on the street), I started making the rounds, but somewhere along the way, I'd become kryptonite. Suddenly, no one wanted to talk to me, no one returned my calls. I'd walk into a place, introduce myself to a chef or an owner, swing into my jive and watch the lights go out behind their eyes.

Normally, I'm unshakable when I'm talking. I can slap backs, buy drinks, make hard jokes and still come off charming. I know the language of cooks and kitchens and the right answers to every question a chef or owner can throw at me. I'd never been more than a couple days without work before. Not once I started looking in earnest. But this time around the block it was harder, so after the first dozen or so no-thank-you's (and a few stop-calling-me's), I started getting desperate and sniveling. I would laugh too loud and try too hard and basically come on like a drunken skank at a rodeo bar—leading with the tits and sequins but too quickly resorting to offering clumsy hand jobs in the alley to anyone who'd take me home. It was ugly and bad and embarrassing, and having seen this same kind of sick neediness in other guys coming through my door when I was the one doing the hiring—shattered survivors of something that I didn't even want to begin hearing about—I knew how bad I must've looked. Walking in the doors of these restaurants, I must've been like poison on two legs, and by about the second month I wouldn't have hired me either. Actually, I knew myself pretty well. I wouldn't have hired me on day two. Much as I wanted it, much as I *needed* it, I was a little bitter and a lot tired by this point—seriously burned out and not-so-secretly sick of picking up the pieces, starting over again. FNG one more time.

On the downward spiral, I used fake names and applied for work at bars and diners and strip clubs featuring twenty-cent hot wings and all-you-can-eat prime rib on Tuesdays. I tried to go ethnic, asking for jobs on the line at the kinds of places where the strip-mall Italian menus of spaghetti and meatballs and chicken-parm sandwiches were rounded out with Chinese egg rolls, tamales, pad thai and samosas, but was thwarted by being unable to speak Russian to the owner or Mandarin to the kitchen manager.

Laura and I started fighting even more than usual. Which basically meant that we were in the ring going flat-out, bare knuckles, every minute we were together. It got so bad, we should've had managers and cut men standing by and someone to ring a bell just to lend some false semblance of civility to what was essentially a nonstop death match. We called each other every name we could think of. And when the English language proved too gentle and lyrical an instrument, we just started making up things to call each other. When our creativity was exhausted, we resorted to throwing stuff.

One of the good things about being poor? You don't have much to throw. And those things you do have are generally lightweight and poorly made. A woman simply cannot do that much damage to her loving man by beaning him in the head with a promotional plastic Batman cup from the 7-Eleven, you know? Though all credit to Laura, she did certainly try.

WHEN I FINALLY GAVE UP and applied for unemployment, I thought I'd hit bottom. It was my first time—first time I'd ever even *considered* it—and driving to the office, I thought about calling my mom and asking her what she thought I should wear. You know, first impressions and all.

Come to find, though, a whole superloser subbasement was dug out beneath the unemployment office. And while standing in line, nervously clutching a stack of paperwork in which I'd been forced to dissect my every failure as a human being over the past five years, surrounded by a shuffling legion of wastrels, check scammers, bums and people like me forced to beg nickels off the state just to keep the lights on, might've *seemed* like the bottom, it wasn't. Not quite.

Applying for unemployment is bad. What's worse is being denied. What's worse is standing before that little goddamn window, feet itching, hoping, *praying*, for a check because you don't have money to buy toothpaste, running uneasy fingers across the shelf in front of the window and thinking how much it reminds you of a galley pass rail, then having some hatchet-faced spinster with bouffant hair and the smell of mothballs and death on her look over your information, shake her head and hand you back the computer printout that says, essentially, "The State of New Mexico cordially invites you to fuck the hell off."

"What's this?" I asked.

"Your denial. Next, please."

"Wait a minute. My what?"

"Denial. You haven't worked long enough in New Mexico to qualify for unemployment, Mr. Sheehan. Next!"

"Wait. How long do I need to have worked here?"

"Minimum of a year."

"And how long does that say I've been working here?"

"Ten and a half months," she said, her voice clipped like the sound of papers being squared up, tapped neatly on a hard surface, filed away and immediately forgotten.

"That's not enough, then."

"No, Mr. Sheehan. It's not."

I felt the pit opening beneath me, smelled its heady vapors, closed my eyes and went in headfirst. Screw it, I thought. Fuckup like me? I don't really deserve the help anyhow.

"Now if you'll take that form over to that office over there, they'll help you apply for out-of-state relief."

I opened my eyes. "Out-of-state what now?"

"Unemployment insurance payments from New York."

"Really?"

"Next, please."

I COULD'VE KISSED THAT BEAUTIFUL OLD CRONE. Kissed her right on her embittered, shriveled-up, Curse of the Mummy face. Because what she was telling me was that instead of collecting unemployment on the nine dollars an hour I'd been making at the Ranch, I'd be collecting against the executive-sous-chef salary I'd been drawing at the hotel in Rochester. In thirty seconds, I'd gone from too broke to buy soup to being the richest gringo in my housing project. I pretty much danced through the next line, filled out the new paperwork with a song in my heart and went home to tell Laura the good news.

"Look, honey. The State of New York is going to pay me to sit on my ass and watch cartoons all day!"

She was so proud.

WAR STORIES

Once the money started arriving, I started sleeping all day. I watched talk shows and ate cereal for lunch. I used the State of New York's mercy funds to buy beer and beef jerky and stopped even pretending to look for a job. Nights, I'd hang out with Laura until she got sleepy, then duck out for the Waffle House with a messenger's bag full of legal pads, pens and paperbacks and either read or write a little or just sit there bullshitting with the nighthawks—the working girls and car thieves, drunks and crazies, night cooks and Backpack Jack, who lived in the Dumpster corral next to the grocery store across Central Avenue and, for a time, was my best friend. He taught me many important things. Such as how to get blind drunk on Listerine without actually going blind, how to suck eggs and sneak weed onto an airplane and cook corned-beef hash on the engine block of a truck.

I'd been keeping night hours for so long that I didn't know how to live any other way. I think there was something about the smell of the Waffle House flat grill and the grease traps, the open short-order kitchen, the closeness of the cooks when I sat on my stool at the counter right in the middle of the Friday-night bar-rush action, that I found soothing. I never ate there, of course, but I could sit all night with my strange friends on a bottomless cup of coffee and pretend that was some sort of a life. Coming home with the sun, I almost felt like I'd been doing something. Like I'd really made good use of my time.

Most girls don't dream at night of finding themselves a depressed, unemployed ex–line cook to marry when they grow up. I'm pretty sure Laura didn't either. But that's pretty much what she got. There are days that I think she married me just so she wouldn't have to forfeit the deposit on the Treasure Island wedding package; that maybe, right up until the very end, she was hoping someone better might stumble along.

A LOT OF THIS WAS BECAUSE I needed a vacation. Not even a real vacation, but just some time away where I wouldn't have to think about food, talk about food, eat and drink food, dream about food, breathe food, worry about food and cook food twenty-four hours a day until, cycling between the up-and-down crashing high of adrenaline rush and total exhaustion, I would find myself running around like crazy in my own skin even when standing still, trying to run in eight different directions at once and grab for pans with arms that I didn't have.

I wish I could remember who in the restaurant business told me this, but it was good advice: If you're not in your own place by thirty with your name over the door—if you're not at least *on your way* there or in the ranks of the kitchen you plan on staying in for life— just quit. Thirtieth birthday? Just walk away. Find Jesus, rob a bank, blow your brains out or just go and sell used cars like so many other ex-cooks do, but whatever it is, get out. Drop the knife, push back from the board, take one last fond look around, and then head for the door. Because if you're not where you want to be by thirty in this industry, you're probably not going to get there. Being on the line is a young man's game that tends to kill the middle-aged either slowly or viciously fast.

And yeah, I know there are exceptions. Of course there are. But trust me: out-by-thirty is a good rule of thumb. I think that for most cooks, kitchens are what we have instead of plans, instead of goals. Kitchens are what we have instead of a real life.

So I collapsed. Because I could, because I needed to, because I knew that even though I hadn't yet hit that magic mark, I'd already spent too long in the galley to let it go easy. Enough time in that kind of environment and everything else becomes a disappointment. You become one of those poor, dim fuckers who show up at the kitchen door on their nights off because, free for a few precious hours, they can't think of anything else to do with themselves and their hands no longer know any action that isn't weird without a knife or pan attached. It's understandable. I mean, when you've really, truly loved it, what in a normal life can compare? You watch cooking shows. Maybe you read the magazines. You keep to the strange little rituals and superstitions that you knew when you were still in The Life (an AC/DC song on the radio would always mean something bad was about to happen, leaving a cigarette burning on the fuse box would mean that nothing bad could *possibly* happen, and both the chef and the sous-chef stepping out for a cigarette at the same time would bring down the rush like rain). You try to have conversations with people about things that have nothing to do with kitchens and fail somewhere in the middle when you realize that you have absolutely nothing to say about anything that *isn't* about kitchens. You listen to the music you listened to when on the line and it all seems flat, like it's missing something, like it's wrong somehow. And that drives you crazy for a few days until you realize that the thing that's missing is the *clack clack clack* of the ticket printer sounding off. It's the sound you've been waiting for all along.

I started writing around this time to fill some of the dull hours. I'd written before. A little bit. Here and there. When I was a kid, I'd write stories in class rather than paying attention; read them sometimes to friends while walking home. Later, on days or weeks when I'd decided that maybe I was drinking a little too much, celebrating a little too much, I'd cool it out by going to the all-night diner after work instead of the bar, and feeling weird about sitting there alone, I'd bring a notebook with me, a pen. When I'd been sick and broke and bored at my folks' house in Rochester, I'd borrow a few bucks from my dad now and then and hitchhike or walk into the city to sit drinking coffee and scribbling away for a few hours.

But this was the first time I'd laid into it with any kind of seriousness or regularity. I was twenty-eight years old. I wrote kitchen stories, food stories, terrible-night stories and best-night-of-my-life stories. I wrote about other stuff, too, but, like my thoughts, the words kept circling back to food, to kitchens. And there was nothing wrong with that. Writing about kitchens was as good as writing about anything else. The best kitchen stories, like the best war stories, aren't really anything more than stories about people anyway.

BESIDES, since no kitchen opportunities were forthcoming (or at least no opportunities walking into our housing project, trudging up the stairs and knocking on our door while I was awake), I didn't know what else to do. Not until the night Laura hit on a suggestion: Why didn't I try being a writer?

Now, mind you, I don't think she meant this as a reasonable alternative to actually working for a living. And her suggestion wasn't delivered quite so politely or with quite so much chipper optimism as you might think. It was more like a challenge. Or a threat. An option of last resort.

We were arguing (of course) on the night it came up. About what no longer mattered because the fights had all started just blending together: a Whitman's Sampler of guilt and blame and humiliation and neglect. I was a slob, she was crazy. I hadn't done the dishes in a year, she was mean. I was a lazy, inconsiderate, miserable, short-tempered prick who'd never really loved her and was just clinging to her now out of desperation for someone to take care of me because I was worthless and stupid and no one had ever demanded anything more from me than my ability to make a nice cassoulet. She . . . couldn't parallel park.

I've known people out there who claim to have happy, supportive, mutually satisfying relationships. I've listened to them talk about the calm and serenity that their significant other brings to them—the joy of their union, the *strength* of their union. You know what I think when I hear this kind of thing?

You poor bastards.

Because not for nothing, fellas, but you just don't know where you stand with a woman until you've stood there, taken both dialectic barrels in the chest, then come back for more. Forget the stinky-feet/little-dick/never-put-the-toilet-seat-down sniping. That's kid's stuff. Until you see the veins in her neck, until her eyes roll back like a shark's eyes, you ain't seen nothing. It's like what Tyler Durden says in *Fight Club*: How much can you know about yourself if you've never been in a fight?

Try falling asleep next to an angry woman who, just a couple hours prior, threatened to stab you with a barbecue fork. That's like taking a nap in the polar-bear cage. While nine times out of ten you might be okay—the bears might just totally ignore you—that tenth time you're going to wake up, open your eyes, and see her there, hovering over you, nose close to your nose, and she's going to say something like, "Do you have any idea how easy it would've been for me to kill you just now?"

Laura and I are two angry, opinionated, stubborn, smart and damaged people who have never backed down from a fight in our lives, never been able to leave well enough alone, never had a scab we didn't pick at until it scarred. And yet through it all, we've loved each other with a fierceness born of absolute honesty. She knows I'm never going to leave her. And when I come home at night, stinking of cheap beer and salami, it's to a woman who knows exactly what kind of a broken, fucked-up, beaten-down, ill-tempered asshole I am and stays with me anyway.

Until you get there yourself, you have no idea how reassuring a feeling that is. I know what true love is now. True love means never having to wonder who's going to be with you when you die.

Probably standing over your corpse with a smoking pistol and a really good reason.

ANYWAY, at some point during our argument I'd gone off on this self-pitying rant about how I'd dedicated my entire life to food and blah blah blah. I said something about how nobody on the outside—no

civilian—understood what it was really like and how the whole business was screwed up with people who only wanted C-school graduates or guys who looked like the chefs on the Food Network, how no
one *gets it* anymore, you know?

And yeah, it was pretty pathetic. But really, it was just a dodge.
I was just attempting to drum up a little sympathy, get out from under the whole lazy/desperate/unemployed loser offensive Laura had
working—a boxer going into a desperation clinch and just trying to
hang on until the bell. But suddenly, mid-scoff, she stopped and
looked at me.

"So why don't you explain it to them?"

"And another thing, it's not like people . . . Wait a minute, what?"

"Why don't you tell them about it?"

"Who?"

She waved her hand. "These 'people' you keep referring to."

"Tell them what?"

"About food and cooking and the business. Write about it."

I shook my head. "No . . . I've been writing about it."

"No, Jay. I mean *really* write about it. Like somewhere that someone other than you will see it. Because really? I'm sick of hearing
about it but you're obviously not sick of talking about it. So why don't
you look for a job as a writer?"

"I . . . Uh . . ."

She raised her eyebrows and tilted her head and opened her
eyes real wide—this thing she does when she knows she's right or
when she knows she's confused me to the point where I have no fight
left in me.

"Look, Jay. I love you, okay? I'll always love you. But this isn't
about love right now. I'm about ready to kill you. If you don't get off
your ass and do *something* soon, I'm going to lose all respect for you
and punch you, understand? So if you say you can't cook anymore,
why not do the other thing you're good at?"

"You mean mast—"

"No. Not masturbating, you idiot. I'm being serious here. Why not try writing? You do it anyway. Why not get paid for it? Seriously, what've you got to lose?"

So I thought about it for a minute, then for ten minutes. Then I pretended to think about it for another half hour or so just because while I appeared to be thinking, Laura appeared willing to not yell at me and the quiet was nice—like the Christmas truce on the Western Front with everyone's gun close at hand but, for the moment, silent.

She was the one with the journalism degree. After a while, I mentioned this to her and she shrugged it off, waving her hand dismissively.

"That'll only be ironic if you actually make something of yourself. Worry about finding a job first."

Then she pulled her knees up to her chest, popped open another beer and stared straight ahead at the TV, signaling that the discussion on this matter had come to a close.

ON THE OUTSIDE

I got my first writing job the next afternoon at a small weekly newspaper called *Crosswinds*, with a mostly deserted office across town from our apartment. It wasn't a good job, but it was something—easy to get, I think, only because I didn't know it was supposed to be hard, and offered to me, I've always believed, only because I'd brought my own pen. And could actually spell. And knew what a semicolon was, more or less.

In any event, I was (rather ridiculously) given the title "investigative reporter" and offered a freelancer's rate of ten cents a word. I had no idea if this was good or bad but figured that it had to be a step in the right direction since I'd already written some words in my life and no one had ever offered me a dime apiece for them before. The only serious complication was that after being dismissed from the editor's office, I had no idea what I was supposed to do next. I poked around the bull pen a little, went out in the parking lot and smoked a cigarette. When it became apparent that no one was actually expecting me to do anything at all, I went out and got drunk at the dim sum restaurant with Laura.

As far as first days of work go, it was nice.

THE DAY I SAW MY FIRST BYLINE IN A NEWSPAPER, I had to walk to the gas station on the corner to see it because our car was broken in nine different ways and I didn't have the money to fix even one. Backpack

Jack was there, panhandling for change and cigarettes. He was a big man, loud and powerful, charming in his way provided one didn't stand too close. I showed him the paper and he clapped me on the back so hard I thought he would break my spine.

"So now you're famous!" he barked. "You gonna forget about all us now?"*

I WROTE ABOUT DRUG-DIVERSION PROGRAMS for homeless people because I knew a little about Albuquerque's homeless population and called some of its bums my friends. I wrote about organic-food labeling because I knew about food, and I wrote about the city's preparations for the Route 66 festival because it was a big deal there and because I was personally offended by efforts to sweep all the drug dealers and prostitutes and night creatures off the street. I mean, this was the Mother Road, America's main line. In my opinion, the street-level weed dealers, pubescent Vietnamese hookers and screaming-drunk homeless vets belonged there more than some bunch of fat, pasty, car-cult tourists from Boise did. Shit, you want to see where the American Dream of westward expansion led? You check out Central Avenue at midnight on a hot summer Friday when the tuners are out and the moon is up and the wind has been blowing a steady breeze of crazy up from the desert all day.

For this, I earned a column called "The Curmudgeon." Because I was only twenty-eight, I took the title as an insult. I wasn't curmudgeonly. I was pissed off. And there's a difference. About a month later (and just two weeks before our families were supposed to be flying out to Vegas to witness Laura and me getting hitched), 9/11 hap-

---

*The byline was at the top of a feature story on organic foods, ironically enough, and the new definition of the word *organic*, which had taken the federal government years to decide on. I can remember reporting and writing the story in a complete terror—having no idea what I was doing, what, exactly, I was *supposed* to be doing, and afraid throughout that sooner or later someone would just come out and ask me what made me think I was some kind of journalist. I mean, shouldn't a person have to have at least some kind of training before being loosed on the world with a micro recorder and a deadline? A degree, maybe, or some basic notion of how the job is done? Apparently not. The learning, in this case, was in the doing, and the only preparation I'd made was renting *Absence of Malice* from Blockbuster and falling asleep halfway through.

pened. Laura and I watched it on TV for three days straight while eating nothing but cheesecakes. We discussed postponing our nuptials,
then decided to go through with it anyway, knowing full well that if
we put it off once, we'd just keep putting it off forever.

Obviously, 9/11 was the biggest news story of the year, of the
decade. I just sat there in my underwear, slack-jawed, staring at the
television, watching that same thirty-second loop of tape over and
over along with everyone else in the world. I never even thought to
call my editor. To take notes. To get out on the street in those first few
crazy hours when it seemed as though the entire world might be coming to an end. Once the dust settled, it occurred to me that perhaps I
wasn't cut out for traditional journalism.

Which was okay because I'd recently picked up a second job,
writing about food for a small regional food-and-travel magazine
called *La Cocinita* and was angling for a third: restaurant critic at the
Weekly Alibi in Albuquerque. The only reason I hadn't yet quit the
other paper outright was because I was owed several hundred dollars
and knew that if I just up and left, I would never see it.*

Getting the job at *La Cocinita* had been equal parts luck, bluff
and excellent timing. Again, not knowing any better, I'd simply
walked into the offices one afternoon and asked to see the chief. I
had no résumé, no experience (beyond my work for *Crosswinds*,
which I was loathe to admit to at the time), no clue how one was supposed to properly go about securing actual *paying* work as a writer
for a respectable organization. I didn't know about clippings, had no
references, hadn't even bothered calling first. I treated newspaper
work the same as I'd treated finding kitchen work: you showed up,
asked for the boss and hoped for the best.

The one prescient guess I'd made was that, somewhere along the
line, someone would probably want to see a sample of my writing be-

---

*In the end, I never did. It was a wonderful introduction to the world of professional writ-
ing—my boss holding out on my paychecks week after week to get me to write more,
those checks then being held as well. There are still days I want to rent a big truck, fill
it with rabid wolverines, back it up to the offices in the middle of the night and empty it
through one of the windows. Not that I'm bitter or anything.

fore offering me a job. As with the restaurant business, where, even today, a guy has to have cooked at least one edible meal before he gets to be called chef, I assumed that eventually I would have to produce proof that I did, in fact, know the English language and could put an actual sentence together without hurting anyone.

To that end, I'd spent the afternoon prior to my ambush of the editor in chief sitting at Milton's (my favorite diner in the city, serving my favorite breakfast burritos in the world) eating a #13 with red chile and inventing some writing samples. I wrote an essay about what it was like during those cooking classes I gave to look up and see fifty stick-thin, health-conscious suburban housewives squirming uncomfortably in their chairs and watching with mounting horror as I added pound after pound of high-fat European butter to my sauce, about all of them staring at me with equal parts lust and revulsion—as though I were up at the front of the room chopping up kittens for stew, but then dipping the kittens in yummy, yummy chocolate.

I wrote another about Mother's Day at La Cité and how fast things can spin out of control even in a good kitchen when someone cuts his finger off, another about *glace de viande*, another about the power of food memories: that first time Laura'd cooked for me in Philadelphia, at her parents' house, and the smell of crushed thyme on her fingertips that night.

The next day, there I was—sitting in the office with my writing samples clutched in sweaty hands, wondering what the hell I was going to say when (and if) the boss agreed to talk to me. There's no handbook out there for trying to bluff your way into a job you're totally unqualified for. No set of best practices. It's the kind of thing you just have to improvise, and my plan was, if necessary, to simply beg. A lot.

The chief, Sergio, had been in an editorial meeting when I'd shown up. Luckily for me, that meeting was going on behind a closed door very close to where I'd been told to sit and wait, and the chief had a big mouth. I could hear everything. And when I heard him smack a hand down on the table and loudly state that what the magazine really needed was "one of those Anthony Bourdain motherfuckers,"* I could feel all the jittery nerves, tension and anxiousness suddenly spin out of me like water down a drain. Right then, I knew I was golden. Quickly, I shuffled up my most bizarre, gonzo, loud-mouth sample,† and laid it on top of the stack. When the door opened, I walked right up to the chief, stuck out my hand and said, "I'm Jason Sheehan, and I am your Anthony Bourdain motherfucker."

IN A LAST-MINUTE BRAINSTORM, I'd made up some dates and the names of a bunch of fictional publications and slapped them on the top of each of the pieces I'd written just before printing them out on my home computer printer and heading out the door. At the time, I thought this was genius. With just a few keystrokes, it suddenly appeared as though I'd been writing about food for years.

It wasn't genius, though. It was stupid to such a degree that, even today, I can hardly believe I got away with it. My bogus clippings were already chock-full of bad language, vile insults, bizarre digressions and, in one case, a long aside about how all moral vegetarians ought to be rounded up into camps and studied until a way could be found to turn them into delicious pork chops. I was already hanging myself pretty far out there on a ragged and bloody edge. But no matter how good I was (or how desperate the magazine might've been), a lie like that would've killed me at *La Cocinita* had anyone ever thought to check on even one of these totally specious references.

But luckily for me, no one ever did. Sergio actually read my first two samples standing right there in the hallway. A half hour later, I had the job. I was assigned an editor (Peri Pakroo, the first person who actually sat me down and explained to me—over lunchtime beers, of course—what I was supposed to be doing for a living), who gave me one column a month on whatever the hell I felt like writing

---

*Anthony Bourdain being the chef turned writer who wrote the wildly successful *Kitchen Confidential* and the man to whom I more or less owe my entire career.

†It was the one about the butter—about doing the cooking class and making a super-high-fat French Sauternes sauce—which is just another proof of the old cook's adage about the only thing better than butter being more butter.

about (my debut being that butter story that'd gotten me the job, if I remember correctly), then another that was more specific and traditional: recipes for Thanksgiving leftovers, Valentine's Day menus for two, how to eat on the street in Juárez without dying.

UP UNTIL SEPTEMBER 11, I'd been kind of looking at this writing thing like a dodge, as something to do to fill the days until I could find another kitchen, another brigade—easier than digging ditches, safer than stealing, but a career side trip that I would absolutely not cop to once it was over. On my best days, making a living as a writer (even if it wasn't much of a living) felt dirty. Like I was getting away with something, like I was just using the computer to print modest stacks of cash in very small denominations and, sooner or later, would have to be caught. The rest of the time it felt like a betrayal of something, even if I couldn't quite put my finger on what.

I could live with it, though, because I saw it as temporary. I was a cook. Writing was just something I was doing to keep the collection agents off my back.

All that summer, I'd just been a guy who couldn't find a job. After 9/11, though, there were no jobs to be had. By anyone. At least not in Albuquerque, in the restaurant industry. Everyone remembers what September 11 was like. The planes, the towers, the shock of it—like waking in the middle of the night on the couch with the television still on, unsure in those first few blurry moments whether what you're watching is news or a movie or maybe a little of both. But afterward, in the days and weeks and months that followed, the shock only deepened. Fun stopped and travel stopped and entertainment stopped. And food? No. People ate a lot of mashed potatoes, a lot of cold sandwiches. They ordered in lo mein and pizza and uncorked that bottle of '76 Lafite they'd been saving for a special occasion because now the special occasion was being alive. Meals were taken in penitence, gilded with private extravagance, and mostly at home. No one was going out anywhere.

Albuquerque's was a tourist-driven restaurant economy. And

with no tourists, there was no economy. The cull was brutal. I heard from friends and friends-of-friends that most staffs had been cut in half, that all new openings had been canceled, that some restaurants were just shutting down entirely for a month, maybe two. No one knew when the panic was going to end.

So all of a sudden, writing *was* my career—a default vocation because it was the only one I had. I never meant for it to happen this way, certainly didn't plan it. It was just circumstance. People ask me sometimes how I got into food writing (almost always meaning—but not asking outright—how *they* might get into food writing, too), and that's what I tell them: circumstance. I became a food writer because, for a few weeks in 2001, everyone in the United States was too sad to eat dinner out.

A WEEK AFTER THE TOWERS CAME DOWN, I asked Gwyneth Doland, the food editor at *La Cocinita*, for the critic's position at its sister paper, the *Alibi*. I was informed that there really wasn't a critic's position per se, and I said make one so I can have it. She said that the paper hadn't done regular or formal restaurant reviews in a while and that no one had seemed to notice much. I told her I could change that— promising, if nothing else, that I'd make the readers notice me. She said she'd think about it and get back to me.

In the meantime, Laura and I drove off to Vegas in a rented car to make the whole mess of debt, poisoned history, psychological disorder and recrimination that composed our relationship legal. The Strip was probably as close to empty as it'd ever been since being just a few acres of high desert scrubland and a Mafia wet dream. All the good restaurants were shuttered. At the chapel, we were told that our booking had been canceled because everyone else who'd been scheduled to wed had already called up to cancel themselves and the wedding coordinator had just assumed we'd forgotten. We said no, we'd very much like to get hitched, please. And in the end, the Treasure Island did right by us. There were no pirates, but Laura's immediate family and mine flew in to stand as witnesses and play the nickel slots. Flowers, candles and a cake from Freed's (Robert Goulet's favorite bakery) were procured. A reverend was located—a white-haired, rheumy-eyed old man with the whiskey shakes and breath that could've stripped paint, who was either a retired or defrocked Baptist, I can never remember which—and we told him to keep his part short, sweet, and to leave God out of it.

We'd written our own vows. They were far from traditional. Ten minutes after the processional had played Laura in, Etta James singing "At Last" played us back down the aisle as man and wife. In the eyes of the Nevada Gaming Commission, we were in it together now, for better or worse, till death do us renegotiate.

We used the same six-dollar rings Laura had bought back in Rochester and ate at In-N-Out Burger to celebrate.

She's still waiting on that honeymoon on Monkey Forest Road.

When we got back to Albuquerque three days later and I called the office, Gwyneth told me I had the job. I was a restaurant critic now.

WHAT MATTERS IS WHAT YOU DON'T KNOW

Grim fact: writing about life as a writer is not nearly so interesting as writing about life as a cook. As a cook, there are knives and fire, battles, drama, fistfights, death, revelry and shit blowing up, all of it spaced out by odd moments of quiet and pure, unfettered joy. Being a writer, on the other hand, is mostly just about sitting still and typing. The minute I set aside my Henckels and picked up a pen, I became a tourist in the cooks' world.

I made a deal with myself when I took that first critic's gig at the *Alibi* that, to the best of my ability and within the bounds of the possible, I would fully inhabit every word I wrote about the industry I'd loved and loathed, lived in and, ultimately, left. I would always be there—lurking, present. There would be no act, no persona, no evasion beyond that which I quickly learned was required by the spy-versus-spy realities of the job itself. Above all, I would always tell the truth.

Not journalistic truth, necessarily. That part was a given, even if never exactly easy. My promise (mostly kept) was to a smaller, more intimate, more controllable truth—one of the self and the experience, of preserving the scene, which has become such a large part of dining out these days, and also all that which went on *behind* the scenes, in the kitchen and on the line, in the crush of service and at the bar once all was said and done. No matter how bad, no matter how embarrassing to myself or those around me, I would tell my stories and, through them, try to illuminate the intricacies of the job going on out of sight of the public. I would try to explain how it was different in every conceivable way from what the civilians were being shown on the Food Network, in celebrity interviews in the glossy food mags where chefs were being treated like Hollywood idols, like the rock stars we'd all once secretly dreamed of becoming. We—meaning my as-yet-nonexistent readers and I—would not be eating at the French Laundry or El Bulli or La Tour, after all. It wasn't Batali or Ripert or Bocuse or Boulud in these kitchens.* It was guys and girls just like me, who'd lived and worked like me and understood the same kind of high joys and ugliness I did.

Who better, then, to tell their stories than me? To write of their triumphs and defeats, the draw of The Life: *La Vida Cocina*, this thing of ours. I imagined being lauded as a hero, as a clear and true voice of the proletarian white jacket. And it was easy, of course, because I hadn't yet had to actually *do* anything. In my imagination, everything that followed from my first day as a critic would be free pie, lobster tails and blow jobs.

Needless to say, that's not quite how things worked out.

IN ALBUQUERQUE, I found myself for the first time confined to the other side of the swinging doors. That idea of telling cooks' stories? Not so easy as I'd thought now that I was supping with the enemy, sitting in pretty dining rooms, eating the food rather than cooking it.

Since I already knew all the tricks and shortcuts, no one could cheapjack me or get away with anything. I could taste the dulling hint of freezer burn, smell a fish that'd already been a grandmother when it came off the delivery truck. I knew what a confit was supposed to taste like when it was done right, the difference between right and rushed, ultimately the difference between rushed and just wrong.

---

*I should say here that it wasn't these guys until much later—until I got to a point in this new, second career where I actually *was* writing about guys like Paul Bocuse and trading e-mails with Eric Ripert.

Every plate set before me, the critic, was like a signed confession by the chef. I knew every motion the guys in the kitchen were making, every pass of the knife, every flip of the pan. If I closed my eyes and concentrated, I could reproduce them in an imaginary kitchen in my head—moving deliberately through the steps of prep and final plating, a little bit of meditative cook's tai chi.

But what I hadn't figured on was then having to kneecap my former friends, contemporaries and fellow travelers for fucking up the duck. I hadn't expected the perfidy, the requisite insolence of talking shit about some poor line dog's chow mein or *desebrado*. I learned quickly that there are no small betrayals in life. That no one gets to sell out just a little.

I also learned that no one really cares what the fish tasted like. No one (except maybe another chef, and only then with an eye toward stealing) wants to read a rote recitation of ingredients: *The breast of hobgoblin was pounded thin, salted, peppered, topped with a sauce of hobo wine and crankcase oil, then, finally, cilantro.*

The food in food writing is set dressing for a story. In criticism, it is causality: I have come to this place because there is food here. In the best cases, it is scenery that rises almost to the level of character, like light in a Bergman film, the optometrist's billboard looming over every downfall of Jay Gatsby and his pals, a menacing couch in a Stanley Kubrick costume drama. But the food itself cannot ever really be a character in full because that honor must, in decency, be reserved for those who grew it, prepared it, served it, ate it or fought about it later that night. The essential, maddening and ironic disconnect in writing about food is that the writer is sent to the places where the food is and then, if he knows what he's doing, writes about everything but. Food has no story. It just is. It is the light, the billboard, the menacing couch. The story is in what was done to the food, with the food, near the food. The story is almost always about food's history (at least a little) and *always* always about how the food made everyone feel.

So, fine. Once I'd learned these three lessons (that being on the floor necessarily cuts you off from the kitchen; that this, in turn, makes the food your single connection to the cooks on the line and the chef in his office; and that the food, though the ostensible reason for your being on the floor, is almost always the least interesting thing to talk about), I was left with only one option: to talk about myself. This was a relief because at least when I was talking about myself, I controlled the story. I could still be a critic, could still say that the veal was good, the baked Alaska frozen, and describe how the waiter put his thumb in the soup, but I could also place it all in a context. Did I know a few things about veal? You bet. And I knew even more about thumb consommé because there was this one place, back in New York, where I had this captain named Johnny . . .

Quickly, this was what my weekly missives became: me talking about myself and talking about food and talking, mostly, about food in relation to me. I became a highly subjective, biased and personal lens through which food in general and certain restaurants in particular were seen. Everything became autobiography because, in my mind, anything else would either be trite (*The omelet was toothsome and had an excellent mouth-feel . . .*) or a shallow lie.* And, of course, autobiography also served my original purpose of offering honesty and genuineness to people who maybe had no idea where their dinner was actually coming from. Maybe I couldn't write about the bad nights, terrible tragedies, blood, dope and ecstasy in *other* chef's kitchens, but I sure as hell could write about all that'd been done in my own.

There was a price, though, because there is always a price. Like a savings account, one's past is a finite commodity. Even Proust, after eating that fucking madeleine, ran dry eventually.

---

*Obviously, when talking to the press, one wants to put one's best food forward. One wants to talk of one's rigorous training, delicate artistry, the calm and competency of one's crew. What one will never admit to on the record? That the grillman is banging the hostess, where the mysterious $2.5 million in start-up capital came from, that your cooks' paychecks all bounced last week, every purveyor in the city has you on COD, and that even while you're talking to me, you've got your dealer on line two just waiting to take last night's profits off your hands in trade for a couple grams of Bolivian marching powder.

I figured I had enough material—enough past—to cover me for about a thousand years. After that, though, I was gonna be in trouble.

"WHAT MATTERS IS WHAT YOU DON'T KNOW. That's where they'll get you."

My current boss, Patty Calhoun, at my current job as critic and food columnist for *Westword* newspaper in Denver, told me that shortly after I came into her employ. It's probably the single best piece of advice I've ever gotten about writing, and up there, I think, in the top ten for life in general. What Patty didn't know when she hired me? Pretty much everything that's in this book. But I'm okay with that. I think the odds are good that she'll never read it. She's already had to put up with me and read nearly every word I've written since 2002, and that's a lot to ask of anyone. As she would be the first to tell you.

What matters is what you don't know. Patty was talking about food and writing about food; saying that, yeah, yeah, it was great, all this cooking experience I had, all this *stuff* I knew. But what was important was the hundred universes full of stuff I didn't. When the bastards are after you, that's where they'll trip you up. And the bastards will always be after you.

THE CRITIC'S JOB at the *Alibi* was wonderful. It was educational and liberating, more fun than a sackful of monkeys and whiskey, certainly easier than standing a fourteen-hour sauté shift at some lost-outpost fusion restaurant making coconut mussels with galangal root or fillet of yak with a side of Styrofoam packing peanuts, and so delightfully, deliciously weird that it hardly ever got dull.

The one thing it wasn't? Well paying. I was getting seven and a half cents a word for eight hundred and fifty words a week, then an additional ten cents a word for twelve hundred words once a month.

Yeah. Do the math.

This put Laura and me in the interesting position of going out on a Friday night in our party duds to eat caviar and filet mignon (or tacos, churros with chocolate, dollar sushi, *pupusas*, moussaka or *bastilla* and thimbles of cinnamon-spiked Turkish coffee, all depending on the week), then spending the next six days eating ramen noodles and oatmeal. My budget for review meals was about forty bucks—not even enough to do a half-assed job, let alone a whole-assed one—so I ended up spending what little I was making off the writing to tack on additional working dinners so I could write better reviews, so I could make more pesos, so I could eat more dinners . . .

We were living right on the edge of the combat zone in 'Burque, in a two-and-a-half-room walk-up, paying rent with Laura's paychecks and eating off mine, but the balance sheet quickly went into the red. Even minor emergencies like running out of beer were enough to send us into a financial tailspin.

So I compensated by taking my final cooking job as (I assume) the only colonial-French-trained chef and published food writer ever to work the short-order line at a Waffle House.

Yes, this was the same Waffle House where I'd been punched in the face for the blatant faggotry of reading on a Friday night, the same one where I'd been a regular since arriving in the Land of Enchantment. For all the months I'd spent looking for work, this was the one place I hadn't thought to try until I walked onto the night-shift line one evening to help out a friend and liked it so much I just decided I'd stay.

It was a great job, the best send-off the industry could possibly have given me. I had a plastic name tag. I wore a paper hat like a 1940s soda jerk. I worked right out in the open, just on the other side of a high counter, with no checks and no dupes—just called orders from the waitresses for hash browns, scattered, smothered and covered, shouted over the din of a cramped bar rush; a half dozen egg pans all going at once, grits boiling over on my flattop and sweet-smelling waffle batter scorching in the tiered ranks of presses. I did my own dishes, hustled the drunks, poured the coffee, hung out with the nighthawks, and, in the dead zone between four and six in the morning, wrote out most of my restaurant reviews longhand, hunched over in the farthest back booth, scribbling with a cup of thick, double-brewed, trucker-strength coffee in one hand and a cigarette in my teeth.

I worked both the *Alibi* critic's gig and nights at the Waffle House pretty much until the day I left Albuquerque for Denver. As a matter of fact, my writing for the *Alibi* and for *Westword* overlapped by a couple weeks in July of 2002. I was commuting six hours, back and forth across the Raton Pass, handling final details in 'Burque for four days, then spending long weekends in and around Denver, eating and trying to get my legs under me in yet another new city. Even after settling in Denver, I moonlighted a little under an assumed name— covering my absence in Albuquerque with a pseudonymous me who never admitted to being hundreds of miles gone.

So, sometimes, it's *who* you don't know that matters, too.

I'D ACTUALLY APPLIED for the *Westword* job over Memorial Day weekend 2002. Laura and I, both sick to death of working split schedules (her on days, me on nights) and of seeing each other only over work dinners, when she was always tired and I was always bad company (focused on memorizing menus, details of the decor, our waiter's name, or trying to figure out why my crème brûlée tasted like ham), had decided to take an eighteen-hour vacation to Boulder. We'd drive up, get a room, go to Juanita's (a divey, cheap and storied Mexican restaurant on Pearl Street, where, once, we'd spent some time together falling in love), drink too much, eat some flautas, then stumble around drunk on the pedestrian mall for a while, watching the buskers and eyeballing the trust-fund hippies.

And that's just what we did. We made the drive, got the room, settled in at Juanita's and started knocking back Coronas and shots of tequila until the world had gone just the right kind of blurry. We had a little something to eat and tried to relax once more into each other's company. It started raining, but when we were ready, we headed out into it anyway, oblivious. The storm had chased just about everyone else inside, and we had the Pearl Street Mall almost to ourselves so walked along it arm-in-arm, leaning on each other, kissing in the dry spots under awnings or in doorways—playing at being in a love story quite different from the one we were living. Sweeter maybe, and certainly more kind.

Because I am a gentleman (though often latent in my manners), I eventually ducked out into the downpour to grab Laura a newspaper to hold over her head. There was a profusion of free weeklies to choose from. *Westword* just happened to be the one I grabbed.

Sobered up somewhat and soaking wet, we drove back to the hotel. Laura and I have always been good in hotels. They are our truest element.

While I was taking a shower, she lay on the bed flipping through the paper we'd carried in with us. She was the one who found the box ad saying that *Westword* was looking for a new restaurant critic. She was the one who said, "Hey, you should apply for this." I had other things on my mind.

I don't remember much else after that. But apparently, during the night, I'd crawled out of bed and started writing a letter. Hungover the next morning, riding south again with Laura behind the wheel, I finished it. And that night, with a few fresh beers in me, I typed it into the computer and fired it off as an e-mail to *Westword*. It was a cover letter, more or less—nine pages long with no résumé attached, no clips, no nothing. Once again, to say that this was the wrong way to go about applying for a job would be a colossal understatement. There is a process, with newspapers, as in any trade, a dance as formalized as an Elizabethan galliard. I'd come in doing the Lindy Hop.

What I didn't know was that Patty—my soon-to-be chief—had already more or less made up her mind on who she was hiring for the critic's job. She'd narrowed down hundreds of applicants* to three

---

*Most of them knuckleheads, thumb-suckers, idiots or worse, but some serious contenders, too—middleweight tradesmen, both local and national. Just so I wouldn't get a big head about it, one afternoon Patty showed me some of the candidates I'd bested: ones who'd handwritten reviews in pencil, who'd misspelled the name of the newspaper they wanted to write for, the chef who'd reviewed his *own restaurant* just so he could say what a genius he was, and the guy who actually wrote that an appetizer at a particularly loathsome chain restaurant had "blowed me away."

strong contenders and was planning to make her final decision after returning from a journalism conference. She was on the road when my ridiculous, ranting cover-letter-slash-curriculum-vitae arrived at the office and got it forwarded to her the next morning.

She wrote back to me directly, asking for writing samples and a résumé as quickly as I could get them to her.

I sent her some samples (including the butter essay, which I now considered a good-luck charm) but, for reasons I can't explain even today, refused to send a résumé.

Patty wrote back, telling me she *really needed* a résumé, like, immediately. "I don't care what's on it," she stated. "I just need to know what you've been doing for the past ten years. Were you in jail? Abducted by aliens? Not that either of those would disqualify you from writing for *Westword*. I just need to know."

So, embarrassed, I banged out a résumé, miserably trying to stitch together a skein of names and dates and places, to cover all the blank spaces where I'd been sick or wandering or unemployable, to organize the thirty-odd kitchens I'd worked in into some semblance of a life. Though not a deliberate attempt to mislead—just from poor memory, zero record keeping and a fervent desire not to look like a schnook on paper—the thing was a total work of fiction. But I sent it to her anyway. There were phone calls, I think. I was called up to Denver for a face-to-face over beers and fat steaks at a restaurant that I hated. But most of what came next was just waiting.

For a month. Just long enough to forget. I'm no better at waiting now than I was when I was fourteen, but at fourteen I hadn't yet acquired the bad habits and cushion of disappointments that make waiting easier. I settled back into my routine of review dinners and night shifts—waking to late-afternoon sunlight streaming through the windows, walking across the street to the 7-Eleven for beer and beef jerky, smoking the rag ends of joints and lying on the couch watching old Czechoslovakian hard-core porno tapes that I'd picked up somewhere, *Apocalypse Now*, *Repo Man*.

Sometime around the Fourth of July, I got the call. It was after-noon. I was sleeping, the ringing of the phone penetrating my dreams like a lancet through the skin of a boil. Staggering and still half-asleep, I found the cordless buried under a pile of papers and laundry near the computer and listened while Patty told me the job was mine if I wanted it: salary, health insurance, 401(k), *very* generous expense account, an office. I blithered out some kind of thank-you, said I'd be there tomorrow if she needed me to, then hung up the phone before I either said something to make her reconsider or fell down.

Which was good because in my cotton-headed, half-dreaming haze, I'd thought she was calling from a restaurant, was a manager or HR person telling me that I was finally going back to the trenches again. For a minute or two, my only thoughts were about my chef jackets, my knives, my gear. During one of those bad months, I'd packed it all away somewhere just to get it out of sight—probably the only cleaning I did that entire time. I started shaking, pissed that I couldn't remember where I'd put my knives, pissed that they were gone, pissed about everything.

I sat down on the couch, lit a cigarette, switched on the TV. *Repo Man* was in the VCR. Rubbing my head, scrubbing my fingers through my recently shortened hair, I slowly pieced things together. I didn't need my knives, my jackets. I wasn't going back. I was going away again, to Denver. I looked around at our crappy little apartment clut-tered with all our crappy thirdhand, pawnshop and discount-store stuff. Down in the parking lot were two broken cars suffering from more vehicular maladies than we had credit to fix. I understood, in a postmodern sort of way, that this was supposed to be one of those moments when I took a deep breath, looked around, and realized that I really loved all my things, my home, the trappings of Laura's and my combined poverty—the broken cars and cracked dishes and thrift-store chairs.

But all I wanted was to burn the place to the ground with every-thing in it, push the cars off the edge of the mesa and walk away clean. I just wanted to get *gone*. Because, fuck it, being poor is only noble when you're not. It only looks good in movies. In real life, all you are is hungry a lot and walking.

IN MY DEBUT COLUMN FOR *WESTWORD* (which was supposed to be a catchall restaurant-news and industry-gossip roundup, like Page Six but with foie gras) I wrote about myself. I told the story about the strawberries and punching the produce supplier, talked about my likes and dislikes, my pet peeves, about sneaking sushi in the parking lot at Wegmans when I was a kid, how much I hated celery (except in mirepoix) and what dried blood smells like crusted on a chef's whites on a ninety-degree night. All I was trying to do was introduce myself to my new city, my new community of chefs and food people. I thought it was actually rather restrained. My first proper review was a lightweight knock-around of a popular neighborhood Italian restaurant in which I wrote primarily about the handmade lobster ravioli, growing up on the East Coast and the anti-Semites one table over.

> We were seated next to a couple sharing what appeared to be their 130th wedding anniversary and very loudly discussing the trouble with people of the Jewish persuasion. Only they weren't using the word *Jewish*, but rather a slur rhyming with *bike*. Charming, right? Actually, only the husband appeared to have problems with bikes; the wife seemed merely embarrassed by the mention of them. I should also add that [Laura], coming from a family of partly bike-ish descent, was ready to put a cocktail fork in this gentleman's eye, and a gross display of physical violence was barely averted by the timely arrival of our server.

The death threats* started arriving a couple days after my first review hit the stands. I took the phone calls and thought it was funny until it wasn't anymore. The letters and e-mails we ran in the paper.

"This is good," Patty told me. "Now you've got their attention."

---

*This is not an exaggeration. I received more than one.

I wrote about green chile and zombies and punk rock; about fusion cuisine and bull testicles, fish eyes and roasted field mice. I ate sliced sea cucumber and cold pig's-ear salad at a blowout Chinese New Year feast that I'd gotten myself invited to incognito. I worked anonymously, with reservations made under the names of long-dead character actors and a wallet full of credit cards obtained under various noms de guerre. I never went in for disguises, for elaborate ruses. I've always been a big fan of writers like John le Carré, so modeled my tradecraft along the lines of the Cold War spies: going for misdirection over costumes, crowds over cover, and sowing befuddlement among the enemy by the expeditious use of false identities, penetration agents and overt propaganda.

With a rented tux, borrowed shoes and a pocketful of business cards that identified me as a wine importer from New York, I infiltrated a Les Amis d'Escoffier* dinner where the chef had spent thirty hours straight prepping and cooking a multicourse dinner in strict accordance with Escoffier's recipes—not an easy thing to do under the best circumstances since the big man tended to demand ludicrously intricate prep work, nearly-impossible-to-procure supplies (such as caul fat and baby starlings), and had a Frenchman's obsession with minuscule detail. Still, it was the best *potage queue de boeuf* I'd ever tasted (oxtail consommé filtered through three different rafts), the best *pigeonneaux en compote*. I was seated across the table from two chefs who I'd recently mocked in my column for their bad business practices and retarded cruise-ship cuisine, then drank my way through nine of ten flights of wine, capped off by cigars, dirty jokes and nips from a bottle of century-old bourbon. I had to call Laura to pick me up. When she did, I was three-quarters unconscious, sitting on the curb on Colfax Avenue singing old Irish drinking songs to myself.

---

*Les Amis is a relatively harmless organization of chefs, restaurant owners and other food-industry people who get together in half-goofy secrecy to slap each other on the back, drink ridiculously expensive wine and eat meals prepared by guest chefs who must work in strict accordance with recipes and preparations laid down by Escoffier himself. It's a guys-only group (the women have their own organization, Les Dames d'Escoffier) and basically just an excuse for a bunch of like-minded hedonists to get together, drink too much, eat too much and behave badly in private. You know, like the Elks club. Or the American Communist Party.

It had been the bourbon that put me over the edge. But what was I supposed to do, say no? Not on your life. I'd had the same problem at a Vietnamese restaurant some months prior, having gotten into a conversation with the owner and the cooks, then hanging around late after the place had closed, eating a shift meal with the crew and drinking. When the owner went behind the bar and pulled out the bottle of snake wine—a literal ball of snakes, preserved in the bottom of a bottle of what tasted like kerosene—I knew I was going to have a bad night. I also knew I had to drink, because this was something special, something *extra*—an opportunity that might never present itself again. Out of this came a sort of mantra for the way I would ever after do the job and live the life: Always drink the snake wine.

WORKING FOR *WESTWORD* was like being an East German CIA station chief crossed with a crime reporter working the Chicago city-hall beat in the 1920s. I made a lot of unusual friends, knew more than I could ever put in print, and was watching more pies than I had fingers to stick in them. I had informers in some of the best restaurants in the city, commando eaters who could be sent in on a moment's notice to do my recon for me, and took a lot of phone calls in the middle of the night from numbers that came up blocked on my cell phone.

"Is this Sheehan?"

"Yeah. Who's this?"

"Get a pen . . ."

At the center of all of it, though, was me. Me and Laura. Me and Laura and a solid core of mercenary eaters—most of them former chefs, bakers turned used-car salesmen and crazed gastronauts doing it for the free meals and booze—but mostly me and Laura. We were our own best field agents, out on the town so often that many weeks our refrigerator held nothing but Styrofoam take-out boxes, beer and fifteen different kinds of mustard. In our busiest weeks, we were eating more than a dozen meals out, keeping track of our reservations and plans on a calendar marked with restaurant names, aliases, times, party size and method of payment so we wouldn't use any one card too often. I had restaurant owners who were trying to follow me around for a picture, who offered bribes for a face-to-face meeting, who hired private investigators to tail me. It's the kind of job where you learn as you go—dirty tricks, dodges, escape and evasion and covering your tracks. I still fuck up now and then, get caught out, make mistakes. But I get a little better at it every week. And I'm still learning.

THE JAMES BEARD AWARDS IS THE BIG ONE—the Academy Awards for food people, minus the gift bags and the red carpet. There are two ceremonies, one for writers and media people, another for chefs. Early in 2003, I was nominated for my first Beard Award for restaurant criticism, for three pieces I'd written during my first couple months on the job in Denver. It was funny: I'd never made it to the Beard House as a chef, *wouldn't* ever have made it while cooking—not in a million years. But apparently the minute I took off the whites, I was able to sneak in the back door with the journalists and hacks. Actually, I'm not sure whether that's funny or just a little sad.

Laura and I flew out to the coast together, then drove into Manhattan for the awards gala. Having never before been to a gala and unsure what one was supposed to wear (tux? chaps? would spats and a top hat be too much or not enough?), I'd called up one of the other nominated writers who'd been before and who was up against me in the criticism category that year. With complete innocent earnestness, I asked him what the appropriate attire was.

"Oh, you don't need to dress fancy," he'd said. "It's a bunch of writers. It's not like everyone's going to be in tuxedos or anything."

Taking my cue from him, I'd bought a twenty-dollar dress shirt at JCPenney and a tie to match. Laura wore a suit, black on black on black. Walking into the lobby of the Grand Hyatt, where the shindig was being held, we (of course) saw everyone in jackets and ties, polished shoes, half the men in penguin suits. I grabbed Laura's arm and held on tight as we plunged in, whispering in her ear that it was her duty as my wife to hunt down that other food writer and kill him should I die before I had the chance.

We knew no one, were known by no one. I was wearing this ridiculous-looking NOMINEE ribbon that made me look like I'd just won third place at a grade-school spelling bee. We each had one drink, sat in a corner, and were totally overlooked. So much so that no one even noticed when we ducked out and went across the street for sushi and tea, making it back just in time to find our seats in the ballroom as the ceremony (and dinner) was starting. Because we worked for the same company, I was sharing space at table with the guy who'd told me I didn't need to wear a jacket. You know what he was wearing? A fucking jacket.

But let me say this. There is one thing that can make a twenty-dollar button-down from Penney's look *good* in a room full of expensive suits and ball gowns. Can you guess what that thing is?

A fucking James Beard Award.

When they called my name, I went up onstage, let them put the medal around my neck (it reminded me of the closing scene from *Star Wars* where Luke and Han Solo and Chewie are all getting their medals), thanked Laura, and got the hell off before I said anything to embarrass myself. By the time I got back to my seat, Mr. Don't Dress Fancy and his date were gone. I kissed Laura, then we ate their desserts.

THERE WERE NO LIMOS AND NO BIG PARTIES after the awards were done. Or rather, there probably were, but none that Laura or I knew about or were invited to. Geeks at the prom all over again. As everyone was making for the doors, I did manage to shake hands with Ruth Reichl from *Gourmet*. She's an incredibly short woman with a charming, shy smile and a formidable mass of curly hair like a show poodle trying to jump straight off her head. She congratulated me, which I thought was nice. She also called me Jerry, but that was okay. After that, there were photos to be taken of all the winners. Because I worked anonymously, I stood proudly among my peers with my back to the camera, my medal draped between my shoulder blades. In the final picture, it looked like I was trying to sniff David Rosengarten's armpit.

While walking back the few blocks to our hotel, Laura and I stopped like tourists to stare up at the gleaming spike of the Chrysler Building and to kiss in its presence. In the fullness of its reality and closeness, it was no less impressive than it had been in my imaginings—in those dawn moments years ago when I could feel it looming just over my possible horizon like a dare, like proof of all I hadn't accomplished, and never would. I was still a couple weeks shy of my thirtieth birthday, and finally, for at least a few minutes and even if no one else noticed it, Laura and I owned Manhattan. It was a nice feeling while it lasted. When all was said and done, we rode the elevator up to our room.

A SHINY MEDAL and a couple souvenir programs weren't the only things Laura and I brought back to Denver with us.

For a couple years, we'd been discussing what we would do about names if Laura ever got pregnant, either by accident or design. Our first thought was to sell the naming rights to large corporations as a way to finance the child's eventual college education and/or bail bond. While we understood that it might be rough on this wholly speculative kid to go through life saddled with a name like Kotex Wondermop Sheehan or Coors Light Presents Starbucks Invesco Sheehan, we figured that eventually he or she would come to understand.

But what if no large corporations were willing to pony up? we wondered. Well, our backup plan had always been to name this purely hypothetical child after the place it was conceived. You know, Denver or Mohave or Camry.

As things turned out, my lovely daughter ought to have been named Manhattan.

I told you Laura and I had always been good in hotels.

THE CHILD ARRIVED RIGHT ON SCHEDULE: in the middle of a snowstorm, on Super Bowl Sunday, and only after seventy-some hours of labor and three days and nights when neither Laura nor I slept a wink. The doctor was about fourteen years old and behaved as though he'd never seen a vagina before. Not even in pictures. And Laura had, insanely, decided on delivering naturally—which meant no meds, no painkillers. Not even for me.

But she did it. And I was there, watching, amazed. It was the greatest magic trick ever. One minute, there's my wife. The next minute, poof! Some terrified-looking Cub Scout is pulling a baby out of her like a rabbit from a hat.

We named her Parker Finn. She was the second most beautiful girl I'd ever seen, lying swaddled, with a tiny hat on, in a bassinet set beside the full-size bed where the first most beautiful girl I'd ever seen lay drooling and snoring like a ripsaw. I read to Parker from Jacques Pépin's book *The Apprentice*, while Laura slept. I watched my daughter as she drifted off, had her first dream; more in love than I'd ever thought possible even if she did smell kinda like veal.

PARKER WAS SMALL AND VORACIOUS, always hungry, and I found it odd that my lovely wife—who had, for so long, shared this food-obsessed life with me—had suddenly *become* food, breast-feeding everywhere for a child who was never full. Laura had also become (in my opinion) an ascetic. No coffee. No booze. No raw food or Indian food or weird cheeses or truffles. I would never have been able to make the sacrifice, which is just one among myriad reasons why I'm really glad I was born a boy.

I also found it fascinating that Parker had been born into this world that was only mine by forced adoption. She experienced her first fine-dining meal at two weeks old, lying in her car seat between Laura and me at Clair de Lune in Denver, watching with fascination as we ate. Sushi bars and Ethiopian restaurants, basement dives and shiny strip-mall cafés—these are her natural environments, the places where she grew up. She came with us to so many work dinners, so many bars, on every plane. She had more airline miles behind her before her second birthday than I had had by the time I was twenty-five.

I knew she was a good kid, a smart kid, and I knew she was *my* kid because she has my stubby legs, my freakishly thick neck, and because, at three years old, while out playing with me one day in a pet store, she looked up at a cage full of parakeets, pointed and asked, "Daddy, what do those taste like?"

I told her I didn't know, that I'd never eaten parakeet before and didn't know anyone who had.

She thought about this for a minute while watching them flutter around their cage. I waited beside her.

"We should find out," she finally said. "Buy me one."

I didn't, but I really wanted to. Instead, I told her that if she was really interested, then maybe when she was older (the parent's classic evasion), we could find out together. She accepted this and put her little hand in mine. We walked away, to go and debate what the guinea pigs might taste like—something with which I did have some experience.

So it's not only what you don't know that matters. It's also what you're willing to someday learn; what you might not know right now, but will. Life never gets dull so long as you're prepared to one day eat the parakeets.

EPILOGUE: TEN THOUSAND NIGHTS

t's six-fifteen. I'm pulling a clean shirt out of the closet. I'm half-brushing my teeth. It's dinnertime, showtime, time to go to work. Reservations at seven: Vigoda, party of four. I'm checking Map-Quest, my wallet, hustling Laura along as gently as I can: "Mother-fucker, come on! We gotta go *now*."

It's four in the afternoon and I'm changing in my car, middle of downtown, rush hour heating up. A nice button-down oxford and a tie that almost matches, my summer-weight sport coat with the spot on the sleeve where the cat barfed that's almost-but-not-quite-completely unnoticeable unless you're looking for it. The cop rolls by me slowly, wondering what the hell I'm doing, wrestling to get my arms in the sleeves—looking at me like he's seen nothing weirder to-day. I tuck my shirt in by the unmanned valet's stand, crush out a cig-arette, bypass the smiling hostess and meet my boss at the bar. Drinks, herring *amuse*, smoked salmon done white trash–style with a coffee can full of hardwood chips and an oven door jammed open with side towels, more drinks. The skate wing is not good. The *loup de mer* is. City-council people eating fried potatoes at the bar, politi-cal operatives by the windows. An impromptu martini-tasting breaks out. I step outside for a smoke and run into the mayor. He's a good guy—an ex-bar-and-restaurant guy, veteran of more years than he'd probably like to admit—and I like him. He reads my columns some-times so I like him double. Standing there, I tell him a funny story about getting loaded on the job in Boulder last weekend and falling asleep on a display of Southwestern carpets at the import store next door to the restaurant. I don't know why he wastes his time listening to me, but he does, and when I'm done, he laughs, so now I like him triple. He makes a crack about how, being mayor, he has a driver now so doesn't have to worry about that kind of thing, but I've heard stories about back when he was in The Life. We shake hands. He goes in. I finish my cigarette, make for the bar, and eat a whole lobster. Two-hour dinner turns to four. When I leave, there's a parking ticket on my car. Later, I'll try to expense it. It's been a good night.

It's ten in the morning and I can't seem to peel myself up off the couch—sleeping in last night's clothes, red-eyed, mouthful of cotton and a headache like a vise on the back of my neck. I smell like sake, like stale smoke and spilled beer and worse. I feel like a character in a cartoon, like if I were to cough right now, all that would come out would be cigarette butts and bottle caps and maybe a piece of sushi or two. "Have fun last night?" Laura yells down from the top of the stairs, smiling down at me like the avenging angel of hangovers. I think about that for a minute. "Fucked if I know," I say, but obviously, yeah, I did. Vague recall of sashimi with real Japanese wasabi, ridiculously expensive, and arctic char on a powdered waffle and arguing across the bar with one of the sushi rollers. A box of wooden matches rattles in my pocket, memento of where I'd been. What I don't recall is getting home.

It's eight o'clock at night, nine, ten, and I'm just trying to get home, so wracked by food poisoning I have to pull over every couple miles to throw up and hurting so bad I want to die until, accidentally, I almost do—heaving so hard I pass out, tumble from the car into a gutter filled with slush and running, icy water. I lay there for twenty minutes, slowly freezing to death, until I'm awakened by my bowels letting go. I shit myself volcanically. Humiliating as it is, I'm sorta thankful because at least it woke me, maybe saved my life. So many people who've known me have already assumed that someday I'd be found dead in a gutter. Dragging myself back into the car, I'm just happy to fucking disappoint them.

It's one in the afternoon, *machaca* on the patio by the waterfall while the mariachis play. It's three in the morning, upstairs in a room above the bar, drinking high-priced tequila and passing joints with Hollywood's B-list. Another story I'll never get to tell. It's ten in the morning and I'm at the bar already—breakfast beers and a whole afternoon ahead of me as visiting dignitary in a friend's kitchen. My buddy Ian comes forward from the galley, wipes his hands on a side towel, looks me over. "Let's get you dressed," he says. First time I've worn a chef's jacket in years. It's big on me, but they all are. Putting it on feels like slipping back into my own skin.

It's eight o'clock. I'd taken my last clean shirt from the luggage, my party jeans, my dad's old cowboy boots, polished to a cinnamon gloss, and my leather jacket. Putting on the costume, I'd told Laura I was going out for a little bit, asked her if she wanted to come along. She'd waved me off, laughing incredulously as if to say, "You *must* be kidding." We were just back from Manhattan again, Philadelphia, Rochester—a whirlwind tour. She was exhausted. Kid had the sniffles. I was only starving.

So alone, standing outside the restaurant in the snow, soft, silent flakes powdering me like confectioners' sugar, I watch the gardemanger inside the warm square of the window laying his weight against the works of a candy-apple-red slicer, humping it, with forearm pressed to the guard and free hand waiting beneath the spinning blade for that one, perfect, wisp-thin piece of prosciutto to fall. I watch a girl with mauled line cook's fingers and the grace of a concert pianist roll and cut handmade pasta, the fine hair on her arms furred with flour. The neighborhood foot traffic ebbs and flows, forms currents, whirlpools around bums, parking kiosks and me—standing riveted, finishing my cigarette, watching a vision as ancient as cuisine: the rise of a bottle of olive oil in a cook's hand tilting it, and the thin stream of green-gold oil splashing across the plate. In the snow, everything is muffled, soft. I can hear the metronome of my own heart, the hiss of my breath escaping, smoke laddering upward in the still, cold air.

Through a door, another door, down a broad, sweeping flight of stairs and to my table. Glass of Corbara in the sudden damp warmth and noise of a busy floor; *crochette*, a ball of *buratta* as big as half a baseball and a plate of prosciutto di San Daniele; another glass of wine. I sit by myself at my table, happy, eating with my fingers, leaving greasy smudges on my wineglass, leaning back comfortably against the leather banquette. In the back, by the kitchen door, I see a cook pass by. A young guy, baseball hat turned backward, dressed in a white coat that doesn't fit him quite right. Busy, this kid. Focused. Wrestling with a sheet tray covered in resting balls of milky-white pizza dough.

I finish my wine, lay a curl of prosciutto on my tongue and wait for my body's heat to melt the soft marble of fat. I shift position, crossing and uncrossing my legs, rubbing the back of my neck where, now, a weight of weariness has settled. My feet hurt in these ridiculous boots. The collar of my shirt bites at my throat.

The kid, the cook with the backward baseball hat and check pants, pops out the door again, moving with a dancer's confidence, a veteran's conservation of motion—twining his way through a knot of people, tapping a *rôtisseur* on the shoulder, ducking down, coming up again with a change-out tray filled with provisions. Flash of a smile—a quick, private joke passing that I can't hear—and a fast, agile shift in his weight, bumping a door closed with his hip somewhere out of sight. There are raised voices, beleaguered station chefs calling for resupply, and the cook is lifting his burden, moving back toward the kitchen, stopping—a stutter step, just an instant—to turn and look out over the room, the floor, the thrilling, thrumming, high buzz of a busy night when everything is going right and everyone is being fed and everywhere echoes with laughter, muddled voices, the tink of silver on plates.

In that moment I dream I am flying—back, suddenly, and away from this place, this basement; away from Denver, through Albuquerque; past ballrooms and buffet lines and cramped galleys; a flutter of Jolly Rogers and knife wounds and pan burns (remembered pain so sweet once it's gone) and joints, snowy alleys and wine bottles, past Florida, Jimmy's, Buffalo, La Cité, Rochester; snatches of favorite songs blowing out behind me, flurries of tickets on the slide, a thousand smiles, ten thousand nights, blood smeared on an apron, mussels in the pan, butter smeared on fingers, Angelo's arms dusted with flour, his strong hands holding mine, moving them. "Like this, Jason. Like this . . ."

Full loop. I'm back again in the restaurant, the basement, heart hammering, swollen with love. And I'm standing, dreaming, walking across the floor, tearing open my dress shirt, buttons popping and scattering like shrapnel, pulling it off, dropping it, stepping out of my uncomfortable boots and kicking them clear, wriggling out of my party jeans, pushing through the swinging door into the back of the house, the locker room, to find once more my death-smelling work boots, my T-shirt, CHARLIE DON'T SURF, my white coat and cook's checks, my Sharpies, cigarettes, knife kit; saying, "Chef, I'm here. I'm back. What do you need? What do you need?"

ACKNOWLEDGMENTS

"Are you kidding me?" Laura asked. We were sitting on the couch watching TV, and I'd just asked her if she could help me with the dedication and acknowledgments for this book. "You've been working on your Academy Awards acceptance speech for twenty years, but you've never thought about this before?"

I admitted that no, I really hadn't. Never satisfied with what I have and perpetually longing for those things I never will have, I've given some thought to what I would say when presented with my Nobel Prize (for cooking, of course), my Oscar, my Latin Grammy. But this? Not so much.

In the end, Laura did help—jogging my memory and reminding me of some of the people who, over the years, have helped me come to this weird place where I now find myself; people who deserve so much more than mere acknowledgment, who are owed blood and sweat and bone and (in some cases) money. Lots and lots of money.

First and foremost, there's my folks, Mike and Cindy Sheehan, without whom I wouldn't exist. I'd like to thank them for making me, raising me well, instilling in me a love of words (especially the four-letter variety) and for not just tying me up in a sack and tossing me off a bridge even when the option must've been very, very tempting.

Ellis and Kathy Serdikoff—thanks for doing the same with Laura. If not for one fateful night in Ithaca, New York (and several fateful nights that followed), I would no doubt be standing on a hot line somewhere, watching the sauce, sweating through my whites and wondering what could have been. In a very real way, none of this would've happened without your daughter. So again, thanks for that.

Thanks to *La Cocinita Magazine* for giving me my first real writing gig, and to Peri Pakroo for explaining to me exactly what it entailed; to Gwyneth Doland for making me a critic and to Patty Calhoun for turning me into an actual writer. Chief, I owe you so many beers . . . Thanks to Jane Le, copy editor extraordinaire, for teaching me that there is a right word for everything and for knowing stuff about early eighties punk music, zombies, French gender, Chinese ducks, Sleestak and everything else that goes into the construction of a proper restaurant review.

A special thanks to everyone at *Westword*, particularly those on the editorial side, and especially Dave Herrera and Amy Haimerl. While I am very thankful for the help, support, bummed smokes, afternoon beers and kind words offered by all the ink-stained wretches with whom I daily labor, DH and Amy have been there from the start.

I'd like to acknowledge National Public Radio, where once upon a time host Jay Allison and independent producer Dan Gediman let me write a three-minute radio piece about barbecue for their project, a resurrection of the Edward R. Murrow program *This I Believe.*

David Dunton of Havey Klinger, Inc., heard the piece during its original broadcast and was moved enough to drop me an e-mail asking if I'd ever thought of writing a book. For that, I can never thank him enough.

It's been a lifetime of luck and good timing and weird coincidence that has led me to this point. I've got to thank my editor, Paul Elie, for taking a chance on me (and helping me find a title).

Finally, I'd like to acknowledge all the cooks and chefs, waiters and dishwashers, owners, partners, dealers, fixers, suppliers, motherfuckers and friends who make up the cast of this book. During the jagged course of my career as a white jacket, I did time in something like thirty different kitchens. Some of them are described here; some of them are not. Names have been changed, timelines screwed with and, undoubtedly, hundreds of small details lost over the years. But good, bad or horrific, there was never a post stood where I didn't take something away with me or learn a valuable lesson.

I firmly believe that, like the title of president or general or convict, the title of chef is granted for life. No matter what you do or where you go, it follows you, because being there, in the heat and fire and madness of the moment, changes you forever. You are never the same person again. And this book was written with that in mind. Even if nothing else comes of this, I am just happy to have been a cook and a chef of no renown in the dawning of the age of the celebrity chef, to have been a fuckup able to stand proud among an army of fuckups and call them my friends.